Diversity and Inclusion

C000111381

Series Editor

Thomas Köllen, Institute of Organization and HRM, University of Bern, Bern, Switzerland

The book series 'Diversity and Inclusion Research' examines the facets of diversity in a variety of contexts, as well as approaches to and perspectives on diversity and inclusion. It presents organizational research on workforce diversity, and covers diversity and inclusion-related issues within communities, cities, regions, nations, and societies.

The series welcomes functional and intersectional perspectives on diversity, as well as constructivist perspectives on processes of "doing" or "performing" diversity. In terms of inclusion, it welcomes research on broader initiatives (such as generalized diversity management approaches), as well as on practices of inclusion that focus on specific dimensions of diversity; these can include age, appearance, ethnicity, disability, gender, gender identity, nationality, race, religion, sexual orientation, sex, or any other characteristic or demographic in which persons can differ from each other, or, conversely, which they share.

The series publishes research from the broad range of academic disciplines within the social sciences (e.g. economics and business administration, linguistics, political science, history, law, psychology, sociology, geography, and education) and humanities (e.g. philosophy and religion). It strongly encourages interdisciplinary and transdisciplinary research, as well as critical perspectives on diversity and inclusion-related issues. By welcoming research from a variety of sectoral, national, and cultural contexts, the series will make an essential contribution to shaping the academic discourse on diversity and inclusion.

Anthony Smith-Meyer

Unlocking the Potential of Diversity in Organisations

The Governance of Inclusion in a Racialised World

 Springer

Anthony Smith-Meyer
Bereldange, Luxembourg

ISSN 2662-5997   ISSN 2662-6004   (electronic)
Diversity and Inclusion Research
ISBN 978-3-031-10404-6   ISBN 978-3-031-10402-2   (eBook)
https://doi.org/10.1007/978-3-031-10402-2

This Springer imprint is published by the registered company Springer Nature Switzerland AG
The registered company address is: Gewerbestrasse 11, 6330 Cham, Switzerland

The writing of this book was sparked by the deaths of African-American citizens at the hands of law enforcement officers in 2020 and the #BLM protests that followed. These victims deserve recognition, as do the millions of other victims of discrimination and abuse throughout my lifetime, but also through the centuries.

Many individuals have stood up to oppressive power at significant personal risk, often paying the price of courage through assassinations, imprisonment, or other forms of suppression. The heroes of our past are joined by the activists seeking justice and truth today, including those journalists who risk everything for the right of free speech and the right to know.

This work, practical as I have sought to make it, is my contribution to try and honour their sacrifices, as much as to help those who have the courage of their convictions to make a difference for justice: privately, professionally, and politically.

However, my special dedication of this book goes to those two persons who provided me with the determination to pursue this work. My mother, Violet, who always viewed others for the good they represented, and my father, Anton, who never lacked courage for standing up for what he believed was fair and right. Without their instruction in empathy and the pursuit of justice and purpose, this book would not have been written.

Anthony Smith-Meyer

Foreword

Many of us do not become aware of, let alone engaged with, the social inequalities around us until we directly experience injustice. However, other humans are on the harsh end of these inequities due to the accident of birth. Such inequities include how their pregnant mothers were treated by the healthcare system, the quality of housing available to them as children, the assumptions lecturers make about their attainment at university, or their lack of access to the social codes required to navigate higher tiers of professional occupations.

Many management students and business leaders are not taught about how such historical or current disadvantages and privileges impact business today. This book is especially for this group. It offers provocative insights and practical guidance for how those with relative structural privilege can wield their power for greater collective benefit. Readers of this book will encounter research and frameworks across disciplines such as management, law, sociology, politics, and psychology. Readers will also be exposed to the insights and experiences of employees belonging to historically marginalised communities. Of the many messages in the book, a key takeaway is that achieving equity and inclusion is not easy, 'ordinary', or 'natural'. The 'business case' is not as simple as is often presented (i.e. 'greater diversity = better business performance'). This book spells out the work inherent in the 'equals' sign. Business has responsibilities to employees and shareholders beyond a simplistic bottom line. My hope is that readers, guided by Anthony, will reap the breadth of diversity and inclusion outcomes. Such non-financial outcomes, including engagement, creativity, and innovation, are associated with higher performance and value creation.

Collaborating with Anthony on this project was a living case study of the labour (and benefits) of the 'equals' sign: a British female academic and consultant of Nigerian heritage in partnership with a business professional, teacher, and European male of Anglo-Scandinavian descent. Our different social positions meant we came to this project with different lived experiences. We grappled with how to surface and disrupt implicit assumptions and stereotypes rather than perpetuate and sustain them. We explored the best ways to communicate understanding for those new to equity work whilst acknowledging the impatience and pain of those who have done this work for decades. Anthony and I dealt with disagreement in the understanding and acceptance that our ultimate goals and underlying values were aligned. We learnt to 'practise what we preach'. Our collaboration is pretty much the 'playbook' of our request to readers—to do the work and unleash the benefits of diversity.

Like many book projects, it is hard to quantify the intellectual, emotional, and material resources that resulted in this work. Our output is offered in the hope that its contents are deemed worthy of your time and engagement. As you read, I invite you to tune into the emotions that may surface. Where you notice discomfort, anger, or anxiety, make a note. Lean into this discomfort with curiosity—it may be your subconscious signalling a critical learning moment. When you are done reading, apply your learning by doing something different no matter how small, to champion equity and inclusion in your sphere of impact. If, when you are done with the book, you are still not sure what you can do differently, turn back to the first page and start reading again. Then, let this be your sole intention—to identify one action from this book to help create a culture of equity in the space you occupy in the world.

East Midlands   Doyin Atewologun
UK

Preface

Social injustice has always exercised me. It does many people, but what have we done to confront it, fight it, rectify it? I might break people down into five categories.

1. The Oblivious: People who do not care as long as they are not on the receiving end of injustice. They are content with the status quo and do not 'experience' or recognise injustice within their social networks.
2. The Complacent: Individuals who acknowledge the existence of social injustice, tut and shake their head in moral indignation when it is apparent, and may speak up when provoked to proclaim their outrage.
3. The Activists: Those who actively campaign and intervene individually or as a group to fight for justice and equality.
4. The Dispossessed: Those, often minorities, subject to injustice, discrimination, and exclusion. People whose voices are often dismissed as unqualified or without merit.
5. The Cynics and Deniers: There are people, both amongst the more and less privileged, who see the world radically different from the above and deny a discrimination problem. They believe that we live in a world where success is essentially down to the individual, where privilege is earned, and that those who feel excluded only have themselves to blame.

For most of my life, I would have to admit being in the Complacent camp, with an occasional flirtation with Activism when confronted with injustice impacting my family, friends, or colleagues under my responsibility.

- When I became a father of daughters, I cared more for gender equality.
- When I discovered I had friends and family who were LGBT+ and appeared to be amongst the Dispossessed, I cared more about LGBT+.
- When I interacted with colleagues and acquaintances of colour, I challenged myself to be fair and open as with any other nationality or race. Still, racial discrimination was not something that touched me personally. I have to admit that for a greater part of my life, I existed in a bubble: a predominantly White bubble.

It is in the nature of 'social bubbles' that they define what we should care about. The ethics of our bubbles dictate to us what we should be outraged by. It takes shocking events, inspirational leaders, or teachers to shake us out of our ignorance or complacency.

2020 was a shocking year. Perhaps, it was the particular cocktail of Coronavirus lockdowns mixed with the horrific stories and videos of racist violence in the USA. Police killed Breonna Taylor in her bed in a mistaken raid; Ahmaud Arbery was hunted down by self-anointed vigilantes whilst out jogging; Atatiana Jefferson was shot by a police officer from outside her bedroom window because she had left her front door ajar; not least we witnessed the traumatic and slow death of George Floyd at the hands of police officers. The sense of systematic injustice and discrimination in a country that, for so many years, was looked to for leadership in the free world was palpable. Europeans looked on aghast, and when US cousins started their #BLM protests, they felt it necessary to join in any and every local protest taking place in their support—irrespective of COVID-19. It was only subsequently that more Europeans started to look over their colonial shoulders and reflect on racism in Europe.

During the past 11 years, I have had the privilege of teaching university students from the Mid-West of America who had ventured over to Europe to explore our culture. They enjoyed many of the experiences they hoped for with trips to Barcelona, Berlin, Venice, and Vienna, amongst many others. Their pictures filled their Instagram feeds whilst I taught them about international business, management, and organisational behaviour. However, my main objective with this young group of students was to demonstrate to them, to make them understand, that there are no absolute 'truths' in this world; there are merely many different perspectives of the 'Facts'. In an Indian parable, we are told of the seven blind men confronted by an elephant. One feels the tail which reminds him of a rope; one feels the trunk, and he thinks of a snake; one touches the side and compares it to a wall; one the tusk which he likens to a spear; and so it goes on. In the end, they meet to describe what an elephant is like. In the words of the poet John Godfrey Saxe. It ends thus:

> And so these men of Indostan
> > Disputed loud and long,
> > Each in his own opinion
> > Exceedingly stiff and strong,
> > Though each was partly in the right
> > And all were in the wrong!

Thus it is with our view of the world. We are raised in the shadow of conventional truth, definitions of mores and norms bounded by the social restrictions, or opportunities that encompass our 'bubble'. As I started this book, I watched the TV series *Little Fires Everywhere*, based on Celeste Ng's book. In it, we observe a world co-inhabited by a Black artist and single mother on the one hand, and the wife and mother of an 'ideal' all-American White, suburban family on the other. Would they ever understand each other?

The events of 2020 energised me to be more active in the fight for racial equality. In doing so, I add my voice to all aspects of social injustice that my understanding of the world allows me. In her book *Caste: The Origin of Our Discontents*, Isabel Wilkerson redefines US racism in terms of a social caste system: not immediately recognised as existing in the USA, but which lies at the core of ongoing discrimination on racial, sexual, and religious grounds. According to Wilkerson, Black Americans are relentlessly identified with slaves of centuries past; slaves in turn are identified as an underclass—much like the untouchables of India. It is perhaps easier to understand how social injustice becomes so stratified and so rigid when viewed through the lens of the caste system.

If we want change, we have to become activists. To be an activist, you can join and support the efforts of activist leaders. You can speak up when in the presence of unfairness or injustice, or you can leverage your abilities and launch your own initiatives. This book is my attempt to contribute to this struggle for social justice. My objective in addressing you, the reader, is to bring you a call to action: to read, reflect, and act.

People ask me how I plead to the charge that I am (undeniably) a 'privileged White male' and consequently incapable of addressing what is primarily a problem facing 'unprivileged BAME minorities'. To the former, I am guilty as charged. My youth and my career have evolved in the context of being a member of the privileged majority. Yet, my experience, traits, and interests combine to persuade me of the need to learn and adapt to the injustices and the absence of universal fairness around me. To the second, I have to disagree fundamentally. To successfully diversify and overcome discriminatory behaviours, let alone create inclusive cultures, requires (1) authentic self-awareness and openness on the part of the privileged and (2) the cultivation of trust and openness amongst those who have reason to be distrustful. The voice of the minority all too often being dismissed by the majority, my voice— that of a White peer in Western society—may be more easily heard amongst the privileged in certain countries. Additionally, my role as facilitator and bridge-builder between communities will, I hope, help all parties to embrace openness more willingly.

To this end, I bring my grey hairs of experience in a multi-cultural world, my knowledge of governance, organisational behaviour, compliance, ethics, change, and people management. In addition, I have researched, explored, and discussed racial topics with members of minority and majority communities and present what I have learned in these chapters. In particular, I am grateful and indebted to Dr Doyin Atewologun for her insight, comments, and encouragement as she has advised me on this work.

My intent with this book is to explain the challenges and some of the drivers of the issues confronting D&I and racial discrimination. I endeavour to set out the beginnings of actions that can start a process of greater inclusiveness in organisations. I do not pretend or claim to provide a handbook of 'how to' accomplish the vision of equality, diversity, and inclusion. What I hope is that the reader will discover some of the pertinent questions to be asked, and the concepts and governance tools available to help answer them.

In fine, my objective is to help those who want to help themselves and their organisations face up to and change their past prejudices. I hope it will form the basis of courses, articles, speeches, and webinars. I will try to convince you, the reader, that change is possible, that we can establish new norms of equality and justice across races, religions, sexual preferences, castes, and other human-made social structures, and that we can change the narrative and consequently our reality.

Nothing ventured, nothing gained.

Bereldange, Luxembourg   Anthony Smith-Meyer

Acknowledgements

The writing of this book has been what I can only, somewhat clichéd, call a journey of discovery. My starting point was governance, ethics, and culture management. My destination was a better understanding of why discriminatory behaviours remain so intractable within the walls of our institutions and social groupings; this, despite our best efforts and knowledge of organisational behaviour. Unoriginal as it may sound, the whole experience was not unlike a journey.

In the first stage, I had to understand the nature of the seas, winds, and currents that I was to traverse. I had to map the seascape of race relations, racial bias, and cultural confrontation. What questions needed answering? Where could I find the answers? I had to navigate through a lot of research. Most of it was academic or from the world of the major consulting companies and other practitioners. I consulted quite broadly. To find my way to the best and most illuminating sources, I listened to many podcasts such as Hidden Brain, Throughline, as well as many-various history and BBC, NPR, and NRK current affairs radio documentaries. The number of sources that gave shape to my musings and instincts is too many to mention here, but do take time to peruse the citations of this book. Many learned and intelligent people have considered the challenge of racial exclusion and inclusion, and I have learnt a lot from them.

At a second stage, I consulted and discussed my plans and conclusions with friends and colleagues from the academic and professional worlds of human resources, diversity and inclusion management, governance, and ethics management. During the pandemic, we came together across frontiers via private online video conferences to discuss and debate. Their reflections and comments have influenced my 'take' and presentations on all aspects of the obstacles we encountered along the way. We had a lot of fun, and I was both encouraged and delighted by the continued interest in this work shown by my partners in this regard. I would particularly mention and thank Sue Egan, Zarine Jacob, Sally March, Julie Nazerali, Michael Shackleton, Turid Solvang, Michèle Sormani-Nielsen, Fritha Sutherland, Carsten Tams, Gudrun Timm, Rachel Treece, Ludo Van der Heyden, and Sharon Ward. Some conversations may have been one-to-one, others as part of our little troop, but each in their way have influenced my choice of topics or approach in writing about them. I am deeply grateful for their interest and contribution.

Finally, I had to bring my conclusions and manuscript safely into harbour. This was the piloting stage where the efforts of Dr Doyin Atewologun as colleague, advisor, and consulting editor have been so valuable to me. In addition to sharing her works and thoughts on the subject, Doyin has encouraged me to challenge both myself and the subject matter. More frequently than I like to admit, Doyin pointed out passages where my own assumptions of 'normality' required deeper thought and explanation and steered me clear of the more obvious remaining rocks of prejudice and reefs of stereotype that might have remained in my path. With Doyin's help, I have managed to improve the completeness of my work, brought more of my own experience to the surface, and clarified and explored notions that have added to the value that I hope this book represents. Before this collaboration, we did not know each other. I am grateful to Doyin for her constructive wisdom and agility as a discussion partner. I hope for, and look forward to, the continuation of our cooperation on future projects.

About the Author

Anthony Smith-Meyer, IoD.Dipl, is a specialist within governance, compliance, and topics relating to organisational behaviour. Currently, he is the Executive Director of the Institute for Financial Integrity and Sustainability in Luxembourg and is founder of a not-for-profit idea-creation and collaboration network known as theGovernanceProject.org. Previously a member of the Group Executive Committee of Compliance and Control at BNP Paribas, Anthony has been extensively involved with compliance and ethics matters since 2003, as Division and later Group Head of Compliance at Fortis Bank. Anthony holds the UK Institute of Directors Diploma in Corporate Direction, is a Certified Director of the Institut Luxembourgeois des Administrateurs (ILA), and is an independent lecturer, trainer, coach, and advisor in matters relating to corporate governance and compliance. He has authored the book *Surviving Organisational Behaviour*, was founder and editor-in-chief of the *Journal of Business Compliance*, and regularly authors articles on ESG topics. This book, themed on the governance of inclusion in a racialised world, is only his latest venture in this sphere.

Anthony has been a regular faculty member of ILA courses on company direction since 2012, as well as for the European Confederation of Director's Associations (EcoDa) in Brussels. He has served as Adjunct Professor and lecturer of International Business and Management at the European Campus of Miami University of Ohio for over a decade.

Anthony's career spans over three decades working for UK, N. American, Scandinavian, Benelux, and French institutions in a wide range of activities including relationship-driven banking, as well as product area trading room activities, structured, asset, and project finance. His work reflects a combination of practical experience with academic acumen that provides lucidity to the subjects he addresses, blending clarity to complex matters and a practical approach to the identification of solutions.

About the Consulting Editor: Dr Doyin Atewologun

Doyin is a psychologist, scholar practitioner, a regular media contributor, and multi-award winner in recognition of her innovative methodologies and pioneering work in promoting inclusion and excellence in organisations. She is Dean of the Rhodes Scholarships at Oxford University and concurrently Director of Delta Alpha Psi, a niche leadership and inclusion consultancy. Doyin was previously Director of the Gender, Leadership and Inclusion Centre at Cranfield School of Management and Reader (Full Professor). Doyin has worked with many of the FTSE 100, United Nations agencies, legal and other professional services firms, and the UK Civil Service, and she adopts an evidence-based approach when working with business leaders to advance inclusion. Doyin is a member of the Health and Wellbeing Response Taskforce for COVID-19 NHS staff and Inclusion Adviser on Regional Talent Boards for the NHS as well as the Academic Adviser on the Parker Steering Committee led by Sir John Parker into ethnic diversity on FTSE350 boards.

Doyin was recognised in *People Management* magazine's Top 20 Diversity and Inclusion 'Power List' for 2020. She won Inspiring Board Leader of the Year at the Precious Awards in 2019 and has won numerous other awards for excellence in academic publications. Doyin has extensive experience in coaching, executive education, programme design, and research advising and has over 35 scholarly and professional publications. Doyin is Honorary Fellow at Trinity College, Oxford University, and has held visiting faculty positions at Queen Mary, University of

London; Lagos Business School, Nigeria; and the University of Pretoria, South Africa.

Doyin has addressed global audiences and has been invited to industry judging panels to amplify underrepresented talent and help identify and evaluate outstanding work in academic publications with practical evidence-based impact.

Introduction

We need this debate.

In my foreword, I explain my reasons for writing this book. That is as it may be, but the topic that we will explore, the questions we will try to answer, and the solutions we are going to suggest are not for my benefit—they are to serve you, the reader. If you have picked up this book, it is because you recognise there is an issue that requires resolution. You acknowledge that there is prejudice, bias, and discrimination in society, your organisation, and your personal life. You may be a company director or executive, a manager, an academic, a student, a member of a community discriminated against, or a relative, friend, or colleague of one. Still, you have not yet found the answer as to how to help turn things around. You have listened to the good intentions expressed by political, civil, and business leaders, yet understood that words are not enough, that training and policy documents alone do not change behaviours.

Too many management executives struggle to understand the nature of the equity, diversity, and inclusion ('D&I') debate, both in terms of its impact and intractability. Indeed, the very notions of equity (generally concerned with fairness in outcome), as opposed to equality (the provision of a level playing field), can lead to a confusing distraction. If we add the notion of belonging, then many individuals less schooled in social sciences and psychology begin, themselves, to be on the outside of the debate: excluded by jargon and specialist terminology. That is why I have decided to use the term "Diversity and Inclusion" as the reference term in this book. The proverbial nut we are trying to crack is D&I; equality is part of the solution, whilst equity and belonging form part of the desired outcomes.

This book seeks to explain why majorities dismiss exclusion as the fault of the excluded, and how prejudice and bias can lead to self-defeating defensive behaviours by those who feel their impact, in turn aggravating racial divisions at work and within society. Using a mixture of applied academic theory, practical examples, and experience from the real world, we will explore the issue of D&I from four angles.

Part I Why diversity and inclusion matters. We have to understand what discrimination looks like, and what the consequences of exclusion are. How do we define, even discover, what systematic or institutional discrimination is? Why, when the evidence shows that reasons for investing in diversity and inclusion are significant, both from a moral and economic perspective, is this path so often rejected by the community we live in?

Part II The forces of exclusion and isolation. Having established the dysfunctional impact of socially led prejudice and bias in Part one, we will examine the drivers of our individual destructive behaviours. The natural instincts that drive us apart are strong, as the trail of failed D&I programmes throughout decades can testify to. We shall try to understand why our traditional risk management approaches struggle against the emotive fears and hopes that trigger discrimination and exclusion.

Part III The imperative conditions of change. We will discover the three essential implementation conditions necessary for sustainable culture change within an organisation. The path that leads to continuous learning and improvement is paved with the power of leadership, an organisational culture of trust, and a living dialogue within the firm.

Part IV The organisation of the cultural transformation process redefines the mission and scope of governance. From the positioning of the D&I function and ensuring a dynamic social capital within the firm to the measurement of cultural change, governance frameworks need careful engineering. We explore the best practice standards of the governance of D&I and review brief case studies of how two major corporations (Microsoft and EY USA) have approached D&I to learn from their examples. Finally, we will review established industry standards of best practice and evaluate their impact on the design of D&I programmes.

The task of addressing all of these aspects is enormous. Some may describe this work as a book of two halves, or two books in one binder. The first deals with the drivers and outcomes of inter-relationship dynamics. The second addresses the needs of the business practitioner looking for answers and solutions. The organisation seeking to find the appropriate response to the D&I challenge needs to understand both these elements to succeed.

This book was inspired by the #BLM movement of 2020. Consequently, the more significant part of my research references the plight of Black communities in the face of discrimination. This emphasis is not to undervalue the challenges facing Asian, ethnic, religious, or other communities that form part of the 'outgroup' to any dominant society. The principles discussed and presented here are relevant to the inclusion of any minority facing the prejudice of an 'ingroup'. The topic is not exclusively one of Black inclusion in White society. Still, in our racialised world, it is one that appears most prevalent in the face of political correctness and social taboos.

At the end of our story, we shall hopefully understand how the time for being a bystander in the D&I debate is over and how the changing expectations of tomorrow's consumers are writing a message on the wall, telling of the necessity for change we ignore at our peril. This book is a contribution to the critical conversation on how to make those changes within organisations.

The Constant Struggle

Difference is the essence of humanity. Difference is an accident of birth, and it should therefore never be the source of hatred or conflict. Therein lies a most fundamental principle of peace: respect for diversity.
John Hume, Nobel Peace Prize 1998

John Hume was considered one of the principal architects of the Good Friday Agreement that brought an end to hostilities between Nationalist Catholic and Unionist Protestant forces in Northern Ireland. His focus was on religious differences, but his truth was universal. Differences are the essence of humanity—it is what makes us unique and what makes getting to know one another new and exciting. He secured peace in Northern Ireland through mutual respect, understanding, and a process of reconciliation. These words contain lessons we need to learn.

Left to our own devices and in a safe environment, our social instincts are to get to know the stranger standing next to us. Through our interaction, we discern the signals that indicate we are in the presence of a friend or foe. More often than not, we pursue a path of friendship based on the discovery of commonalities between us, thereby satisfying both our curiosity and mutual desire for safety. Ironically, it is only upon the introduction of social groupings and established institutions intended to provide predictable security that our behaviours change. No longer responsible for ensuring our own security, we rely on strength in numbers, or the law courts to protect us and our property. We choose to rely on the rule of law to provide future stability and predictable outcomes for our investments.

If our civil establishments are open and optimistic, we may welcome and integrate newcomers. In the words of the President of the EU Commission, Ursula von der Leyen, the aspiration is that 'The rule of law protects the people from the rule of the powerful'.[1] If society is fearful and defensive, the law's purpose quickly becomes one of protecting privilege and buffering against any competition. In his book *The Tyranny of Merit*, Professor Michael Sandel convincingly argues that the rule of law functions to protect the status of the wealthy and powerful by creating a 'merit aristocracy'. Merit becomes a byword for traits and qualifications that perpetuate the status quo and defends privilege against new challengers who, in truth, might be more deserving.

Populism is the political expression of the protection of privilege and the exclusion of anything or anyone who might challenge our comfort zone. The more our societies shrink into narrow interest groups, the greater the inclination to see 'others' as a threat to be confronted and suppressed. The tools in this struggle are stereotype,

---

[1]Tweeted by @vonderleyen at 12:48pm on 30 September 2020 on Twitter.

bias, and prejudice. Throughout history, our societies have swung between optimism and pessimism, confidence, and fear, leading to sporadic periods of negativity in the form of nationalism or populism. So far in the twenty-first century, we have been in the grip of regional wars, international terrorism, irrational exuberance, financial crisis, austerity, global pandemics, and a looming climate crisis. People have been fearful, and populism has gained traction by identifying 'external threats'. In the Muslim world, the threat has been Western permissiveness; in the Christian world, it has been Islamic fundamentalism; in the USA, it has been the declining dominance of White citizens relative to People of Colour; in Europe, it has been the arrival of a mixture of economic migrants and Middle and Near Eastern war refugees. Populism has proffered 'easy' solutions and 'obvious' enemies. The majorities who elect them to power behave in ways that rationalise and justify their choice, including the deliberate denial of rights to minorities.

Turning the Tide

Suppose fear, ignorance, and discomfort in the face of change are the main drivers of creating divides between cultures and peoples. In that case, we also know that we can redefine and correct such destructive and potentially dangerous conflicts by addressing them. Such behaviour between nations ignites wars. In urban centres, it produces riots. In our organisations, it pushes away talent and potential, and diminishes value creation.

Executives and board members have only a minor ability to influence behaviours in broader society, although they have some. However, within their organisations, it is entirely within their powers to create a safe environment for experimentation and trust to develop between majority and minority groupings. Companies can establish frameworks that encourage openness and constructive dialogue to help all employees understand the impact of their conscious and unconscious behaviours. We can recruit leaders who focus on a new future and do not base discussion on past and present differences. We can enable managers and employees to tackle uncomfortable subjects better and include minorities in the everyday business of pursuing the corporate mission. It requires commitment, endeavour, and courage. By the time we end this book, I hope you will find the inspiration, the motivation, the tools, and the conviction to make the change.

As Archbishop Desmond Tutu of South Africa is reputed to have said:

Do your little bit of good where you are;
    it's those little bits of good put together that overwhelm the world.

Sidenote on Terminology

In researching the subject of racial discrimination, diversity, and inclusion, I have discovered that the topic is replete with jargon. Like much academic language, constant references to concepts and specialised conditions render the argumentation and logic difficult for the layperson to follow. In this context, I identify company directors, executives, managers, and employees as laypeople. In addition to academic and consultancy jargon, there is the additional risk of changing associations with much of the language used. For example, the working title for this book was 'Governance of D&I in the Age of #BLM'. At the time, BLM meant 'Black Lives Matter'—it was a humanitarian issue. To be woke meant to be aware of social justice matters. A footballer 'taking the knee' before a game was a gesture of solidarity with colleagues across sport experiencing racial harassment. In the relatively short time frame from initiating the book project to its completion, that same footballer is derided by his own fans for supporting #BLM, in turn labelled by the social media as a Marxist attempt to destroy the police. To be woke is increasingly interpreted to be vandals of national pride rather than truth and justice-seekers. In the struggle for cultural control, language and terminology have been weaponised.

Even the name of the issue at hand is a goalpost on the move. Is inclusion more critical than diversity? Should we then refer to an inclusion and diversity policy? Is equity considered central to the debate? We may then refer to EDI. What then of equality? Can we achieve equitable outcomes without ensuring equality of opportunity for all first? Is D&I too technical or process-oriented a description? DIB adds the concept of belonging to the equation. In naming our subject, we must consider what messages it conveys. To an audience of academics engaged in organisational behaviour, the inclusion of equity and belonging can lead to lengthy and thought-provoking debates; to board members focused on non-financial reporting and practical solutions, it may merely serve to be a distraction from the objective at hand. For the purposes of this book, I shall use the term D&I, but this is not to deny the importance of equality, equity, and belonging, all of which I discuss in the book.

The world of prejudice, bias, and discrimination is replete with generalisations and presumption. Leaders not immersed in the subject of diversity and inclusion are quick to adopt suggested sound bites crafted by wordsmiths from their policy or public relations departments. However, words matter, and the use of phrases that appear to the orator as elegant or well-meant might hide nuanced offence. What exactly is meant by minority ethnic? Some categorisation is helpful if only to make policy development possible, but it is not accidental that in this book, I do not reference the 'BAME community'—at the very least, this particular round hole must be acknowledged to be an aggregation of a number of communities in the plural.

I apply several descriptives to reference those impacted positively or negatively by racial discrimination. My inspiration for writing the book originated in the events leading to the resurgence of #BLM in the summer of 2020. Much of the available research focuses on the US experience of being a member of the Black Asian or other Minority Ethnic communities. However, the message I seek to convey is broader than the US BAME population. It applies to discriminatory relationships between Asians in Asia, Indigenous Peoples in Latin America, and all Ethnic Minorities across the world, including Romanis in the EU and the Sami in Norway. It also extends to all those discriminated against due to the strength of their faith or any aspect that identifies them as 'other'. In certain countries that would include members of the lower echelons of a caste system, or simply members of society considered as less worthy by a privileged, elitist establishment. Words like the 'unprivileged', 'minorities', the 'outgroup', or the 'excluded', 'disadvantaged', and even the 'suppressed' will be found in the text. Some are chosen to accentuate a divergence of social standing or power; others, frankly, avoid the repetitive use of common phrases. Sometimes, I want the word to shock. I do not wish to upset or harm anyone. If this proves to be the case, I apologise in advance.

Contents

Part IV   The Governance of D&I: Best Practice Standards

Part I

Of Diversity and Discrimination

Exploring racial diversity and inclusion is intricate, emotional and politically sensitive. Often, the task is further complicated by having to deal with various combinations of diversity. Referred to as intersectionality (overlapping social categorisations of any mix of race, gender, sexuality, religion, disability and more),[1] each category is subject to bias and discriminatory forces stacked one atop the other. The conventional "inappropriateness" of someone being accepted as an equal or not is compounded by the perception that the person is also of another culture, an outsider often regarded as "inferior until proven otherwise".

To speak up on racial issues is challenging and uncomfortable. Unconscious bias training has been prominent in Diversity and Inclusion (D&I) training for many years without eradicating more than superficial racial behaviours. There is no "easy fix" to the issue of D&I in a racialised world, hence the writing of this book in four parts.

- Discovering the Meaning and Impact of Diversity and Discrimination
- Exploring the Causes and Drivers of Prejudice and Discrimination
- Identifying Keys to Unlocking Diversity and Inclusive Cultures and Behaviours
- Organisation, Governance and Best Practice

To manage inclusion, we have to understand what it is to be excluded. To promote diversity, we have to see its potential. To alter behaviours and mindsets, we must master the levers of prejudice and group dynamics. If we are to achieve culture change, we must equip ourselves with the necessary tools for the task. Managing a sustainable transformation process requires a rewriting of the mission and re-focusing traditional risk management governance. The assurance of effective monitoring and decision-making no longer suffices. If we wish to manage culture, we must track sentiment and experience also.

---

[1] "Demarginalising the intersection of Race and Sex: A Black feminist critique of antidiscrimination doctrine, femininist theory and antiracial politics" by Kimberlé Williams Crenshaw. University of Chicago Legal Forum, 1989.

#TheSinsOfOurFathers

1

1.1   Is the World Your Oyster? Discovering Discrimination

Elisse Daley is a musician who describes herself as having big nostrils and curly hair. She is "not sad" that she is Black, but casting agencies and judges tell her she does not really "fit the criteria" or that they do not think she will be able to perform because of "the way you look". Furthermore, they would never say anything about her talent. So Elisse asks herself, "why aren't you judging me based on my talent?"

David Chukwujeku grew up in Glasgow, Scotland. He comments: "There are so many barriers that people pretend don't exist, but you're constantly hearing them; then everyone tells you they don't exist, and you're worried whether the problem is you. Being Black is asking questions and having people shout you down instead".

Melanie Onovo describes herself at school as "I was a big Black girl, which meant I was picked on a lot, but teachers wouldn't see it as bullying. I would be the one deemed to be aggressive and the complainer. I felt massively gaslighted[1] about the kind of person I was, which did a lot to diminish my sense of self-worth and self-esteem".

Chieka Okadigbo takes care when walking down the street. "You think, 'How do I look to other people?' Because you're tall and don't want people to feel intimidated. Being Black means to continuously not be 100% yourself".

Jack Callow finds opportunity in community: "Being Black in the UK gives you a sense of belonging. There's a level of respect the Black community gives each other. We all kind of have that caring nature towards each other because we need to have it".

Liza Bilal sees a silver lining on the cloud. She concludes: "Black people, wherever they go, are so innovative. I think Blackness means innovation. It means resistance. It means persistence".

---

[1] "Gaslighting is the process of causing someone to doubt their own thoughts, beliefs and perceptions". Dictionary.Cambridge.org, accessed 29 October, 2021.

Dylan Kawende displays the kind of courage and optimism needed to get ahead. "Teachers told me I wasn't going to Oxford or Cambridge, and I should give up on that idea. Now I'm an incoming student at Cambridge University. Whenever I had the opportunity to do public speaking at school, I was met with a combination of praise and cynicism, like: 'Who does he think he is, looking at him trying to be White?' It was because I was articulate. It was the idea that to be well-spoken, articulate, confident—those aren't qualities that are to be associated with a Black man. So even then, it was clear to me that this is the kind of obstacle I'm going to have to overcome on a regular basis, where I'm having to defy perceptions and redefine what it means to be a young Black man". It should not be so difficult.

These testimonies come from an interactive series on UK racism on the Guardian's online platform [1]. Their stories differ from the horrendous reports of police violence in the USA that sparked worldwide #BLM protests. They demonstrate the perpetual imposition of exclusion on those deemed to be different, and the impact this has on the emotions of those touched by discrimination, feelings of rejection, disappointment, self-esteem and simmering resentment.

By definition, most of us belong to the "majority"; we do not know what it is to be viewed as a minority, let alone a minority viewed as "inferior", whom the majority consider it normal to marginalise and suppress. Jack Callow takes comfort in the sense of belonging generated by being part of a discriminated minority. Anyone who feels threatened will pull together with others who find themselves in the same situation; this does create a community of sorts—but a community apart. Liza Bilal explains how constant headwinds make Black people more persistent and resistant. These may be qualities that help students like Dylan Kawende get to Cambridge University, but is he the exception that proves the rule and does it encourage the openness and collaborative behaviours needed to belong in greater society?

Reports and newspaper columns like this appear in all too many countries. It is not just a story of schoolyard bullying, either. It continues through careers, family life and retirement.

1.2   Uniqueness: Discovering Inclusion

Is it possible to know the meaning of inclusion before you have discovered the emotion of exclusion? What does it take to shake off the shackles of self-perception; the image we all have of ourselves that is the cornerstone of our self-esteem and confidence? Is it possible to practice empathy without having the courage to question your fundamental assumptions of justice and fairness? It can take a lifetime to learn the lessons of diversity and to master our handling of it. In my case, my first conscious lessons came at the age of 12.

I walked into the classroom in India, where my new teacher greeted me with a polite smile and showed me to my desk. All eyes were on me. Not only was I the new boy, but I was also from a different world, of a different culture, the foreigner. One year later, the same thing happened, this time in Norway, my homeland. The classroom, the teacher, the eyes—I was different; a curiosity. I was a foreigner once again. I was learning small lessons on exclusion that, nonetheless, have stayed with me ever since.

Moving to Mumbai was a big move. My father took up his post, and I started a new school. I recall stepping into the school classroom. I was the only White boy[2] (all the others were at boarding schools back in Europe). I suppose I was nervous; are not we always when we start a new school or job? I guess I was excited. There was a lot to take in, including the misery of having to wear the prescribed black leather shoes under a scorching sun. At first, I did not feel that others regarded me differently. Teachers and fellow pupils were welcoming and friendly. They taught me the basics of cricket in the playground, although the reward for an extended innings was the increasing discomfort of burning hot feet on the asphalt playground.

I settled in. I have no particular memory of otherness; except one. I recall one specific break time when it struck me—an actual moment I have never forgotten—that everyone was overly "nice". Was it something someone said about how being my friend made him more important in the eyes of others? That I held an apparent esteem that rubbed off on those associated with me. I knew my father had status in his job; I never imagined I shared in that, or that others sought it from me. Yet, there in the schoolyard, a peer suddenly appeared friendly to me not because of my person, but because of my status as the White son of a diplomat. It is not without irony that I reflect on how the realisation that I was considered of high status made me feel. I felt disappointed that our relationship was based on image rather than personality, and objectified as a representative of another world; that there was a barrier to being at one with those I considered my friends. From that moment on, I would be slow to confide real trust in others I met; it was a lesson in staying alert to flattery or ingratiation. If such a benign experience is still with me 50 years later, how crushing must it be for those whose experience and emotions are triggered by the denial of opportunity or oppression on a daily basis?

A year later, I returned to my hometown, Oslo, in Norway. Coming from Mumbai, it was a different world, but I was back in my fatherland, with my people; or was I? At the start of the first lesson, the teacher asked me to say a few words about myself. I looked up, stood up and pushed my chair under the desk. I explained who I was, then pulled the chair out and sat down. The class was silent. All eyes were on me, and all mouths were open in astonishment (at least that is the image I still have in my head). Rather than answering while remaining seated, I had acted according to the custom practised at my last school. That trivial moment marked me as "different". I spoke Norwegian like my fellow students, I was blond and blue-eyed like most, but I was not "one of them". I was a third-culture kid. It was the start

---

[2] There is a debate surrounding the capitalisation of the "B" in Black when referencing African Americans and other Black communities. The New York Times has adopted the practice, a.o. The inference is that the term, when used in a racial context, like Irish, Norwegian or Asian, carries with it emotional and historic connotations that are too important to "trivialize" with a "b". I am persuaded by the argument, but then also choose to use a capital "W" in White when highlighting the legacy of racial discrimination and prejudice.

of 2 years of unwanted attention from the male "influencers" in the class. To cut a long story short, I love my country, but I could never fit in.

So what? I am a White European in Europe, and I have learnt to be at ease with being different; others seem at ease with my being different. I would never lay claim to having suffered from systematic discrimination or institutionalised injustice. But I have experienced the indignation of being marginalised, gained the alertness born of being bullied, felt the exclusion from social circles I wanted to be a part of due to nothing more than different behavioural expectations. These moments did not last long, but I can, and do, recall them. Surely, we can all remember a time when we were on the outside, or in a vulnerable minority, feeling threatened. We, the privileged, dismiss them as temporary aberrations; but imagine for a moment if that was your everyday. For a large section of our society, it is.

1.3   Diversity: The Good and the Difficult

There are many forms of diversity. There are many differences of mind; scholars argue at least eight of them [2]. In addition, we have differences in upbringing and schooling, national cultures and religious faiths, which mould our expectations of what is normal or disruptive. Finally, our experiences of success or trauma pre-wire us to be exploratory or prudent. Not least, we learn from our observations of the fate of others and alter our opinions and perspectives accordingly.

Diversity is also physical or genetic. We have differences in sex between male and female and a range of sexual or behavioural preferences based more on DNA than convention. Some have highly agile and athletic abilities, while others require enabling solutions to live a normal life. Diversity is all of the above and more. Gardenswarz and Rowe explain the multitude of conditions and influences that construct our personal diversity with their four layers of diversity model [3].

1. DNA personality traits: Aspects of our personality determined by our genetic make-up.
2. Internal/given traits: Non-neurological inherited characteristics such as gender, skin colour, sexual orientation or physical or cognitive abilities and disabilities.
3. External/evolutionary traits: Conventions conferred on us by background and education, including cultural traditions, religion and lifestyles dictated by geographic factors.
4. Organisational dimensions/framework: Influences on our diversity by observation and experience resulting from our own choices. This would include chosen education, skills developed, career choices, mobility and exposure to other cultures.

It is sobering to note that each of these four aspects carries with them stereotypical and prejudicial views as to worth, ability, merit and hierarchy.

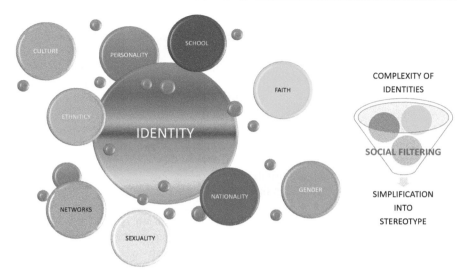

Fig. 1.1 The stereotyping of diversity

Square Pegs in Round Holes

If we are to understand the individual across the table from us properly, we need to apply the full extent of our listening skills, emotional and cultural intelligence. If not, our understanding of our conversation partner will increasingly be a simplified reflection of our prejudice. We will process the uniqueness of the other through a filter of confirmation bias (Fig. 1.1).

In the absence of personal contact, we can alter our stereotypical images and prejudiced presumptions through study and education. However, without impending need, our neurological mind will much prefer to adopt the less strenuous process of stereotyping square pegs into the round hole categories of LGBT+, Black, Asian or Minority Ethnic, Moslems or Christians, to name but a few. Considering the multitudes of unique aspects hidden behind each of those letters or categories, it is easy to understand the reluctance of any individual to be labelled in any way. For example, a lesbian of mixed heritage with an Asian appearance raised in the USA is unique in a way that only she can be.

What Is the Problem?

There is something about human beings that makes us curious, to ask questions. How we react to those questions can be placed in two buckets: We have answers that (1) entertain and amuse us, even deepen our knowledge and increase our self-esteem, and we have answers that (2) disrupt us, imply a need to revisit our behaviour and presumptions. Disruptive questions infer that we may be wrong in our views and have done wrong in the past as a result. Our curiosity might not kill the cat, but it may damage our self-esteem as much as increase it. What then are the nature of these questions we might prefer not to ponder?

What is your view on diversity in your social circle? How do you define it? What is your reaction when unorthodoxy intrudes on your life? Do you find it curious and exciting, or sense danger and conflict? Is diversity an opportunity to grow or a threat to our comfort?

What is it to be a minority? Do we feel different when we are in the majority? Are we predominantly in one or the other camp? Do those who feel ignored or discriminated against in one setting recognise when they are excluding an outsider in another? Does the habitually privileged individual wonder at the advantage and luck they have been born into? Do they, too, feel the outrage of injustice when not respected?

Racism is bad … discrimination is unfair … exclusion is cruel. Most of the world's population will agree with these statements—but do they act accordingly? Do we see the "beam in our own eye or only the splinter in the eye of our brother?" We throw stones, barely conscious that we lodge within a glass house. Change is frequently considered as a negative. We are encouraged to not "rock the boat" or "change horses midstream". Do we batten down the hatches when we sense the winds of change coming? Avoiding turmoil is our basic instinct. Change is either uncomfortable or potentially disruptive and fear-inducing.

1.4   The Identity Tension: Identities and Society

What is diversity if not a diversion from the conventional, a challenge to our established thinking and behaviours? We can either ignore it and exclude everything it represents, or we can embrace and explore it: potentially altering our view of the world and how we navigate our way through life. Once it is manifestly present, diversity cannot be ignored. If we do, we lose control. Diversity will alter the composition of those around you and with it the impulses and influences you are subject to, thereby impacting us in unforeseen ways. The only way we can keep control of our existence is either to banish the effect of diversity or to learn from it—adopting that learning in a way that serves us. As humans, we want to control. To stay on top of our lives, we need to be proactive. The question is, which is the best way to deal with incoming change? Attack it as a threat or embrace it as an opportunity?

Optimism and hopefulness are, happily, traits common to most people, irrespective of race or gender. The more confidence we possess and the higher the sense of safety, the more we strive to "find ourselves". Some cultures have a high tolerance for these demonstrations of "Self", making it easier to experiment and maintain an open mind. Ultimately, the individual will progress from identifying Self with, arguably stereotypical, socially defined categories such as LGBT+ or BAME to being at one with their own uniqueness. The end of that voyage is an expressive society that is continuously evolving and learning. Other cultures demand

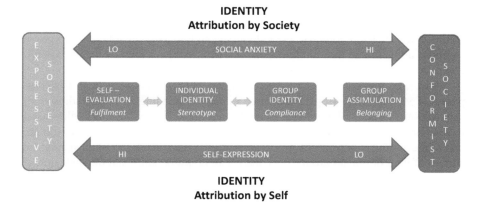

Fig. 1.2   The identity tension

conformity and compliance, leaving those who dare to change ostracised. Through social pressures composed of benefits and punishments, the individual may be persuaded into complete acceptance of group ethics and expectations in return for a safe harbour of acceptance and belonging. Conformist society offers security but demands loyalty and adherence to social conventions in return.

Society experiences individualistic behaviours as disruptive to its mores and norms, even potentially as a threat to the established order. In general, social pressures require members to conform to conventional behaviour and opinions, which we might call group or social ethics. The more members of society deviate from those norms, such as by embracing and exhibiting their uniqueness, the greater the friction between stability and change. Conformist society attributes esteem and success to those who abide by conventional ideas of good behaviour and merit. Suppose an individual wishes to be an accepted member of a conformist community. In that case, the cost of entry is to cease questioning group definitions of good citizenship and to alter behaviours and opinions to align with group expectations. Unless the individual prefers to be an outsider, a nomad wandering between communities, they have simple choices to make: which group do I wish to associate with, and to what degree do I want to belong? I can remain with the community I was raised in; I can migrate to one that requires me to change my persona; I can migrate to another, which identifies more closely with how I visualise myself. The ease with which these changes can be made is determined by the degree society identifies as expressive or conformist. Only in an expressive society where two or more communities are entirely tolerant or accepting one of the other will I be able to coexist in both as a unique individual.

In Fig. 1.2, we can see how tension arises when the individual and society strive in each of their direction. The individual in a conformist society can move from the safety and belonging provided by the community to a point where some individuality can be expressed, yet still remain within the limits of social norms and expectations. Once the individual moves beyond the restraining forces of convention, they may experience a greater sense of Self and individuality, but at the price of stereotypical labelling by conventional society, rendering the individual an outsider. Finally, if the confines of society are released, the individual can look beyond adherence to group identities altogether to find fulfilment on their own terms—a journey that is easier to complete in a society that would itself identify as expressive.

Society, be it expansive or conformist, is not entirely homogeneous. It is composed of various sub-groups, each more or less demanding in their traditions or expectations. Usually, the pressure to conform to these groups' norms applies itself independent of any power balance between communities. It matters little if you are part of the dominant or minority grouping. A person who decides to swim against the current of their dominant group peers and speak up for equality and the inclusion of outgroup minorities risks exclusion by those parts of privileged society that fear such change. Likewise, a member of an excluded minority who appears to invest themselves strongly in the ways of the majority culture may be viewed by those who fear the gradual erosion of their culture as a betrayal of their origins.

Father Michael Lapsley, a White ANC activist in apartheid South Africa, lost both his hands and an eye in a targeted letter bombing by the South African secret service in 1990. He is the living example of how "other White people thought of (me) as a race traitor and rebutted (me) because they saw my choices as a judgement on those they failed to take" [4].

1.5   Choosing Diversity: Choosing Destiny

Would it not be easier to let the "system" deal with it? After all, we pay our taxes and elect politicians to make the hard choices. The enlightened ingroup might nod their heads in support of social justice. The disadvantaged outgroup might accept the limitations placed on them, live in hope for changed circumstances for their children, and take comfort in their outgroup communities.

At the core of systemic racism is systemic apathy. In all societies, we allow our prejudice to get in the way of our best intentions, and when it does, we rationalise and justify our words and actions. In most societies, injustice against minorities causes hurt and pain leading to outrage and anger. Over time, most angry and ambitious victims of discrimination learn that their emotion only results in more obstacles, tears and rage. Discrimination safeguards the privileges of the dominant majority and removes agency from those who want to be recognised as equals. Systemic discrimination reduces or removes status in a broader, privileged society. At its worst, life for those so disadvantaged is safer and more comfortable when they temper their ambition, adopt compliant behaviours, and keep a low profile. It does not need to be so.

Some leaders inspire resistance to such pressures. Inspirational civil rights campaigners who set aside personal comfort and pleasures to pursue justice. Such people become leaders of conscience, some famous like Martin Luther King, Nelson Mandela, Father Michael Lapsley, and Rosa Parkes, who force through political and institutional change. Others, parents, teachers, officials, doctors or nurses, act as role models and change the lives of individuals, creating aspirations and the confidence sometimes required to break conventional expectations. Challenging the norms and expectations of dominant majorities is to swim against the current. It is not going to be easy.

In society, discrimination against those who offer different perspectives is a lost opportunity to grow and learn. To deliberately underestimate the abilities and contributions that individuals can make based on their skin colour, gender or sexuality, or the foreignness of their name or religion is to deny ourselves the value of their contribution. To change such attitudes in society is a mammoth task that will take a generation or two to achieve; within an organisation, it remains challenging, but not an impossibility. This book tries to explain why there is reason to hope, to try and to succeed.

The Organisational Opportunity

Organisational behaviour theory makes reference to human and social capital. Human capital concerns the capabilities and potential of the individual members of an organisation, or employees of a company in terms of their growth potential and value contribution. A worker is not "just like any other" worker. The individual is unique, and their specific qualities can be put to a "best use" in one or another role. In short, it considers the potential of diversity.

Equally, social capital is the environment in which that individual operates. It is the study of how to organise best to enhance the performance of the individual. To understand social capital is to understand how social interaction is influenced by organisational structure, to the point where it will hinder or facilitate collaboration between individuals. The social infrastructure that is in place frames the environment.

In a community of individuals, be it a village, town or city, there exists a social infrastructure. In a village, it may be based around religious centres or between landowners and tradespeople. In a city, it will be more complex and involve more and less wealthy communities split and classified according to a hierarchical class system. There will be many cultural collection points, and even ex-patriate communities may congregate around certain schools or traditional neighbourhoods. Organisations are not any different, but they are simpler to manage. For example, the Board of Directors can establish values and recruitment policies can selectively target candidates who agree to these values. Remuneration and reward systems can regulate and monitor behaviour, incentivise and punish contrarians, in a way that no free society would accept.

Those Who Dare, Win

Companies and organisations have a choice. They can follow the inclusive path of change and unknown opportunity or the path of least resistance, remaining within the known parameters of tradition and past success. The easiest route is the latter. We prefer the company of those who make us feel confident and secure; people of a similar disposition, background and politics. To break free of such instincts requires conviction, determination and courage.

If we choose for diversity, it will be a variety of reasons. Amongst them are fundamental principles of human rights and social justice, but also (as we will explore in Chap. 3) creativity, innovation, value creation and long-term success. We require determination and courage to take on the diversity challenge as diversity will bring change, and change will result in conflict.

Organising for Conflict

A student once replied to my question, "What is a conflict?" citing his grandfather: "A conflict is when you have two people in the same State". In other words, when you have two independent minds engaging, one with the other, and when the acts of one might impact the environment of the other, there is a conflict of interest.

Unmanaged, and without the right kind of leadership, differences in culture, upbringing, and even information sources will lead to a perception of conflict of interest. Often, there is a zero-sum game presumption where one will suffer if another is to benefit. As the majority group forms, they define the minority group. The dynamics between them will rest on the respective size and power that resides within them. The more powerful group will impose their will and define their laws in such a way as to diminish the real or the imagined threat of the less powerful. Michael Sandel argues that, in the USA, the so-called American Dream is a cruel illusion [5]. The privileged have defined merit in terms that build on what is already in their near-exclusive possession. The dominant group will fight to keep their advantage and suppress or distract the dominated. Consequently, those denied access to the "Dream" will look to each other for support and belonging instead. The lines are drawn; each group views the other as an adversary, and we start to search for differences to increase the gap between them, not to bridge it. As the Norwegian playwright, Henrik Ibsen, once said in his book, Peer Gynt: "To live is to war with trolls".

From Algorithm to Compassion

If our narrow interests lead us naturally to a path of conflict, we can progress past such strife by altering our understanding of our interests. Yuval Noah Harari argues that the ongoing Humanist Revolution in attitudes has redefined the formula for acquiring knowledge and understanding of our emotions and ethics [6]. He defines it as:

$$\text{Knowledge} = \text{Experiences} \times \text{Sensitivity}$$

He explains that our emotional reactions are triggered by recalling and relating personal experiences to what we observe. We apply memorised sensations with sensitivity (or empathy) to our observations. Harari argues that our past schooling and current mindset is still driven by the preceding Scientific Revolution formula for the acquisition of knowledge and understanding, namely:

$$\text{Knowledge} = \text{Empirical Data} \times \text{Mathematics}$$

Our society has arguably thrived on scientific, Newtonian thinking. Perhaps it has even protected us through its balanced calculation of mutually guaranteed nuclear destruction. But potentially, it has also prevented us from gaining the understanding and knowledge required to overcome fear, bias and prejudice relative to diversity. Suppose we are to see promise in our differences rather than competition and advance to the next level of humanity and prosperity. In that case, we must explore our experiences and emotions to find our answers. It is the task of leaders to open this unfamiliar path of enlightenment and guide us through it.

References

1. Accessed August 16, 2020, from https://www.theguardian.com/uk-news/ng-interactive/2020/jul/29/young-british-black-voices-behind-uk-anti-racism-protests-george-floyd#2
2. Gardner, H. (2011). *Frames of mind: The theory of multiple intelligences*. Basic Books.
3. Gardenswartz and Rowe. (2003). *Diverse teams at work*. SHRM.
4. Lapsley, M., & Karakashian, S. (2012). *Redeeming the past: My journey from freedom fighter to healer*. Orbis Books.
5. Sandel, M. (2020). *The Tyranny of merit*. Farrar, Strauss and Giroux.
6. Harari, Y. N. (2016). *Homo Deus*. Penguin Random House Press.

#TimesOfChange: Where Are We Now?

2

The time was 15:25 on 25 July 2020, close to the Government Quarter in Oslo, Norway. My cousin was seated in his office when a powerful explosion blew out his windows and damaged several ministerial offices around him, killing 8 people and injuring over 200. Happily, my cousin was not seriously hurt. Meanwhile, Reda and his mother were nearby.

> My mother and I were in town. We heard the explosion. Many windows were shattered, and we decided to get home as quickly as possible. On the way home, however, an ethnically White man in his forties came up to my mother and started screaming at her and harassing her, calling her "Terrorist! This is all your fault"; that we were responsible. All the time, I was standing next to her. What was I to do? This was a 40 to 50-year-old man. I was extremely angry, but at the same time so scared. It was the first time I experienced racism. [1]

We can cite examples of racist reactions all over the world. Some countries are said to be more inclusive than others. Norway is considered an equitable and tolerant country, but prejudice and bias surface there like anywhere else when fear strikes. In this case, the violence was perpetrated by a 32-year-old "home-grown" Norwegian White supremacist, who went on to massacre 77 teenagers and young adults at a political youth gathering sponsored by the centre-left Norwegian Labour Party on Utøya.

In such a manner do injustice and prejudice manifest themselves.

2.1 Things Are Getting Worse, Not Better

In the "White" sphere that predominates in the OECD, there is a disparity in how we see the world. The 40- to 50-year-old man who confronted Reda and his mother immediately concluded that a terrorist act must be the work of those of a different complexion and religion to his own. Although the Norwegian and White man who effected the attacks is clearly a terrorist in all senses of the word, it remains hard for domestic commentators to describe him directly as a terrorist. Even on the tenth

A. Smith-Meyer, *Unlocking the Potential of Diversity in Organisations*, Diversity and Inclusion Research, https://doi.org/10.1007/978-3-031-10402-2_2

anniversary of the 2011 attack, a Norwegian professor wrote an opinion piece for Aljazeera in which he fails to label the man directly as a terrorist. Although he references "terrorist acts" and "hate crime" to describe the horror, when speaking of the person he exclusively uses words like "extremist" or "perpetrator" to describe him [2]. This differentiation between White domestic "extremists" and "foreign" immigrant "terrorists" is not unusual. Yet, the oblivious majority of us claim to be "not racist".

The "Oblivious" in our societies say that they are "not racist", yet, as commented on by Professor Ibram Kendi, being "not racist" is a term that "signifies neutrality... [but] there is no neutrality in the racism struggle. The opposite of 'racist' isn't 'not racist.' It is 'antiracist.' ... One either endorses the idea of a racial hierarchy as a racist or racial equality as an antiracist." If so, we have to register that, regrettably, things are not improving for ethnic minorities seeking social equality and justice. While majority groups comfort themselves that they do not witness or "experience" the alleged racism taking place around them, minority groups experience how prejudice and bias constantly erect barriers to their progress and well-being.

For many minority populations to find purpose, love and a sense of belonging, they are forced to congregate in informally segregated communities; inadvertently increasing the feeling of isolation.

Those who believe the problem is surmountable or overstated are comforted by the knowledge that discrimination based on gender, race, creed or sexual inclination is illegal in many countries. They consider that we now compete on an equal footing; indeed, some complain of being disadvantaged due to affirmative action or quota hires as organisations and businesses try to balance numbers to appear more equitable. Yet, against a benchmark of a US Black employed working population equal to 12.3% of the total, only 4.1% of CEOs are Black. This compares to the 88.8% of CEOs who are White (77.7% of the working population). The comparable number for Hispanics is materially worse [3].

Certain professions, such as the law, appear remarkably backward in their diversity, registering only an 8.3% Black presence compared to 83% White. We can continue. At US finance companies, only 2.4% of executive committee members and 1.4% of managing directors are Black, even though 35% of Black Harvard Business School graduates work there [4]. In society generally, it is projected that the median wealth of Black families in the USA will fall to zero dollars by 2050; compare this to White families who might anticipate reaching $100,000 in the same time frame [5].

In most of Europe, even tracking ethnicity evokes memories of the Holocaust and is considered an invasion of privacy. Consequently, we do not have pan-European statistics comparable to those found in the USA. As a result, the racial dimension is far less visible or discussed. Many look at the USA and see a level of racial challenge we do not have in Europe, hence comforting ourselves that "our" issues are not a priority. Yet they are. The European ideals of human dignity, equality and human rights speak of a society without injustice, discrimination or systemic privilege. Unfortunately, the presumption amongst the privileged that words and aspirations are reflections of reality allows too many to practice a "racial blindness" that brushes institutional discrimination under the proverbial carpet. Social injustice is never fair, and an unjust society degrades trust over time—sometimes very rapidly.

Force and Counter-Force

In the twenty-first century so far, there have been few impactful "enlightened leaders" on the world stage; certainly, less than what one might consider necessary to create a "critical mass" able to overcome the forces that divide us. There have been prominent, frightening events such as the 2001 9/11 attack on New York, and subsequently others in Europe. We have witnessed the devastation of "wars against terror" in the Middle East, and civil wars in Syria, the Sudan and Ethiopia. The world has watched the anguish of modern campaigns of ethnic cleansing or genocide against Yazidis in Iraq, Rohingyas in Myanmar, Uighurs in China, and the continued plight of the Palestinians in Occupied Territories. In 2022 we have seen the return of war in Europe swiftly followed by an energy crisis. The financial and ensuing economic crisis of 2008/2009 and the current pandemic have provided fertile ground for political elements that thrive on uncertainty and hardship in otherwise stable societies. Whole countries have swerved towards protectionist and xenophobic policies in an attempt to "regain sovereignty"—to retreat to a comfortable "bubble" where we feel familiar, safe and "in control".

This tendency has manifested itself in a populist political backdrop in the USA and EU that is unusual, but not unprecedented. It produced a US movement that wanted to "Make America Great Again", to which we must ask, "Whose America?". In the UK, a nationalist government won an 80-seat parliamentary majority in 2019 with the promise to "take back control" and close borders to immigrants—a longing for days of empire perhaps, momentarily forgetting the inconvenience of legacy responsibility. Populists in France, Germany, Italy and the Netherlands, to mention but a few, want to reassert what it means to be . . . what? An exclusive stereotype of nationalists? Everywhere, the foreigner and the "other tribes" within society are seen as a threat rather than an opportunity. Some politicians are trying to show inclusive leadership, but the winds of exclusion and fear of change are resilient.

As discussed above, this retreat to the familiar increases suspicion of the less familiar and evolves into defensive attitudes. Sometimes this produces aggressive behaviours such as that evident in US racial and policing policy through the ages [6], the treatment of Syrian and other refugees in Europe since 2015, and White supremacist terror actions in places as far apart as Norway and New Zealand.

Occasionally, however, the usually silent and inactive majority of citizens who only want a "quiet life" see a threat to our rights and liberties in a broader perspective and react.

During the second quarter of 2020, conditions for a perfect storm of outrage formed. The combination of a social media blitz of US police and White violence towards Blacks, the hardship imposed on the underprivileged as a result of the COVID-19 lockdown, and the concurrent availability of time during a pandemic to reflect on what our social priorities ought to be, led to a sense of outrage at police profiling and violence, at racial discrimination and institutional injustice. The

#BlackLivesMatter movement of 2010 re-emerged in the USA and found echo chambers in Europe and around the world. People were justifiably angry; employees, customers, and citizens shouted, "Not on my patch/Not in my time".

In the meantime, observable trends are, as in the past, not showing future promise. Ongoing demonstrations in the USA are demanding change, but there is no public commitment to any concrete plan to alter the increasing wealth disparity between Black and White households. The outrage we witness in #BLM demonstrations and speeches is a necessary emotional reaction that generates counter-outrage and a hardening of discriminatory behaviours. Alas, time is not the healer in this case; it only dulls feelings of empathy and concern amongst those who are bystanders rather than victims. Already, in September 2020, the proportion of White Americans who considered racism a major problem slid from 45% in June to 33% [7]. The support shown, anger expressed; if the issue is not kept front and centre of our consciousness, life returns to normal.

2.2   Society, Organisations and Leadership

If we are to capture the angry energy evidenced on city streets across the world and convert this into a positive force for good, we need inspired and determined leadership. Not destructive and defensive leaders who wish to protect the status quo and defend past privilege against all challengers, but visionary leadership that looks beyond short-term gain or pain to a world that can thrive on diversity and broad-based community. We see some emergence of a new generation of leaders who appear to view the world in terms of opportunity rather than exclusion. Still, the forces they have to overcome remain powerful, fearful of change, and lean towards inertia.

In the absence of transparent and credible political leadership, corporate leaders are called upon to clarify where they stand on #BLM. Most conclude that they have little choice in the matter. In fear of judgement by stakeholders, they have no option but to "take the knee" in acknowledgement of the need to resist racism. However, this time, once they have said all the right things, they find eyes still resting upon them in anticipation of their next steps. The New York Times reported on US CEOs lining up to condemn racism, yet "many of the same companies have contributed to systemic inequality". Amazon calls for the equitable treatment of Black workers but is regularly accused of mistreating their mainly Black and Hispanic low-skilled workers. The US NFL now empathise with #BLM, but just months previously, the NFL barred Colin Kaepernick for "taking the knee" at its matches. L'Oreal tweets in 2020 that "Speaking out is worth it", yet only 3 years before, in 2017, fired their model, Munroe Bergdorf, for making waves against racism. There were just four Black executives in the Fortune 500 in 2020. None of the global financial giants like Bank of America, JPMorgan or Wells Fargo has Black managers in their leadership groups; nor could you find them in Silicon Valley amongst FaceBook, Google or Microsoft. Even Exxon, who boasted two Black board members, had no Black executives [8]. In the UK of 2020, the top 100 companies can only find 10 out of

297 chairpersons, CEOs and CFOs who are Black or Minority Ethnic—indeed, there was not one CEO amongst them [9].

Beautiful words penned by the brand management or public relations departments fall today on sceptical ears—for corporates to feign indignation is a dangerous game. The Millennial and GenZ populations are rapidly taking hold of society, and they are as rigid in their expectations as they are unforgiving. To gain their trust, you have to prove your authenticity; if you lose their confidence, you will struggle to regain it. Brand management is no longer a marketing game; it is a manifestation of character [10].

2.3 Opening Doors to Diversity

Intersectionality is the experience of being subject to overlapping forms of prejudice and discrimination. Imagine for an instant the plight of the Black women trying to make their career in almost every sector in Western society. We have been struggling to overcome gender bias for generations. Yet, mainstream consultancies still publish studies and promote actions designed to balance male and female representation in management and boards. Being Black only compounds the bias and discrimination women face.

In the global tech industry in 2019, women already had a well-known uphill struggle to manifest a presence, registering only 7.5% of the population of professional developers. Imagine then the likelihood of encountering a woman amongst the 3.1% of developers who are Black, or the 7.3% who are Hispanic. Consider the isolation of the Black woman, who in any given meeting can expect to be the only woman present, if not also the only Black person. Ask yourself if that might not subdue the enthusiasm of even the brightest talent to speak up or express ideas that are "out-of-the-box".

A recent study of lawyers, architects and engineers found that whereas only 15% of White men feel they have to work twice as hard as others to gain recognition; 71% of the few Black women employed there do. The argument is that when confronted with Black or Minority Ethnic employees, White spaces are influenced by stereotypical expectations when evaluating their potential. In doing so, a White supervisor may well interpret the behaviour of their subordinate in terms of their stereotypical caricature (e.g. the angry Black woman). Hence, Black women find they need to balance assertiveness with deference to a far greater extent than White women. One Black biology professor commented about her own career experience "Isolation . . . you don't know who you can trust . . . And its alienating—this has been a very lonely life" [11].

Diversity cannot live up to its promise in the presence of isolation; the isolated Black woman has no room to thrive. A 2020 study by the United Nations measured team success as a factor of differing levels of diversity. The all-male teams provided the comparative baseline, indicating the delivery of better quality decisions relative to individuals 58% of the time. Where gender diversity existed, the study showed that the chances of better decisions improved to 73% of the time; teams that were diverse in terms of age, gender and geography outperformed 87% of the time [12].

The Merit Aristocracy

Human Resource departments find the best-qualified candidates to suit the skills and personality profiles needed to meet business objectives successfully. To do so, HR professionals pay attention to profile ideal candidates accurately. It is only fair and just to presume that they do so without any intentional gender, sexual or racial preference.

Subsequently, recruiting managers are entitled to expect a list of interview subjects based purely on merit. However, if this is the case, why do we find so few Black or other minority colleagues in so many of our organisations? An analysis of the UK FTSE 350 prepared for the Parker Review 2020 showed that, indeed, the commitment to increasing diversity is typically accompanied by assurances that this will be achieved by prioritising merit in the appointment process. The presumption is that in placing merit before ethnicity, gender, sexual preferences, religion or skin colour, then bias will be overcome. Would it be that simple? As late as September 2020, Charles W. Scharf, the CEO of Wells Fargo, perpetuated the myth of unqualified diversity candidates when he said, "While it might sound like an excuse, the unfortunate reality is that there is a very limited pool of black talent to recruit from" [13]. Could it be that our definition of "merit" is prejudiced? After all, the HR professional who diligently authors a recruitment profile is producing the equivalent of an algorithm. A skills-based profile is meant to weed out prejudice. There is a problem, however. Whereas an algorithm is somehow presumed to be impartial, the programme is still written by a human who is both emotional and unconsciously prejudiced. As these programmers are dominated by authors who are part of the elite majority using definitions of talent, qualifications and merit accessible only to that elite, the algorithm will perpetuate a privileged view of competence. To coin a favourite phrase: An algorithm is but prejudice expressed in numbers.

The much-vaunted "American Dream" is that anyone who works hard enough can make it to the top. Regrettably, it is all too easy to disprove the thesis. "Merit" entails going to the best schools, having the most influential networks in higher social circles, and access to meaningful internships and expensive graduate education. Thus defined, those who are not born with privilege or parents with means face a ceiling far lower than the glass one so often spoken of in gender diversity forums. Too many minority groups are denied opportunity and upward mobility. Black recruits are still described as "diversity hires" in too many prestigious institutions. Too often, the opportunity to try and break a glass ceiling seems like a privilege itself. Take a firm that repeats the mantra "we only hire the best", do they not mean they only hire from the "best" schools? The Human Resource officer outlining the next recruitment qualification profile does not intend to discriminate against underrepresented talent; they do not need to. The restricted accessibility of the "best schools" that face less privileged minorities does the discriminating for them.

Even the University Entrance Officer selecting the "best students" is not, necessarily, exercising any prejudice against any underprivileged talent that would benefit from a place at the school. Many minority students apply, get accepted then withdraw due to financial or family restraints linked to socio-economic circumstances. To fulfil the American Dream, we need to have a precondition of level playing fields. Some countries are closer to this than others, but only in utopia does it exist [14].

Indeed, it is estimated that only one-third of today's graduates gain access to jobs that directly lead to what one might term "successful careers". What distinguishes these "Sprinters" from students who take longer to build the credibility and experience needed to access these "golden" job opportunities is that (1) 80% had at least one internship and (2) had accumulated less than $10,000 in student loan debt. Students who enjoy less financial support from their families and have to work their way through university, or experience other disruptions to their education, enjoy far less success than their peers. Consider that research shows that Black graduates aged 22–27 are twice as likely as White students to be unemployed, or that in 2017 less than 50% of Black and Hispanic students in the USA completed their degrees in the stipulated 4-year term. A picture of systemic denial of opportunity starts to form. "Merit" is no longer a definition of personal achievement; it is a measure of the quality of opportunity granted to the individual. As opportunity is a matter of privilege, and privilege begets privilege, we can see the logic of the term "Merit Aristocracy" as coined by Michael Sandel in his book "The Tyranny of Merit".

Life on the Career Ladder

Using the analogy of the career ladder, we might describe the experience of the aspiring minority professional: Where there is prejudice or privilege, there is a qualitative difference in the ladder made available to excluded minorities and that made available to the included majority. In some countries, one might even describe the ladder available to ethnic minorities as both rickety and shorter.

Imagine for a moment the life circumstances and social pressures facing a Black professional trying to make a success of themselves in the USA of 2020. Anré Williams, an experienced 55-year-old Senior Executive at American Express, expresses it thus: "at times I feel terrified about the things that could happen to me or to my friends or to my relatives or to my son in a world which sometimes is completely unpredictable. You just don't know how things can go sideways sometimes when they shouldn't" [15].

For any human being to grow and develop, they need to find confidence in their ability and trust that their environment is fundamentally just and safe. As long as we have societies and organisations that have not learnt to be inclusive of diversity, it will be a struggle for the excluded to get a foot in the door. It will require an extra degree of courage and determination for the "outsider" to risk the confrontation caused by facing down stereotypical expectations of the "ingroup". For any excluded minority, it is often considered more sustainable to conform to the majority's behavioural expectations and keep a low profile; it is better to build security than to aim for self-actualisation.

Anré Williams again: "Remaining silent, in a way, is almost an implicit acknowledgement that you're OK with the way things are and you're just going to ignore it. And people aren't comfortable ignoring it anymore or allowing it to be ignored. And that's what's different right now, I think".

References

1. Forklart podcast. (2020, July 24). Fem historier om rasisme i Norge. *Aftenposten*.
2. aljazeera.com. (2021, July 26). *Norway ten years after the Utøya massacre*. An Opinion published.
3. US Bureau of Labor Statistics web site. Accessed October 6, 2020.
4. Mayo, A. J., & Roberts, L. M. (Eds.). (2019). *Pathways to Leadership*. Harvard Business Review Press.
5. Roberts, L. M., & Mayo, A. J. (2019, November). *Advancing black leaders*. Harvard Business Review.
6. *American Police*. An NPR "Throughline" podcast of 4 June 2020. https://www.npr.org/2020/0 6/03/869046127/american-police
7. Henderson, F. A., & Kinias, Z. (2020, September 24). Understanding the origins of white denial. *INSEAD Knowledge*.
8. Gelles, D. (2020, June 6). Corporate America has failed Black America. *NYT*.
9. Partridge, J. (2021, February 3). FTSE 100 firms have no black executives in top three roles. *The Guardian*.
10. Francis, T., & Hoefel, F. (2018, November 12). *True Gen: Generation Z and its implications for companies*. McKinsey & Company Insights.
11. Williams, J. (2020, June 12). Companies have the tools to fight racism. Will they use them? *Bloomberg*.
12. UN Technology Innovations Lab. *Inclusion & diversity: Tech it or leave IT*. Accessed July 10, 2020.
13. McEvoy, J. (2020, September 23). Wells Fargo CEO apologizes for saying there's a 'limited pool of Black talent'. *Forbes.com*.
14. Sandel, M. (2020). *The Tyranny of merit*. Farrar, Strauss and Giroux.
15. Abelson, M., Basak, S., Butler, K., Leising, M., Surane, J., & Tan (2020, August 3). The only one in the room. *Bloomberg*.

#DiversityRocks: Why Do We Care?

3

> *A conversation between a peasant, a priest and a physician*
> *may produce novel ideas that would never emerge from a*
> *conversation between three hunter-gatherers.*
> Yuval Noah Harari
> —*Homo Deus*

3.1 Diversity and Inclusion: Two Words, Two Concepts

Let us, for a moment, consider what we are discussing. In any given organisation, we will generally have members drawn more or less from heterogeneous backgrounds. The degree to which diversity is deemed present or not is determined by the extent to which there is a presence of individuals who think differently from the dominant majority. Female presence on a board previously labelled as "Pale, Male, and Stale" will alter both the nature and content of the debate. Bringing Asian, Latino or African perspectives to an all-White US or European committee will broaden the scope of the discussion immeasurably.

To have an inclusive culture is not defined by diversity, however. An organisational culture can be more or less open to challenge, debate and an exchange of views and opinions. In an autocratic environment, a strong and commanding leader may quash opposing views by punishing any opposition to their ideas and thereby scoring very low on any scale of inclusiveness. On the other hand, if speaking up, challenge and discussion are encouraged and rewarded, the level of confidence and trust will be high, and the culture may qualify as inclusive.

Hence, diversity and inclusion are not symbiotic twins. As depicted in Fig. 3.1, they can both exist separately. Yet to pursue one without the other conspires to promote only the stagnating effects of inertia or mono-directional thinking, whereas the organisation seeks innovation and improvement. In the diagram below, we consider what happens with the various combinations of diversity and inclusion.

© The Author(s), under exclusive license to Springer Nature Switzerland AG 2022
A. Smith-Meyer, *Unlocking the Potential of Diversity in Organisations*, Diversity and Inclusion Research, https://doi.org/10.1007/978-3-031-10402-2_3

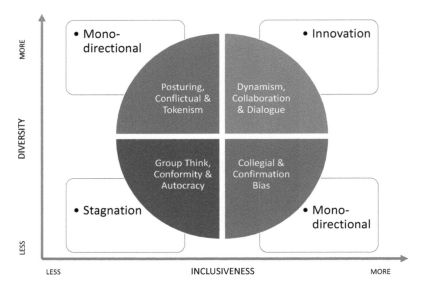

Fig. 3.1 The interaction of diversity and inclusion

- *Groupthink* is the nightmare scenario for any organisational behaviouralist. It is an environment with no diversity and a lack of inclusiveness or tolerance of alternative opinions and questions. In Groupthink environments, the boss' diktats go unchallenged. Immersed in a world that reflects only the thoughts of a narrowly selected leadership, the company will likely have a diminished capacity to identify changing circumstances. Its focus will tend to be on past success. It risks either stagnation and being overtaken by innovative competitors or over-confidently embarking on impulsive and risky projects leading to inevitable accidents.
- *Confirmation culture* is where we still exclude outsiders with their disruptive views, but we enjoy a high degree of trust and collegiality. The greater openness to debate will likely ensure that broader questions will be raised and discussed. Still, with the absence of genuinely different perspectives, the thought process of members will be similar. Despite the greater openness to debate, the communality of prejudices and perpetuation of commonly held beliefs will reduce the incidence of challenge and have little beneficial impact on outcomes. Potentially, external developments and internal problems will be identified and solutions found—however, the bias will be to stay on the tried and trusted track and continue on the conviction born of past success and proven solutions. Falling into the trap of confirmation bias will be easier. Even though stagnation may be avoided, the blinkered vision of an undiversified decision-making group will likely render perspectives and debates mono-directional.
- *Tokenism* is a culture whereby diversity is sought and tolerated for appearances only. Diverse opinions and initiative are not encouraged, and the prevailing

culture of the dominating, non-inclusive leadership will prevail. Diverse elements will adopt customary behaviours or, like their majority group colleagues, be expected not to complain. Suppose a company has decided that there must be an appearance of diversity. In that case, they will probably understand and even accept that different views may well be expressed, but they will pay scant attention to unconventional viewpoints. If the company is less inclusive, then experimentation and creative thinking will not be given room for development and will be stymied. A broader understanding of external changes and the risks and opportunities that diversity brings may help avoid the risk of stagnation and reduce tendencies to act impulsively and recklessly. However, innovation will not be able to flourish, and once again, mono-directional thinking is the most likely outcome.

– *Dynamism* resulting from the encouragement of inclusive dialogue and constructive challenge, along with a highly diverse decision-making college, will take the small gains seen in the Tokenism quarter and open the doors to creativity and innovation. The inclusive environment will encourage the exchange of knowledge permitted in the aforementioned confirmation culture. Contrarywise, now it will be between diverse individuals with mutual respect for each other and who bring different perspectives and understandings to identify solutions sought by the organisation. It is only by encouraging high levels of diversity and inclusion in combination that we will achieve higher rates of innovation and improvement.

Diversity and Inclusion: Go Together Like a Horse and Carriage

Pursuing diversity without effective inclusion is tokenism and potentially worse than ignoring the issue. Some organisations have erroneously believed that the correct response to criticism caused by a lack of female, LGBT+ or Black representation amongst its board members or management ranks is (say) to recruit a token woman of colour. In doing so, they demonstrate that they have understood neither the nature of discrimination nor the value of diversity. What happens? The company determines to address the criticism by recruiting the best-qualified minority candidates available, but does not consider what qualities that employee may bring to the firm. To the company, an analyst is an analyst; an engineer is an engineer. It expects to carry on just as before. This company asks its new minority recruit to adopt the mindset and behaviours of the existing majority and not to "rock the boat" by challenging established attitudes and perceptions. If a Black hire is recruited for diversity reasons, but without any understanding of the need for inclusiveness, there is no room for that person's personal growth, nor any acceptance that different perspectives add value. Indeed, one might argue that the most likely applicant and recruit may be the "diversity" candidate who complies most closely with dominant group behaviours.

Before becoming a successful entrepreneur, Jared Johnson joined JPMorgan Chase & Co as an associate in 2015. His witness statement of his time on Wall Street was: "What they were doing was almost training you to learn the language, learn the customs. We were taught and groomed how to operate in a White corporate world. People are very resistant to give up any elements, traditions of the White corporate American culture to make room for something that looks different" [1]. Jared understood he had to alter his behaviour and mirror the demeanour of the dominant culture to gain acceptance and achieve success, but the need went beyond relationship building. The intent was to hide who he, himself, actually was— it was not to connect with his White colleagues on any emotional level.

If the move to increase diversity is viewed as positive discrimination rather than explained as a strategic shift in mindset and creativity, then the reaction of those now seemingly denied opportunities simply to make room for a previously "uninvited guest" will be one of resentment. Curtis Johnson, Managing Director in Carlyle Group Inc., said of his time at Lehman Brothers: "I think I sort of got rammed down their throat, frankly, as a diversity hire. They were resentful, and it didn't matter that I was talented and as ready to work as anyone. I walked into a situation where I felt very much attacked and disliked from the beginning . . . it was really unwelcoming".

3.2   "Time to Change Course, Captain": Introducing Change

In 2019, a United Nations report remarked on the role of diversity and inclusion in the world of information technology as follows: "Smart for your business today, vital for your success tomorrow" [2]. This report, focusing on IT, is only one of many that highlight the benefits of exposing minds to ideas derived from different perspectives, backgrounds and traditions. The numbers may vary, but they all point in the same direction, be it relative to financial results, financial stability, employee engagement or innovation [3].

Although the notion of "lower quartile" indicates non-diverse companies, it is a relative term and may still include companies that enjoy a degree of diversity. A thought-provoking conclusion of McKinsey & Company in its 2020 study was that companies in the top quartile for both gender and ethnic diversity are 12% more likely to outperform all other companies [4]. If the promise of such rich returns is not persuasive enough in itself, the numbers can be viewed from the other side of the coin. If your competition is better at diversity and inclusion than you are, then it is much more likely that your business will fail or be acquired by one of them.

Indeed, recent studies show that the competitive advantage of diverse companies relative to those who lag behind increases over a 5-year period. The disadvantage for the lower quartile, less gender-diverse company, augmented from minus 9% in 2014 to minus 19% in 2019. The premium afforded ethnically diverse companies relative to those less diversified (again top versus bottom quartile) remains even higher at 36% (compared to gender diversity of 25%). Interestingly, whereas the advantage of gender-diverse companies is growing, this does not appear to be the case for ethnically diverse companies. The explanation is likely found in the observation that public sentiment towards diversity on social media is relatively high (52% positive), whereas sentiment on inclusion is the opposite at 61% negative. It seems that the inclusion of women who belong to the same ethnicity face less resistance than the inclusion of other ethnic minorities, be they men or women. The struggle for gender equality, ongoing since granting women the vote, has lasted over 100 years. This compares to the "only" five or so decades since the US civil rights movement's breakthrough. Add the still modest population size of racial minorities in Western industrialised countries, and it is perhaps no surprise that inclusion for People of Colour within White society lags disappointingly behind that of women?

Diversity is not necessarily, if ever, comfortable. When everyone makes the same assumptions and has similar expectations of outcome, decisions and life are more straightforward, but rarely better. In his book "Noise: A flaw in human judgement", the Nobel Memorial prize-winning Professor Daniel Kahneman explores and explains the inefficiency of the decision-making of the single individual [5]. On our own, we are inaccurate and erratic. Combined with others who challenge and offer alternative solutions and answers, we discover that we are more accurate and consistent when acting as a group. Both intuitively and through numerous studies, we can understand that under the challenge of diverse teams, we are more likely to reexamine facts consistently and remain objective. Working with people who think differently will challenge our logic and assumptions, thereby overcoming inertia, surpassing mono-directional thinking and leading to ever-better reasoning and performance. We leave the rationale of "good enough" behind and strive instead for continuous improvement [3].

To Rock the Boat ... or Not

It seems intuitive that it can never be a mistake to "do your best", to "put your best foot forward", or to "be the best version of yourself". Indeed, it seems to be a successful formula for personal growth and career prospects among friends and like-minded colleagues. Yet, how does the "majority" react to talent and wisdom emerging from an unexpected source, one that is "foreign", an "outsider", an "upstart"?

Most societies organise themselves with a hierarchy—in some countries, there is an open reference to class systems. There has been a long tradition in the UK, for example, to reference the aristocratic, upper, middle and lower or working classes. In other countries such as India, there is a formalised and very rigid caste system, ranging from the intellectual Brahmins down to the manual workers of the Shudras and the lowest of the low, the Dalits or the Untouchables. In either social system, these labels impose barriers between the various levels. In any class system, an individual from a lower class who dares to raise their voice against, or even in support of someone from a higher class is considered to have spoken out of turn. The "upper classes" do not expect a person from the "lower classes" to have any capacity or ability to "perform" at an equivalent level to themselves. For a member of the lower echelons of society to raise their voice, therefore, attracts danger. They risk being dismissed as insignificant or even derided as a "pretender". In such circumstances, the "outsider" risks drawing attention to themselves for no gain, or worse, even being bullied or punished for their audaciousness.

Yuval Harari introduced me to the term WEIRD countries: Western, Educated, Industrialised, Rich Democracies. It is not only an attention-grabbing play on words, but one can discern how WEIRD values, customs and traditions have dominated, and continue to dominate, the global discourse on perceptions of right and wrong. Unfortunately, this also extends to our prejudices and stereotypical expectations of what is conventional and natural. We welcome creativity and imagination as long as it emanates from sources we feel close to and comfortable with—but when it emerges from unexpected quarters, it is often perceived as threatening and disruptive.

3.3   Citizenship . . . But for Whom?

WEIRD societies often claim that values of equality, brotherhood, justice and human rights are universal and applied without bias. At least, they boast legal provisions to protect against discrimination. Yet, even in 2020, social media is replete with observations of "mansplaining" put-downs of better-qualified women, of male-dominated panels of experts, of glass ceilings and gender-based differences in pay scales. If this is still the case for women in WEIRD countries, we can surmise we have an even greater distance to go for people who identify as LGBT+ or People of Colour.

In a society where there is a division between the majority who are "naturally" in charge and a minority who are not yet considered "worthy" of inclusion, not only will the interests of the "outsider" be less represented, but they will also be less willing to take the risk of exploring them. Therefore, it is only a natural survival strategy to stay out of the limelight when in unfamiliar or unfriendly territory and express confidence and creativity only within the confines of "your own community".

A closed and conformist society upholds the status quo. A society that is expansive and confident in its ability to absorb and make the best of new ideas is generally regarded as an "open" society, willing to embrace new ideas and perspectives. In such an environment, new ideas and voices are encouraged; even from unexpected, minority sources. It is somewhat ironic that many countries frequently perceive themselves as "open", yet erect barriers to change. Under the guise of promoting the stability and predictability associated with long-term prosperity, society often pass laws and pursue policies that encourage the maintenance of the status quo instead, introducing an institutional bias against change and acceptance of "the other". Do those who hold institutional power favour upholding values supporting the status quo by closing the door on new entrants, or leaving it open to new but potentially disruptive ideas?

If the "minority voice" feels safe expressing its ideas, we might expect its volume to increase. A US study looking at the number of patents filed by Black inventors between 1870 and 1940 showed that during the many periods of increased racial violence and lawlessness, Black inventors registered significantly fewer patents than in periods of relative racial tolerance. To paraphrase the author of the study, Lisa

Cook, "if there is something that impedes the rate of arrival of ideas, you're going to impede progress. It's not just for a short period, and it's not just for Black people. This is a cautionary tale for all economies and businesses". If we agree that invention and innovation are generally good for prosperity, financial success and social well-being, then any obstacle preventing such progress is damaging and undesirable. In short, openness to new ideas is beneficial; hence exposure to new perspectives derived from the inclusiveness of diverse opinions should be welcomed. Why then, are we so fearful of change?

Better Safe Than Sorry?

Daniel Kahneman, popularised the dual processing theory: the assertion that the human species has a two-speed brain that applies two systems to decision-making. System 1 is the most primitive, unconscious and automatic part of the brain that drives most of our behaviour and physical activity. We might call it our wits; it is what we depend most on for survival. System 2 is the "rational" part of the brain that develops both ideas and logic. It requires consciousness and, therefore, more time to process the complex notions it is designed for. The theory stipulates that System 1 dominates and executes the majority of our decisions. We might hope that when System 2 is activated, it would use its cognitive and logical ability to override the possibly prejudiced urges of System 1. Kahneman concludes that more often than not, System 2 seeks to rationalise System 1 preferences instead by creating a narrative that suits it [6].

Consequently, if System 1 is the primary driver of our decision-making, itself designed to detect things such as the danger in the outline of shadows and tone of voice, then we have to understand that bias is built-in to the workings of the brain as it responds to the stimuli that trigger a reaction. The less we have to think about our observations, the more deep-seated or unconscious our bias will become. Neurological researchers have made it their business to uncover how our deductive abilities are influenced by the manner it receives information; indeed, it is changing how both products are marketed and how political ideas are presented to us. The stimuli recipes of persuasion are alarmingly simple, triggered as they are by self-interest, a preference for clear-cut and straightforward choices, and emotions inspired by images or personal desires (amongst others) [7].

Hence, it is not surprising that our natural preference is to be prudent and make sure we do not lose what we already have. If we are to be persuaded to take the risk of opportunity, our primal senses need to be excited at the prospect. We need to view the path to opportunity as unobstructed and clear, and our evaluation of benefit over cost must be straightforward. The rewards and gains of diversity may be argued using studies and complex statistical calculations. However, the images of Islamic terrorism, cheap foreign labour "taking our jobs", or the greedy "1%" are far more captivating concepts to our primal brains.

3.4   Forces for D&I: The Focus on Change

So far, in this chapter, we have looked at the benefits on offer from diversity and inclusion ("D&I"). We have also sought to explain why it seems unnatural and difficult for us to take advantage of something that, intellectually, appears attractive. Fear of the consequences and the discomfort of change dominate individual attitudes. Accepting diversity is to open the door to strangers who might challenge our personal advantage for promotions, attention and even love. To be inclusive of their ideas will complicate our mission and disrupt our stability. As individuals, we risk losing our reputation as go-to experts in the organisation; we may have to learn new concepts and adopt new attitudes in our problem-solving. That we experience resistance to change is not unexpected, yet gradually we see D&I growing as an organisational priority. It warrants a moment of consideration to understand why; and where it is taking us.

Basic Change Management Theory explains that change requires impulses either from inside or outside the organisation. For example, internal drivers of change relative to diversity might include a real need for fresh ideas or a push from demographic changes in employee attitudes; perhaps a rising intolerance of observed injustice on the grounds of gender, sexual preference, race or physical ability. External drivers might include the opening of new markets or an increasing clamour by consumers or investors for corporate responsibility, action against pollution, climate or human rights. The driver may even be new legislation and regulation introduced by politicians sensing a change in electoral views and expectations.

Currently, we have an increasing number of stakeholders demanding greater transparency and evidence that business is delivering products and services without incurring disproportionate, if any, harm to the environment or society. Simultaneously, the meaning of environment and society is expanding both in terms of scope and reach. Anti-pollution measures or carbon emissions are no longer being measured for local impact only, but now is viewed in terms of global impact and deforestation, recyclability of products and water management. Social impact is no longer limited to the welfare of employees and the satisfaction of customers. It also concerns communities near and far, including the non-discrimination of gender, LGBT+ or race, and accessibility and fairness for those previously considered non-target clients.

This demand for accountability is forcing organisations to conduct social auditing of their activities.[1] Accusations of "window-dressing" or "green-washing" have raised the call for transparency to evidence claims previously made in slick advertising or public relations exercises. If it is not already, "green-washing" is a strategy soon to be consigned to the history books. Companies are also having to engage in social accounting to meet requirements for non-financial reporting and other

---

[1] A Social Audit focusses primarily on non-financial issues, is prepared for all stakeholders (not only shareholders) and is largely voluntary, although regulation and legislation for quoted companies is becoming more normal.

Environment, Social and Governance ("ESG") standards being introduced. Invest-ment analysis reports and legislation such as the European Union's Non-Financial Reporting Directive have made this a reality [8]. However, more than being viewed as an imposed necessity, increasingly companies are beginning to understand that not monitoring and addressing environmental and social performance is risking the displeasure of a broad range of stakeholders. The information gathered in a social audit is becoming helpful in identifying business risks and other potential problems that can harm the organisation and its stakeholders [9]. Millennials and Generation Z are influencing their parents' opinions and raising the bar of accountability of firms in terms of impact on the planet and people. As a result, the risk and cost of reputational loss are rising; to a point where the price of auditing, transparency and repair is worth paying.

Arguments against social auditing often refer to inadequate information systems, poor quality or insufficient information. This objection no longer holds water. The surveillance economy is not only directed at consumers but also at producers. Where we find a reluctance to introduce social audits, we will find those who are lagging in risk management practices. Still, at its heart, we will also find a fear of consequence and discomfort at the prospect of being obliged to make the necessary changes resulting from social auditing [10].

Times; They Are a-Changing

In a report written in November 2018, McKinsey breaks down the trends in consumer behaviours by generation, underlining a message that marketing circles have been discussing for the past decade [11]. I am of the Baby-Boomer age. We were raised to respect authority, to focus on the greater good rather than personal profit. To an extent, we might have been classified as naïve idealists too prone to believe what those in authority told us. When respected brands told us that their washing powder washed whiter, we tended to give them the benefit of the doubt. We had a positivity bias that emboldened us to believe that, even though we knew that the advertising we saw was intended to sway our purchasing decisions, a brand would not brush the harm a product might cause us under the carpet. Surely, the company we trusted would never act in a way that would be detrimental to its clients?

Generation Z (those born post-1999 to the present day) are different. They see a world that has been damaged economically by global actors who were supposed to be well-educated and responsible leaders. Financial geniuses failed to protect their old age pensioners and retail savers from financial harm, leading to the 2008/2009 financial crash and a decade or more of austerity. Politicians mandated to care for our future well-being appear to have had more concern for their careers and retention of power at the next election. A generation of industry has led our planet to the edge of environmental and climatic disaster. GenZ has due reason to be concerned, sceptical and demanding. McKinsey describes this future generation of consumer power as anchored around one principle: The search for truth. Sean Pillot de Chenecey wrote the 2019 book "The Post-Truth Business" around this phenomenon [12]. The writing is on the wall.

> GenZers value individual expression and avoid labels. They mobilise themselves for a variety of causes. They believe profoundly in the efficacy of dialogue to solve conflicts and improve the world. Finally, they make decisions and relate to institutions in a highly analytical and pragmatic way.
>
> (Francis & Hoeffel [11])

Where Baby Boomers are described as romantic, revolutionary and collectivist, McKinsey labels GenZ as in a limitless pursuit of uniqueness and ethical outcomes. In addition, they signal a shift in the priorities of Millennials whose hereto hedonistic tendencies are being turned. Perhaps it is an increasing concern for the future looming for their children, or even just enlightened self-interest in, for example, saving the planet and our democratic freedoms. Any company looking out for its future success has to realise that if they cannot address the piercing questions of GenZ, and increasingly those of the Millennials, while others do—then they are condemning their organisations to oblivion within a decade.

> Marketeers used to concentrate on the four P's, i.e. Product, Promotion, Place, Price. . . .
> Now marketeers need to focus on the three E's:
> – Engage (Listen to what they tell you. Be part of the conversation. Be a presence in your fans' lives),
> – Equip (Give them reasons to talk about your products and service),
> – Empower (Give consumers different ways to talk and share).
>
> (Pillot de Chenecey [12])

Perhaps it is time to listen to the younger generation; before the competition does?

References

1. Abelson, M., Basak, S., Butler, K., Leising, M., Surane, J., & Tan (2020, August 3). The only one in the room. *Bloomberg*.
2. UN Technology Innovations Lab. *Inclusion & diversity: Tech it or leave IT*. Accessed July 10, 2020.
3. Rock, D., & Grant, H. (2016, November). Why diverse teams are smarter. *Harvard Business Review*.
4. Hunt, V., Prince, S., Dixon-Fyle, S., & Dolan, K. (2020, May). *Diversity wins*. Mckinsey.
5. Kahneman, D., Sibony, O., & Sunstein, C. (2021). *Noise: A flaw in human judgement*. Little, Brown Spark.
6. Kahneman, D. (2011). *Thinking, fast and slow*. Farrar, Straus & Giroux.
7. Morin, C., & Renvoise, P. (2018). *The persuasion code*. Wiley.
8. *The Non-Financial Reporting Directive – Directive 2014/95/EU*. European Union taking effect in March 2021.

9. Crane, A., & Matten, D. (2016). *Business ethics*. Oxford University Press.
10. Williams, J. (2020, June 12). Companies have the tools to fight racism. Will they use them? *Bloomberg*.
11. Francis, T., & Hoefel, F. (2018, November 12). *True Gen: Generation Z and its implications for companies*. McKinsey & Company Insights.
12. de Chenecey, S. P. (2019). *The post-truth business*. Kogan Page Publishers.

Part II

Identifying the Scale of the Challenge

In Part I, we visited the conflict between social order and individual self-expression, between society's demands for community-led compliance, uniformity and stability, and the potential benefits that can accrue to the individual who is allowed to seek personal fulfilment. However, creating room for diversity is not the same as being inclusive. Indeed, the pressures within society and organisations to establish order and stability tend to define group norms in ways that often lead to exclusion.

For the discerning and thinking person, this reality is hard to comprehend or accept. Surely, we reason, the informed man or woman on the street will recognise and act against unfairness or injustice when it occurs. It is in our self-interest to ensure others are treated fairly if we wish to be treated fairly ourselves. Yet, prejudice and discrimination persist, and onlookers remain passive. Suppose we are to change behaviours and mindsets. In that case, we must understand the drivers of inequality and the apparent conscience-free discrimination we witness about us— if we choose to see it. In this Part II, we shall be exploring the causes and drivers of prejudice and discrimination that appear to thrive despite our claims to high ethics and conscience.

The individual's understanding of what constitutes ethical and expected behaviour is the product of many influences. Our moral values as individuals are born of our background and upbringing. It comprises what we have been taught and what we have observed as real-world values that impact our lives and relationships. This primary and individual ethical perception will change over time in line with our knowledge and experience. However, the most critical influences on our beliefs and behaviours will be those imposed on us, firstly by society and secondly by those organisations and groups we interact with. Hence, we experience a continuous exchange of influences between the individual, community and organisations, the three dimensions of ethical values constantly in competition with each other.

In the following discussion, we will consider the societal elements that drive ethical behaviours and consider them in the light of their implications on the creation of an appropriate approach to formulating an effective D&I governance, strategy and policy.

BirdsOfaFeatherFlockTogether: Living Apart Together

4

4.1 The Barriers That Separate Us: See, Hear and Speak No Evil

Ms. Ursula Burns qualifies as a success for most people, irrespective of background. As CEO of Xerox for 6 years, she was the first Black female CEO of a Fortune 500 company, is the chairwoman of the telecommunications company, VEON, and a member of the board at Uber [1]. Yet, despite having been welcomed into the executive ranks of leading companies, it is apparent that Ms. Burns still feels an outsider within the society into which she is so closely integrated. At Davos, Switzerland, in 2018, she stated: "I dress like the one per cent. I drive like the one per cent. I wear watches and jewellery like the one per cent. (Yet) I worry every day if a policeman is near me. They look at me as first and foremost a threat to their place in society".

By dint of her qualifications and experience, Ursula Burns meets all aspects of merit, no matter who defines what that is. She slides easily in and out of corporate settings, irrespective of gender or race considerations. Ms. Burns is accepted as an equal and valued member of the groupings she works and socialises with. Within the organisational context, her professional avatar is safe, yet, outside this safe space, societal prejudice is so strong, the division between "them and us" so prevalent, that she is nervous around officers of the law. Our instinct to stereotype is so powerful that we cannot rationalise our way around it. So we have to ask ourselves, why?

The Communication Barrier

It is human nature to seek like-minded people with whom to bond. The more alike we are, the more probable it is that we share the same opinions and seek similar outcomes. We know that to meet a challenge, "two heads are better than one", just as we know that "two people in the same State is a conflict". We also know that we are predisposed to desire specific outcomes and crave evidence to support the opinions we hold. Thus, our instinct is to look for and retain any information supporting our position and reject information that contradicts us. We fashionably call this "confirmation bias"—our tendency to only listen to and recall information that supports our pre-existing beliefs.

In the workplace, this distorts the communication between two people who have different perspectives on their circumstances. Where the more privileged majority sees themselves as "us" and minority voices as "them", more credence is granted to those who are part of the same "family". Chris White speaks of his time on Wall Street: "Two people could be saying the exact same thing. In one case, someone's given the benefit of the doubt. They're believed. They're trusted. In another case, they're doubted. They're not listened to. They're not heard. And it's painfully obvious to you when you're not" [2].

Social Perception and Information Processing

Good decision-takers know better. They know that bias and emotion may blinker their vision and lead them to misinterpret what they observe. Therefore, it is logical to hope that if we succeed in creating some distance from our immediate emotions, we can adjust for bias by better evaluating our observations, thereby correcting our prejudice. However, this is only to acknowledge half of the challenge. The challenge is not merely how to better assess what we see, but also to recognise that there is much that we do not see.

We all know the analogy that what is visible to us is only "the tip of the iceberg" and that most of the world around us is "hidden beneath the surface". Still, we pay more attention to what we see and underestimate what is hidden from view.

Consider the following neurological limitations that we all struggle with:

1. When we see, our brain does not actually see—it interprets the images it receives from the eyes.
2. When we observe, it is not a continuous process, but a series of observations with gaps between them.
3. When there is too much to observe, our observation powers are limited to our capacity to interpret what we see.
4. When we lack observations, our mind recognises a void and seeks to fill it with suppositions and possibilities.
5. When faced with a question we do not know the answer to, our social conditioning is such that we want to please our immediate associates and strengthen existing bonds in preference to exploring new ones; thereby reinforcing conventional bias.

This thought process and instinct result in behaviours such as "not seeing the wood for trees", "jumping to conclusions" and a reversion to prejudice. It seems that we cannot believe everything we see, and certainly not rely on intellectual reasoning alone [3].

People generally see what they look for,
and hear what they listen for . . .

From "To Kill a Mockingbird" by Harper Lee.

In academia, we speak of the social information-processing model that explains how:

1. We interpret what we observe in a way that supports our expectations, be they desirable or to be feared.
2. We interpret and digest complex information by simplifying the "facts" into more easily recallable, stereotypical biases that confirm the world to be as we have experienced it so far.
3. We memorise best what we believe is of importance to us. Observations not deemed sufficiently significant or immediately understandable are discarded, or imperfectly and partially retained.
4. We recall our memories in order to support our pre-existing beliefs. The context in which we try to retrieve our memory will predispose us to revive our original observations from a particular angle, perhaps even for a purpose that we would not have predicted when first experiencing the event.

Assume for a moment that we all believe that it is in our best interests to fight discrimination, introduce diversity into our environment, and create a welcoming and inclusive culture to benefit from it. In that case, it seems that nature has us pre-wired to be our own worst enemy.

We have considered how often we stereotype certain traits and categorise behaviours accordingly. For example, in a homogeneous society, we may believe that we are good at "reading people"—classifying people we meet into various personality types, or as being trustworthy or not. We interpret social signals; we draw conclusions from an averted gaze; we judge a smile as sincere or not; we recognise hand gestures as indicators of stress or extroversion. We usually do this with relative ease and without much thought, as those we encounter tend to be similarly educated and behave according to the social norms we expect.

Yet, how often do we have to admit that our first impressions were a little too rash—that a reluctance to speak out might be as much a sign of respect as of submission. Did we ever judge someone as arrogant and dismissive when perhaps they were having a bad day or were preoccupied with a very pressing problem? If we can make errors in our evaluation of peers within a uniform social environment, how much more difficult is it to judge the behaviour and expressions of those who originate from a background or culture that is alien to us?

4.2   The Dual Forces of Exclusion

Suppose our cognitive ability to communicate comfortably with one another diminishes the more we find ourselves with people dissimilar to ourselves. In that case, it is more relaxing to seek the company of those who see and experience the world as we do. Those who enjoy majority privilege will celebrate and nurture the customs and definitions of success that have secured them that privilege. If we are one of the dispossessed or disadvantaged minority, we will seek the comfort of those who understand our predicament, recognise the cultural traditions and expressions of community and joy as we do, and judge success on the same achievable benchmark available to us.

Diversity has both positive and negative contexts. Identifying the enemy has been a political strategy to divert attention away from problems at home throughout history. The medieval and modern history of the Jews is littered with examples of pogroms and persecution. During the Cold War, diversity of ideology was undoubtedly not viewed positively as fingers hovered over the buttons of nuclear war. Since the terror attacks of 11 September 2001, the USA and its allies have waged war on terror—a war that has Western society increasingly label anyone of the Muslim faith as a potential threat. History is filled with examples of diversity leading to division, not unity. Why?

In the Blue Corner . . .

In any situation where we have two groups of unequal influence and power, we have criteria of success and prowess determined by the more powerful, most frequently the majority. They are able to define what represents merit and integrity—they decide what conventions are considered normal and ethical and what behaviours and opinions are laudable. They select role models and perpetuate the myths and stories of what represents good citizenship. In too many democracies, it is usually the standards and rules by which the "deserving" gain merit, enabling them to protect the assets and rights they have accumulated: A result that perpetuates privilege in the hands of a few as they pass these benefits on to their children. Those who do not adhere or conform to these criteria are considered less qualified, less worthy, and— as we have discussed before—of a lower social standing or caste; hence, "less deserving" [4].

Any society that cares for long-term security and prosperity will create institutional guardrails that provide its citizens with a roadmap on how to navigate their lives and careers with a modicum of predictability; predictability being key to enabling those citizens to believe and have confidence in the future. This stability is what best serves long-term investment both in commerce and family life. It is natural for a government to protect its institutional framework from any disruption that might destroy that predictability. Hence, we have a political bias to preserve the status quo and deflect forces of change. However, that is not to say that citizens themselves—buoyed by the confidence that their institutional frameworks provide them—are not open to experimenting, developing and growing their broader understanding of the world. The challenge they face is first to learn how to build bridges between themselves and minority influencers, and secondly to understand the role prejudice has in effective communication. Even the most open and well-meaning members of Michael Sandel's "Meritocratic Aristocracy" will struggle to avoid three common missteps on the way to cross-cultural understanding.

1. Avoiding potential conflict. The extreme position in conflict avoidance is to reject the notion that there is one, leading to a refusal to engage on the subject. Even in circumstances where the individual recognises that there are sensitivities and a significant gap in experience and world perception, the default response is to remain silent. For example, many White people will avoid speaking about racism with Black colleagues or acquaintances because they fear confrontation or discomfort in doing so; or even just to avoid causing offence.
2. Avoiding blame. Suppose we already understand that the underlying injustice experienced by the underprivileged minority is the result of the attitudes, institutions and even the privileges from which we ourselves benefit. In that case, we are opening up the possibility of attracting blame or guilt by association, at least. None of us likes to feel we are the cause of injustice to others. This is a conversation we would prefer not to get too deeply involved in.
3. Avoiding the appearance of ignorance. There is a saying that a little knowledge "goes a long way" and another that it is "a dangerous thing". Indeed, most of us are better at expressing our own opinion than listening. Asking questions, seeking advice or knowledge, or even remaining silent on a topic is too often viewed as being ignorant or uneducated [5].

In the blue corner of the dominant social grouping, therefore, there is a natural urge to seek esteem and a sense of achievement from others who measure success and celebrate accepted truths and hierarchies similarly—sometimes unquestioningly. To step outside of that "bubble" or comfort zone requires more than simple curiosity. To overcome the fear of conflict or potential discomfort, there must be a promise of reward on the other side of the experience. If we are not entirely convinced, we may express empathetic outrage when injustice is observed at close quarters, but we are more than happy to move on to other priorities once the dust settles [6].

In the Red Corner . . .

Individuals who feel excluded from the dominant group will also seek comfort and support from others with whom they can bond based on shared experiences, worries and concerns. They, too, will unite around traditions and definitions of success that they can celebrate. It may be that such groupings—ethnic, religious or otherwise— prioritise achievements by a different order of priority than that of the dominant group. It may be that some of these are cultural (e.g. community before individual), or they may be imposed by the realities of life due to barriers on the paths of success defined by the dominant classes.

How we react to micro-aggression or worse forms of prejudice is very individual. Sensing resistance to our presence might spur us on to prove ourselves by being "better than they are". The common assertion that women have to be superior to men to advance their careers is symptomatic of that; we hear the same from Black professionals working amongst White colleagues, or openly gay people competing with conservatively minded heterosexuals. But, it can also become demoralising to have to face up to continued oppression. There may be times when daily reminders that others see you as less worthy of respect become demoralising, resulting in a retreat from the toxicity of the society that rejects you, or even to acceptance, defeatism and depression. A situation where the only option left is to turn one's back on that environment and take one's skills and experience elsewhere. Although, an alternative form of reaction identified by researchers investigating gender discrimination is that of denial.

Despite manifest evidence to the contrary, many women and men across 23 countries report that gender discrimination is no longer a problem in their communities. Studies tested the hypothesis that denial (as opposed to acknowledgement) of gender discrimination is associated with a willful blindness to circumstances that would otherwise demand recognition that the person lives in a systemically unfair society. Men would have to concede they are guilty of unjust discrimination towards their womenfolk. Women would have to accept the misery of knowing that they are unfairly denied their potential. In academic words: "denying gender discrimination promotes the view that the system is fair (leading to) higher subjective well-being among women" [7].

Interestingly, we have the phenomenon that in Sweden, a country that ranks amongst the top five in terms of gender equality, men and women consider their communities to be replete with sexism. In contrast, those living in countries where sexism is considered relatively high identify their society as being more egalitarian. The argument is that "denial of discrimination is an individual-level coping mechanism and that, like other self-group distancing strategies, it may perpetuate gender inequality".

In other words, if the burden of fighting what appears to be inevitable is greater than bears thinking about, we find it easier to live with if we refuse to recognise the injustice before us. To live with a manifestly inequitable situation, we redefine the meaning of fairness to regain our self-esteem, confidence and subjective well-being. The same phenomenon can be applied to those who witness abject injustice in their society, but cannot accept the implied cost of eliminating that injustice. Views on slavery in the US South in the mid-nineteenth century might be a case in point. The Confederacy based everything, its lifestyle, business and wealth on the slave economy. Any admission that their existence was immoral and cruel would demand them to change the system: for many, no doubt, such ideas would have threatened livelihood, privilege and . . . subjective well-being. The only way to free our society from such blinkers of denial is to make it safe to remove them. Even then, it demands much courage to admit that previously held beliefs were delusional.

4.3   The Curse of History: The Narrative of Legacy

We must acknowledge the exceptional case that is the USA in this context. The history of colonialism, immigration and slavery have combined in ways that are not recognisable in other Western democracies. In the USA, African-American populations historically belong to a resident slave caste in terms of social standing and hierarchy. Furthermore, the backdrop of laws and enforcement traditions, manifest in the Black Codes introduced following the 13th Amendment to the US Constitution of 1865 that officially abolished slavery, resulted in close to 100 years of overt discrimination and exclusion by White society [8]. Such codes effectively criminalised the already subservient caste categorisation of African Americans as US legislators provided the means for previous slaveowners to reclaim recently liberated slaves back to a state of forced labour, this time as criminals [9]. The legacy of this history is that many US citizens still harbour a common prejudice against the stereotypical image of Black men being a threat to the peace and Black women being uneducated, angry single mothers living in poverty. If this discriminatory profiling of an easily identifiable population has then spilt over to other, working-class immigrant populations of colour, such as many Latinos, it has been a tragic by-product of US history. In the face of such oppression, it is not strange that African-American and Minority Ethnic populations within the USA regard much of the White dominant groupings with distrust.

European democracies have histories and legacies of their own. It was the colonialists who industrialised the slave trade, but conveniently out of sight of those who prospered as a result in Amsterdam, Bordeaux, Bristol, Copenhagen, Lisbon and Liverpool, amongst many others. Their wealth allowed them to dominate and colonise large parts of the Americas, Africa and Asia. Their superiority in terms of organisation and weaponry allowed the European to form the conviction and belief that White people were "superior", even endowed with a God-given duty to "rescue" lesser societies from their plight and lead them to European-style civil values. Compared to #BlackLivesMatter policing issues in the USA, European prejudice and discriminatory problems may seem less urgent. However, this is an illusion and should not be a comfort for dominant groupings to disregard the obstructions and injustice faced by excluded minorities every day. Regrettably, the absence of pan-European statistics prevents the highlighting of everyday racism. However, a visit to the headquarters of most European companies will generally evidence a lack of inclusion similar to the USA.

In Europe, being White is just considered to be "the norm"; being of a different appearance or culture is "merely" being in a category of "other/Foreign" and therefore of lesser importance—somehow less valued. The indigenous European derives self-esteem from their legacy, culture and national narrative; those who do not share this self-worth cannot, therefore, qualify to be included in the privileges that legacy provides. It is not usually a loathing of the foreigner that leads to discrimination. Instead, it is an expression of a hierarchical system where White Europeans see themselves as at the head of the pyramid. Even notions of freedom and liberty, it seems, are not universal [10]. They are carefully crafted colonial concepts that support the freedoms of the "deserving" dominant culture and which are sparingly accorded to those emanating from the "lower orders".

Consider then, if groups of "privileged" ex-patriates flock together like birds of a feather, then how much higher the propensity to do so when you feel disadvantaged, discriminated against, looked down upon? Any individual who experiences a degree of exclusion or threat will tend to seek out others they can relate to. Firstly, there is safety in numbers, but secondly, it is far more pleasant to circulate with people who understand, trust and support you. How often have I not seen and heard members of the majority culture comment and ask why "those people" gather at "their" tables; rather than ask themselves why "they" do not find it natural to join them at the larger table? Defining people by their different origins only creates barriers between us; seeing people as individuals whose uniqueness adds to our collegial team is more likely to remove those barriers. It is at the core of our mission here to formulate inclusion policies for the benefit of the company, and society.

4.4   A Question of Trust and the Fear of Strangers

As an undergraduate in the UK, I observed how many of my countrymen sought out other Norwegian students and kept themselves apart from British and other international students. Some even found it strange that I was more inclined to mix with British students (my natural "group" having just spent 5 years at a UK school) than to hang out with them. I was blond and blue-eyed like most of them, but due to my non-exclusive relationship with my countrymen, I was not entirely considered "one of them". Exclusion can happen to individuals commuting between two relatively similar groups with no known conflict of interest. Consider then the fate of those who seek to cross the divide of male and female environments, religious and LGBT+ communities or different racial groupings in a non-inclusive setting?

How can minorities who have faced discrimination, glances of scorn and dismissal at the hands of dominant groupings feel anything but discomfort when in their midst? Indeed, what is the psychological impact on an individual who is reminded every day that their presence is subject to the good grace and tolerance of a more powerful dominant majority culture? How does it impact hope and confidence when opportunities and support available to others is denied to you as a matter of course? What happens to an individual when benchmarks of success and merit are structured such that you cannot qualify? All because you happen to be of the "wrong" gender, sexuality, religion or colour:

> We don't get paid the same amount for the same work. We've been disproportionately affected in layoffs and unemployment [11].

> I have to work twice as hard to get the same level of recognition as my colleagues [12].

On Wall Street, it's being perceived as not being competent or being too aggressive or not being worthy of leadership based on sight, not on any of the other evidence around you [2].

In a non-inclusive environment, there is a constant concern that those of the "other" group will not properly tend to our needs. In such circumstances, our preference for relying on our "own" communities is strengthened—further dividing society, sometimes in unexpected ways.

People Like Us

The news media is replete with stories of White patients refusing treatment or rejecting the advice of non-White medical staff [13]. Some Minorities fear not being understood or being misdiagnosed when treated by doctors of a different race [14]. Can we trust anyone but our own kind? It is a critical question; regrettably, sometimes based on historical abuse of the unprivileged [15]. What if our simple fear of encountering discrimination results in our not trusting what someone of the "other" group is teaching, advising or informing on? Marlon Wade made an observation of his own behaviours that resulted in an academic study. He needed a new doctor and had over 20 to choose from. One stood out. She was, like him, Black and a practising Moslem. This is what he explains: "She gets me, I get her. We talk about life; we talk about religion. You know, if something is wrong with me, she is going to let me know" [16].

Owen Garrick runs the Bridge Clinical Research, which studies how the US medical system might work better for African Americans. His findings were that when Black rather than White doctors treated Black patients, there was a 72% improvement in the ability of the Black doctor to persuade their African-American patients to take a full cholesterol screening, including blood tests and measuring body mass—and this when both White and Black doctors offered the same level of attention and care to the patient. Interestingly, it works both ways. In his studies, he found that 65% of Blacks maintained that a same-race doctor would better understand them and, therefore, trust them with more extensive preventative medical testing—amongst White patients, the equivalent number was 70%.

If we value perceived empathy in our doctors and teachers above the pure expertise they represent, it impacts our trust in them. In these cases, it affects our health and our learning ability.

Professor Constance Lindsay of the University of North Carolina runs a programme to research the disparities in the academic achievement of African-American students compared to White students. He explains one of his conclusions: "If you're a Black student and you have a Black teacher, on average, you're going to have a higher test score than a Black student who has a White teacher". But, again, the study concludes that this is not due to the teacher's discriminatory teaching practices—the differences emanate from within the student.

It would be easy, but wrong to interpret such results as an argument for segregation; that would be like the doctor who treats symptoms rather than the cause of an illness. The differences observed resulted from an unfounded and prejudiced perception of how we are likely to be treated by individuals who are culturally different from ourselves. On the other hand, if we are accustomed to inclusive attitudes and are able to see the professional value of the person opposite, the fear of non-empathy recedes, and we can start to believe that, indeed, our doctor or teacher does, in fact, care for us—no matter their race, religion or culture.

4.5   If You Can't Beat Them, Join Them

Stereotype and prejudice are pervasive. They visibly act as discriminatory blocks on what the disadvantaged minority can access and therefore achieve. What is also of concern is the less obvious impact they have on the self-esteem and confidence of those subjected to them. If everyone else tells you that women are no good at engineering, Black people are not academic, or White students are outperformed in mathematics by Asians, do not be surprised if, like stress, it influences performance [17]. Studies show that when told that their performance in a mathematics test is to be compared to that of Asian peers, White men are intimidated to the point that their performance deteriorates. Likewise, Black and female student scores fall when they are informed that their results will be competitively compared to White or male peers. Perhaps most tragically, but also illuminatingly, the performance of Black students brought up in the USA is more affected than that of Black students of Caribbean origin.

This phenomenon is known as "stereotype threat"—when performance under the pressure of comparison to a stereotypically "superior" competitor or colleague results in higher stress levels that diminish focus and concentration. This effect is observed as much in sports as in intellectual activity. The fear of confirming a stereotypical perception becomes a self-fulfilling prophecy; some may label it a version of "inferiority complex". Whatever its name, it is clear that what stereotypical expectations say about you impacts your ability to succeed. To break down stereotype is to deconstruct prejudice; to remove prejudice is to facilitate inclusion [18].

Integration and Adaption

Most people have experienced moments when it has seemed more advisable to "blend in with the crowd" rather than stand out and be your natural self. As discussed, if such instances are few and far between, we dismiss them as an aberration, or just another unpleasant episode and settle into our normal comfort zone and social bubble where we feel competent and appreciated for who we are. However, if this instinct to fit in is a constant requirement in the face of stereotypical prejudice and discriminatory behaviour, it becomes a way of life—or at least an alter ego. It is called Code-Switching.

Even in a homogenous community where members have a similar background, education and values, new entrants to a social group, neighbourhood, school, workplace, etc., will quickly detect the "way we do things around here". It will be evident from how people talk, how they address others, the degree of formality in behaviours, and the environment; is it hostile and suspicious or welcoming and curious? These are all expressions of social culture. New arrivals will observe and mirror what they see to gain rapid acceptance within the group. Not doing so risks the individual becoming isolated and excluded.

The strength of the culture may vary. Some student societies, sports and recreation clubs, even adult organisations or communities, may project a powerful credo and ensure new entrants buy into the culture through a series of initiation rituals. Companies will often organise an induction programme for new employees to help them understand its formal rules, codes of conduct and the internal policy framework, and possibly any external regulations the company is subject to. If the culture is strong, most people will slowly change their attitudes and behaviours to fit in, although there are limits. Someone with a solid aversion to particular behavioural expectations, a strong sense of ego with little concern for others, or a strong allegiance to another social group with contradictory norms may decline to integrate and adapt. Instead, they might resist, risking exclusion and rejection by the new group with whom they intended to integrate. For some, such resistance may close doors when no others are open and available; there is no option but to code-switch.

Jone is a 17-year-old Sami in Norway. He wants to be a reindeer herdsman like his father and grandfather before him. However, before Jone pursues this ambition, he wants to finish his land management education at a school no more than 1.5 h from home. Unfortunately, even in twenty-first-century Norway, he experiences the threat of exclusion from his non-Sami Norwegian colleagues. "When I am at home, I can speak Sami and be myself, but when I am at school, I must become a new person, or I become 'the Sami'. It's tiring being two completely different people all the time, but it has become a habit" [19].

The Bribe

The marginalised minority lives under constant pressure to conform. It is, without doubt, the path of least resistance. Not to conform is to demand the dominant majority to accept your diversity, be flexible and willing to listen to your uniqueness, accommodate and be inclusive of your influence as an individual. The price of standing tall in one's diversity is to face the winds of resistance and rejection; then, there is always the offer of "the bribe". Abandon your uniqueness and integrate with the dominant ethic and attitudes. Allow the discourse to ignore obvious inequities in exchange for peace and at least a modicum of success on the terms of the ingroup. Eddie Glaude—Chair of the Department of African American Studies, Princeton University—explains it thus: "We are constantly faced with taking the bribe. And what is the bribe? The bribe is your silence. The bribe is, you know, just pursue your craft and make your money. The bribe is to adjust yourself to injustice. And then, in the context of the world in which we inhabit, that bribe involves the deformation of attention, right? So we start producing work that doesn't capture folks' attention. It actually becomes a part of this white noise that leaves folks' eyes blank, right? It's doesn't force them to do much" [20].

The Metachrosis Effect

Like the chameleon, the "odd one out" frequently finds safety in adopting the behaviours and colours of those around them. Children of mixed culture parentage do it all the time. For example, an individual raised by (e.g.) a White Anglican father and a Black Muslim mother, and who has been in regular touch with relatives both in (say) Liverpool and Nairobi, is likely to be observed switching between languages and cultural behaviours with relaxed ease. Adjusting one's style of speech, appearance, behaviour, and expression will optimise the comfort of others in exchange for fair treatment. Trust relationships and even employment opportunities come naturally and easily if the individual feels that in code-switching, they are simply emphasising different aspects of themselves. Code-switching becomes a shortcut to acceptance and relationships—not a denial of Self. Imagine, though, if this was the only way, not to gain trust, but to be tolerated? Research at teaching institutions reveals that African-American students selectively code-switch between standard English in the classroom and African-American Vernacular English with their social peers, which intentionally elevates their social standing within each circle [21].

Black people disguising their true selves when mixing with White colleagues differs from the code-switch experience of Europeans, such as myself. When I code-switch between English and Norwegian, even to a slightly lesser extent with French and Danish colleagues, I feel I gain something in exchange—an elevation in my trust relationships from fair to good. I remain myself and merely exhibit who I am using different words, syntax and body language. For the person who feels unwelcome as a baseline, the improvement experienced is to rise from a state of rejection or worse to being tolerated. Under threat, the adoption of "alien" language and behaviours is no longer a tool of communication, but rather a form of defence against injustice. Tragically, a transformation of this degree will often feel like a betrayal of their true selves and a denial of the community they emotionally identify with.

"Acting White" is a phrase construed during the era of racial integration in the USA during the 1970s when Black teenagers singled out their peers attending "White" schools in this way [22]. Whatever was the intention of non-integrated Black teens labelling their erstwhile friends in this manner, it signified that African-American students had an uncomfortable choice. To either adopt White behaviours and navigate a White institutional framework that opens the door to academic achievement, merit and success, or "remain" Black for fear that their peers will consider them as "traitors" to their community [23].

Based on informed opinion, there are three main reasons for people to engage in defensive code-switching at the workplace [21]:

- Avoiding stereotypical behaviour, language and opinions associated with negative views related to gender, culture or race such as being lazy, unreliable or unintelligent (amongst others). If the conventional stereotype applied to those of your background is negative, then distancing yourself from that identity will increase the likelihood of promotions or job opportunities.
- Avoiding the stigma of belonging to a group, culture, or race looked down on by the dominant group as "unsuited"; who are dismissed as unprofessional due to appearance, hairstyles, dress codes or language/syntax [24].
- Embracing the dominating culture's interests and conventional viewpoints will increase the chance of being accepted within its ranks. In other words, the affiliation bias of the dominant elite that encourages them to work with individuals similar to themselves opens opportunities for promotion and involvement to those who pretend to do so.

We can already deduce how this form of code-switching denies organisations and society the perceived benefits of diversity. A company may pursue a broader diversification of hires in its recruitment policies. Still, if this is not accompanied by inclusion initiatives, it acts merely as a pro-forma exercise to meet non-financial reporting targets. The harm, however, goes beyond this.

There is stress associated with involuntary code-switching, such as expressed by the City and Wall Street banker, Tessie Petion: "We have to be super-careful about everything, because if it goes badly with me, then maybe the next time they look at a Person of Color then they're like, 'Well, we tried that one, right?'".

My Avatar and I

The excluded minority face a constant dilemma. Do the less privileged suppress their cultural identity for the sake of career success, or should they be themselves?

Research shows that White colleagues perceive code-switching Black peers as "more professional, whilst Black colleagues consider their racial brethren as less professional". A 29-year-old Black female finance professional explains it as follows: "I am in a constant battle of censoring ... watering down my views, thoughts, and personality for the possibility of being looked at differently than a non-Black man or woman in the workplace if they exhibited the same behaviour. It's exhausting navigating an all-White workplace" [21].

The Bind of Intersectional Discrimination

Let us revert to our lone Black woman for a moment. In a predominantly White setting, she has to counter social expectations as to both the character and traits of women, as well as present themselves to fit in with the image of White-defined professionalism, merit and success. Dealing with prejudice may entail remaining non-confrontational when, indeed, confrontation would be constructive. It may force her to accept constant interruptions by male and White female colleagues picking up on her ideas and completing her sentences as if they were their own. Suppose the former Nigerian Finance Minister Ngozi Okonjo-Iweala had changed her "work-name" to accommodate Western traditions. In that case, she may have avoided the February 2021 Reuters headline (later retracted) "No nonsense Nigerian woman to be named boss" for the World Trade Organisation. It is not uncommon for the Black African job applicant to adopt a typically White "nickname", language, accents and syntax to get through an interview. For many Minority Ethnic people, staying silent, smiling or even joining in the banter that reinforces the negative stereotype one is trying to escape from is the only option.

The challenge is the same, even if you are a White female on an oil platform, a homosexual in a homophobic culture, a Muslim amid Christians raging against presumed Islamic hostility, or any minority whose place in society is thought to be amongst those designated to the lower castes. To carry this burden every day at work and still demonstrate your talent, creativity and energy freely is a near-impossible task. If, at the same time, your own community judges you a traitor to your own culture, rather than a role model of success—the professional and personal burden will be too much for many; their positive contribution to work and society lost.

> Women and professionals of colour… are (often) required to perform added, unacknowl-edged, and uncompensated labour and to pay … an inclusion tax, which is levied in the form of time, money, and mental and emotional energy required to gain entry to and acceptance from traditionally white and male institutional spaces. That can include the hours at the hair salon needed to conform to European standards of beauty and the tailoring of clothing to fit within white norms of professional attire. Adding to this cumbersome load is the emotional and mental burden inflicted upon those who are perpetually the only Person of Color, or woman, or person of a modest economic background in the room.

> Tsedale M. Melaku

> August 2019.

4.6   Light at the End of the Tunnel

In a world where intolerance reigns and an evil eye glances towards those who dress or think differently from the mainstream majority, things can indeed turn defensive and ugly. Yet, in the USA, the American Dream is meant to offer the hope that anyone willing to work hard can make it to the top. Likewise, the ideals of the European Union are built upon a celebration of differences, regarding interaction as a way to learn and enrich our lives. Such ideas require us to open our eyes to the many different perceptions of right and wrong in the world, and challenge us to leave the confines of prejudice and accepted truth to discover new opportunities and learning.

It does, however, require three elements:

i. The privileged must consider the less privileged with the openness of a learning mindset.
ii. The newcomer must be willing to respect, if not necessarily embrace, host values.
iii. Both parties must be willing to accept, reconcile and come to terms with each other's differences.

Both parties must seek common understanding and harmony, and work towards the betterment of the community or organisation they have in common. This engagement takes trust and sometimes a little courage.

Professor of Management, Fred Luthans, is famous within behavioural sciences for his work on applied positive psychology. His Model of Positive Organisational Behaviour explains how our perception of self drives individual behaviour in any social setting [25].

Luthans argues that emotional and psychological aspects such as self-confidence, hope and optimism determine our ability to develop and grow and, ultimately, our behaviour. Hence, we can encourage individuals to find the best version of themselves in a form of the Pygmalion Effect (whereby high expectations lead to improved performance). We also empower them to showcase both who they are and what they can contribute to whatever project or organisation they are a part of. Equally, when work and life experiences do everything to suppress or erode belief in Self through the workings of stereotype risk, disempowerment, exclusion and discrimination, then the opposite impact is true. We become a lesser version of ourselves, keep a low profile, adopt the behaviours required to gain greater acceptance amongst those we have to rely on, and fear making our voice heard.

The school of positive psychology agrees. The greatest enemy of the potential gains of diversity is defensiveness and fear of change. The task of the organisation committed to nurturing diversity is to foster a culture of learning and trust, and to promote a common goal in the form of organisational purpose—a banner around which all can cooperate and celebrate.

References

1. Ursula Burns. Accessed October 22, 2020, from www.forbes.com
2. Abelson, M., Basak, S., Butler, K., Leising, M., Surane, J., & Tan, G. (2020, August 3). *The only one in the room*. Bloomberg.
3. Smith-Meyer, A. (2018). *Surviving organisational behaviour*. Kindle Publishing.
4. Sandel, M. (2020). *The tyranny of merit*. Farrar, Strauss and Giroux.
5. Roberts, L. M., & Washington, E. (2020, June 1). US businesses must take meaningful action against racism. *Harvard Business Review*.
6. Henderson, A., & Kinias, Z. (2020, September 24). *Understanding the origins of White denial*. INSEAD Knowledge.

7. Napier, J. L., Suppes, A., & Bettinsoli, M. L. (2020, July 13). Denial of gender discrimination is associated with better subjective well-being among women. *European Journal of Social Psychology*.
8. Wilkerson, I. (2020). *Caste: The origins of our discontents*. Random House.
9. (2020, June 4). *American Police*. npr, the throughline podcast.
10. Stovall, T. (2021). *White freedom: The racial history of an idea*. Princeton.
11. Gelles, D. (2020, June 6). Corporate America has failed Black America. *New York Times*.
12. Williams, J. (2020, June 12). *Companies have the tools to fight racism. Will they use them?* Bloomberg.
13. Kline, R. (2020, February 13). What if a patient wants to choose the ethnicity of their doctor? *The BMJ Opinion Blog*.
14. University of Michigan. (2010, January 8). Race-based misdiagnosis still remains a health care problem. *Science Daily*.
15. Royles, D. (2020, December 15). Years of medical abuse make Black Americans less likely to trust the coronavirus vaccine. *The Washington Post*.
16. npr. (2020, May 25). *People like us: How our identities shape health and educational success*. The hidden brain podcast.
17. McWhorter, J. H. (2000). Explaining the Black education gap. *Wilson Quarterly, 24*(3).
18. Steele, C. M. (2011, April). *Whistling Vivaldi*. W.W. Norton.
19. Ciakudia-Moxnes, I. (2021, October 16). *Jone (17) føler han må skjule sin samiske side: Det har blitt en vanesak*. NRK. no; P3. no. Accessed January 2, 2022.
20. (2021, April 29). *Interview of Eddie Glaude on the throughline podcast, NPR*. James Baldwin's Shadow.
21. McCluney, C. L., Robotham, K., Smith, R., & Durkee, M. (2019, November 15). The costs of code-switching. *Harvard Business Review*.
22. McWhorter, J. (2019, July 20). The origins of the 'acting White' charge. *The Atlantic*.
23. Horvat, E. M., & O'Connor, C. (Eds.). (2006). *Beyond acting White*. Rowman & Littlefield.
24. Melaku, T. (2019, August 7). Why women and people of color in law still hear "you don't look like a lawyer". *Harvard Business Review*.
25. Luthans, F., Youssef, C. M., & Avolio, B. J. (2006). *Psychological capital: Developing the human competitive edge*. Oxford University Press.

#BreakingTheMould: Why Traditional D&I Programmes Fail

5

5.1   The Tyranny of the Unconscious Mind

Humans of all cultures act on bias, which in turn extends to stereotype and prejudice. Our perception of the world is shaped by convention as taught to us by our family, schools, and eventually religions and media. They are reinforced by myths and stories that often are no more than unsubstantiated hearsay. The only time we discard these conventions, "rules", or interpretations of the world around us is when we observe behaviours that challenge our expectations, or if we dare to explore where these ideas come from or who they serve.

Baby boomers, such as myself, grew up watching adverts on TV that stereotyped women as housewives, films depicting Black people as uneducated, and mainstream media indicating homosexuals as somehow deviant. Over time, my education, experience, and observation of real-world behaviours destroyed these conventional stereotypes. I actually had to learn that people who are "different" are neither a threat nor less worthy than myself. What took longer to understand was that the convention and stereotype that I was discarding as an individual remained active as a silent protector of my privilege and relative advantage. No matter how enlightened I might believe I become, I am forever only scratching the surface. The learnt behaviours and assumptions of our society and institutions have to be peeled back, one layer at a time. My conscious behaviour and interaction with those I now seek to treat with respect is, dare I say it, much improved. Still, unconsciously, I remained blind to the many obstacles confronting minorities that ensured that institutional bias continued to tilt the playing field of opportunity in my favour. My worldview takes time to adjust, just as it does with most of those around me.

Unconscious bias meant that in my workplaces, irrespective of my opinion and throughout most of my career, women or People of Colour were considered less emotionally capable or technically competent, less reliable or even less trustworthy. The women, gay or Black colleagues and friends I encountered were the few who had "made it" to my table—the one including the traditionally privileged groupings. Throughout my career, I was rarely challenged by the talents of coloured, female or

A. Smith-Meyer, *Unlocking the Potential of Diversity in Organisations*, Diversity and Inclusion Research, https://doi.org/10.1007/978-3-031-10402-2_5

LGBT+ competition, all of whom have either been absent or maintained a low profile to "survive" under the domination of what we now call White privilege.

As that White privileged male, I have to look back on my career and wonder what my world would have looked like if not for this suppression of minority talent. Optimistically, a collaboration with those excluded may have opened more doors to knowledge, innovation and even adventure. Alternatively, perhaps someone more deserving would have gained those key promotions accorded to me? One can only speculate. I am certain that my work and life experience would have been different, and I choose to believe more rewarding. However, I am not the injured party here. I only have to remind myself what it feels like to be belittled, bullied or viewed as "not one of the locals" to recall the effort required to gain acceptance and imagine what it means to have no "privilege" to wield in that struggle.

When D&I Programmes Fail

A UK Royal Air Force spokesman informed the BBC that "The Royal Air Force has an absolute zero tolerance to racism, bullying and hazing of any kind". The standards of conduct always expected of staff in the RAF are set out in their Code of Practice booklet "Ethos, Core Values and Standards of the RAF" [1]. Yet, so is banter and a belief that mental resilience is a quality that can be built on "teasing". Many who have attended private schools in the UK have had a similar upbringing—perhaps one that encourages stoicism and the famous "stiff upper lip" caricature of the English.

The Core Values of the RAF are Respect, Integrity, Service, Excellence. Embedded in the term respect is inclusivity: "Each one of us has a responsibility to ensure the people around us always feel welcome and included" [2]. The advice given to Kyrean NG, a British Malaysian recruit, by his corporal was, "there's a good chance that everyone will ostracise you. They're nervous about being around you in case they offend you". Not long after that, the same corporal offered up the "banter" sentence, "Your name sounds like the noise you make when you go to the toilet". The comment offended Kyrean; sufficiently so that he recalls it perfectly more than 10 years later. The RAF culture in 2008 was not what its Code of Conduct manual promises today: the story he tells is one where the dominant majority group fear being disrespectful in any formal setting, yet do not refrain from insulting the person to the core of their identity … in the name of friendly banter.

The example is relevant here because it is representative of so many organisational cultures where the intention of respect and inclusion is known and present, but there is a failure to embed the behaviours implied by those values in grassroots behaviour. The postscript to the above story is that the RAF lost the services of Kyrean NG, now an engineer.

We can fight conscious bias—we render it unacceptable and, in the words of the English Football Association, "Kick it out". In an organisation, we introduce so-called zero-tolerance rules where any racist act or word is punished, and the perpetrator expelled from the group. Organisations fight wrongdoing such as corruption, sexual harassment, bullying, and even smoking in this manner. Measures like this are incomplete, however. The subsequent changes in organisational behaviour of a disciplinary approach are based more on fear than conviction. It may treat the symptoms and cure a problem, but depending on the nature of the subject at hand, it will not, by itself, change the disease that sits deep in our culture. Some personalities may indeed discover they prefer to work elsewhere, but smokers will find places to smoke where it is acceptable to do so. Individuals prone to sexist views will hold their tongue at work, but still allow bias to colour their decisions.

We cannot legislate away stereotypical bias and prejudice embedded in our upbringing and conventional social thinking. What comes to us as "the natural order of things" does not get questioned. We "know" that women should always be caring and unthreatening; we "know" that Muslims are against our liberal Western values; we "know" that Black employees are not "executive material". We also "know" that Americans are loud, the English are hypocritical, Germans don't have a sense of humour, Scandinavians are cold, and the French are rude. None of these things is true, and the severity of consequences can differ. Still, until we encounter the very people we harbour stereotypical images of up close and personal, our opinions are hard to change. Our unconscious mind does not question our biases; we generally act according to its knee-jerk instruction.

We already know that there are at least three consequences to our surreptitious unconscious bias in the workplace:

- A suppression of talent and potential born of a lack of awareness of individual uniqueness and how social norms seek to control and suppress individuality.
- The mismanagement of diversified talent and the erosion of corporate culture in terms of collegial trust and organisational justice.
- The altered behaviour and suppression of self-expression enacted by minorities in response to their perceived threat of discrimination and the impact on the self-confidence and self-esteem of minorities experiencing negative bias in any situation.

We have a responsibility as individuals, board members, executives, managers, colleagues and even members of the broader society we live in. In all communities where there is a strong convention supporting a dominant elite, we have to accept that "our way" is only the "old way" and that new perspectives will redefine our horizons and the meaning of "the high way". Until we learn this, we will never be able to define the benefits of a D&I policy, let alone ever implement one successfully.

5.2 First, Tentative Words and the Open Mind

Executives and organisations typically struggle when confronting and embracing bias, be this negative bias towards "outsider" minority groups or positive bias favouring majority, ingroup members. Often, the leaders themselves suffer from the same blinkered vision that they appreciate their employees and company are accused of. All too often, the executive and board members themselves suffer from overconfidence bias and a superior self-image. All too frequently, the apparent solution is to alter the behaviour of others rather than themselves. Why is it so difficult to break free of our prejudice? How must organisations and their members change their approach to implement D&I policies successfully? How significant is the required change, and on whose shoulders is this burden to be placed?

Early in June 2020, Jamie Dimon was pictured "taking the knee" in symbolic support of #BlackLivesMatter. He also stated, "we are committed to fighting against racism and discrimination wherever and however it exists" [3]. These are bold words from the CEO and Chairperson of JPMorgan, who also led the charge for the change in the definition of "Purpose" for the Business Round Table in the USA, discarding predominantly shareholder capitalism for broader stakeholder capitalism [4]. Yet, we still look for significant signs of progress beyond the quick promise to increase Black, Asian and minority ethnic recruitment. Indications of remorse or open discussion of past marketing and lending policies that disadvantage racial minorities have still to be broached by business leaders [5].

The CEO of Morgan Stanley, James Gorman, felt moved to declare that this period in 2020 "will not be easily forgotten in history, and it shouldn't be. God willing, it will be seen as a turning point in race relations". Yet, his audience may be forgiven for folding their arms in anticipation. Like so many of his contemporaries, his bank has a deplorably low presence of Black executives in its ranks despite the seemingly symbolic, immediate promotion of two Black women to seats on the bank's operating and management committees [6].

It is not only in finance. When L'Oreal tweeted, "Speaking out is worth it", it placed their earlier firing of Munroe Bergdorf in 2017 for making statements against racism in stark contrast. They have now rehired her to serve on their newly established UK Diversity and Inclusion Advisory Board, but it seems a very recent change of heart. Organisations can no longer get away with not facing up to years of institutionalised prejudice and White blindness through clever public relation campaigns, photo opportunities, statements and hurried appointments. That time is past. The positive bias of the baby-boomer generation towards institutions and authority is rapidly giving way to the far more demanding, sceptical and negatively biased Millennials and Generation Z [7]. The facts speak for themselves, there is something in the make-up of society, from education and opportunity, through to recruitment and promotions that disadvantages large sections of society, be they Black, Asian, Minority Ethnic, female, LGBT+ or disabled [8].

Charting a New Course

The reality of statistics and observed outcomes amply demonstrate the presence of bias, unconscious or otherwise. If we are prepared to accept that such results are detrimental to our organisations, society and community wellbeing, or merely immoral and fundamentally in contravention of our human values, this inequality should compel any leadership to take action to correct the situation. Even then, the default reaction is often to establish a working group, devise a plan, and a programme to be rolled out into the organisation.

Traditionally, boards and their executives devise and approve D&I programmes to face a problem of racial or other bias. Often, management appoints an individual with a profile reflective of the mission to lead the initiative, such as a member of Human Resources representing the target social group; be this a woman, a member of the LGBT+ community, or a "Person of Colour". Then, with the decision taken, a budget allocated, and the task delegated, the executive focus can return to less taxing issues like financial performance.

Some companies are getting on with it. Following the resurgence of #BLM in the aftermath of the George Floyd killing in the USA, Satya Nadella, CEO of Microsoft, announced plans to double the number of Black managers and senior leaders over the next 5 years. This target forms part of the key objectives of senior management, influencing their pay and promotion prospects [9]. Also, Microsoft intends to double the number of Black-owned approved suppliers over the next 3 years and ask existing suppliers to disclose their diversity status and goals. Finally, the firm announced a $50 million investment fund to support small businesses owned by the Black community. Microsoft is not alone in making promises. In the #BLM America of 2020, many other companies like Google and Facebook pledged to improve the diversity mix in their leadership ranks. Estée Lauder has committed $10 million to racial justice organisations over the next 3 years [10]. The question remains; will these D&I measures prove sustainable? As previously mentioned, Morgan Stanley, JPMorgan, Walmart, Wells Fargo and Slack all stand accused of proffering inauthentic words and promises [6]. What are they getting wrong?

Education and the Marley Hypothesis

Bob Marley fans will know the song "Buffalo Soldier". Some may even know its connection to the Black soldiers who served in the US Army during the Indian wars and who, "in the heart of America/Stolen from Africa, brought to America/Fighting on arrival, fighting for survival". Bob Marley's song uses the term as a symbol of Black identity and resistance. His words, "If you know your history/Then you would know where you're coming from", resonates with a study entitled "The Marley Hypothesis: denial of racism reflects ignorance of history" [11]. At the heart of this study is the correlation between a knowledge of Black history and sensitivity to racist behaviour or statements. Specifically, compared to the culturally aware Black person, a White individual with little understanding of the history of slavery, colonialism and racism, will be slower or even unable to connect behaviours, symbols and words with racist impact. In other words, the researchers predicted a positive correlation between people with higher levels of historical knowledge and their ability to perceive systemic or individual instances of racism. This observation was not exclusive to one group more than any other. It was as accurate for African Americans as it was for European Americans.

Furthermore, whereas ignorance of the history of race relations hampers the individual's ability to interpret current events as racist, the study also found that the more strongly European Americans identified with their cultural roots, the more the relevance of Black history diminished. Once again, the observation was race-neutral. The greater an African American identified with their cultural heritage, the more likely they were to interpret what they saw and heard as evidence of racism, thereby increasing a sense of persecution. This dual effect means that individuals in the majority group are more likely to reject allegations of racism against them as either spurious or as a direct affront to their self-esteem gained from buying into the majority view of the historical justification for their cultural "superiority" [12]. Arguably, supremacism of any kind is an extreme view of self-worth based on narrative; frequently, a rejection of history.

Import these findings into our society. In the wake of the George Floyd protests, there was a clear spike in outrage in the USA and across the world. Yet, while protests continued in the USA, activism on #BLM faded elsewhere—potentially explainable. Europeans and Asians voiced their objection to what they perceive as brazen discrimination and inequality against African Americans, not events at home. Less understandable, however, is the surge of interest and protest amongst White Americans followed by a decline of the share of White Americans who consider racism a significant problem in its aftermath. A YouGov/The Economist survey revealed that whereas 45% of respondents answered this question positively in June 2020, the share had fallen to 33% by early August. On the other hand, 75% of Black Americans said racism was a big problem in both surveys [13].

The Marley Hypothesis implies that dominant majorities less sensitised to the history of discrimination will be inclined to respond strongly to an undeniable instance of injustice, as clearly was the case with the video of George Floyd's killing. The transgression is so severe that despite the incident being "far from home", it awakens a sense of universal outrage against the perpetrators. The fact that the perpetrator is "one of us" is dismissed as incidental. The narrative is constructed that the guilt clearly lies with the "rotten apple" that needs to be plucked from the barrel. Suppose an individual act is vile enough and is so closely tied to our community that it undermines our sense of identity and carries guilt by association unless we act. In that case, we will not tolerate it: "it is not who we are". However, less blatant or brazen events might be viewed as "normal aberration" and thus be afforded less significance and be quickly forgotten as the news media moves away from racial injustice to other stories. But, the traumatised minority cannot move on so easily. Indeed, the short attention span of their White "allies" will likely be viewed as further evidence of the systemic and ingrained tolerance of racial disparity in their society.

There is a second effect underway, however. One that leads to a denial of what seems evident to all others. When the majority feels that their community values and ethics are under attack, it threatens their legacy and sense of identity: "it is, indeed, who we are". The discomfort that the majority—in this case, White Americans—experiences when their "own" institutions, police forces, and sometimes friends and colleagues are accused of being ignoble and unjust places us in an acute dilemma. If the accusations are accurate, we may imagine we are called upon to reject a part of our heritage and network. If we are proud of our heritage, then it is difficult to understand when others point to the unacceptable failures of that culture. In terms of violations against those less powerful, there are accusations a-plenty: A constant undermining of Black voter rights in what US politicians have consistently claimed to be the greatest democracy on earth; the suppression and looting of native rights in the colonies of the greatest empire the world has ever seen; or blatantly anti-migrant sentiment seen in many European capitals as Syrian war refugees sought asylum in our human rights-oriented societies. We want to resist such insinuations; we want to reject the evidence. We will not be ready to confront our community failings until we are prepared to accept that history is only the story told by the victors and that our heroes and role models were ordinary humans, themselves complete with flaws and prejudices. We will not succeed in our efforts to eradicate injustice through policies and procedures if we cannot readily confront our past and accept that current unfairness and inequality are the sorry results of our collective histories. We have to accept that to build a future that we can be proud of rather than ashamed of, we have to face and solve our social problems together. The fight for racial justice, and all other forms of equality, requires a change of mindset. We need to reconfigure our perception of right and wrong and produce new ethical standards to guide us. We need to change the culture within our organisations as well as in our societies [13].

> White people don't know who they are or where they come from. That's why you think I'm a problem. But I am not the problem. Your history is. And as long as you pretend you don't know your history, you're going to be the prisoner of it.

James Baldwin [14]

5.3 D&I Management . . . Just Another Risk?

Our seniors and our management schools teach us that whenever confronted by factors leading to undesirable outcomes, there is a logical process of deliberation to identify its cause and mitigate or resolve it. The decision-making process is only over once we have decided to act (or not), and we have checked that the original issue has been effectively dealt with.

Defining and describing a rational decision-making model is a matter of granularity: How detailed do you want the process description to be? With the proviso that beneath each stage heading, you could devise other, more detailed sub-headings, I have chosen to present the rational model as a five-stage path to optimising the result [15].

The rational decision-making model is methodical and steadfast:

1. Identification of the challenge, problem or opportunity
2. Generation of options and choices to deal with or solve the question

3. Evaluation of the multiple alternative solutions available and selecting one, based on purpose and desired impact and outcome
4. Acting upon the decision and implementing the solution chosen
5. Monitoring implementation and obtaining feedback on its success relative to achieving the intended results, then making any adjustments necessary to ensure an optimal outcome

It sounds relatively straightforward when described like this, but do not be fooled. In outlining your options and making a selection, there is a complex array of factors to be considered, such as:

  (i) Viability, or the degree of difficulty involved in achieving success with a high certainty of probability
 (ii) Cost factors, or issues of available resources, that limit your options or curb your ability to achieve competing goals, or
(iii) The impact of your decisions on the welfare of others, be it clients, partners, society or even personal health and family

The executive or the board's default reaction is to approach an identified problem topic, even as emotional as ethics, harassment or racism, analytically and methodically. To do so, they will establish objective and measurable goals for a policy and mandate a "programme" for implementation. Finally, they will establish accountability by assigning responsibility for the programme with Human Resources, Ethics and Compliance, or another suitably named internal control department.

D&I Policy

A "good" D&I policy will typically include an exposé on the social context in which the firm operates and how these influence its activities and stakeholders. The policy will analyse the distribution of staff by business activity or location and compare diversity ratios at various levels of management. It will evaluate the recruitment policy of Human Resources and select a few values such as "respect" and "be inclusive" to highlight in a training programme rolled out over a (say) 1 year period. The executive will define measurable objectives for monitoring and non-financial reporting purposes. The public relations department will draft statements and press releases to emphasise the seriousness with which the firm is dealing with a hitherto lack of diversity and career progression for Ethnic Minorities.

There is nothing wrong with the above. However, there are three possible approaches to handling and implementation.

- The "Wokewashing" approach is the practice of issuing politically correct statements without any intention to take effective follow-through action. The organisational leadership believes that diversity is not a problem "here" and that all that is required is a brand image campaign to deflect media from criticising the firm.

- The "Delegation" approach, whereby once the assessment and evaluation process is complete, a policy and programme established, and an accountable individual appointed, the problem is considered delegated and dealt with. The board delegates to the executive, and the executive passes the baton to an individual with a title along the lines of "Chief Diversity Officer". Without any rights of recourse to the board, if the board fails to view their work as a priority, the subject matter no longer appears on the boardroom table apart from inside a quarterly report indicating some early quick wins to calm the nerves—both inside and outside the firm.

- The "Ownership" approach, whereby the board assumes full responsibility for any lack of diversity or inclusiveness in the corporate culture, recognises the value of change and invests itself and recruits an executive who shares the aspiration to establish an inclusive culture. In this scenario, the diversity function is empowered with independence, resources and the platform to transform the necessary structures, processes and practices.

Experience has shown that the achievement of an ethical or inclusive culture, even one moulded to your bespoke corporate purpose, is not a quick fix. Time and again, executives have tried to alter employee behaviours by issuing new procedures, training programmes and monitoring, without adopting and engaging in behavioural changes themselves. A new procedure to adjust an operational task can be communicated, taught and checked in a technical delegation exercise. In the matter of culture change, in dealing with human emotions, this is not an option.

Behaviours and attitudes can only be influenced by the observations and conviction of individual employees gained from the attitudes and behaviours of their superiors and the evidence provided by reward and sanction decisions. Members of organisations, from the board of directors to the groundsman, have to be confident that they understand the authentic intent of the organisation, the values and behaviours they are expected to enact and for which they will be promoted or sanctioned. They have to be clear on the desired impact of their decisions that will influence their performance reviews.

Books have been, and are still being, written on culture change. Yet, corporate purpose, values and ethics are not built on solid and unyielding bedrock; they are not castles that provide reliable defences against the onslaught of changing circumstances outside their walls. Rather, they provide the compass and nautical charts needed to navigate shifting sands moved by the changing tides of public concerns. To pursue any other approach than one of ownership is only to tip one's hat to the clamour for corporate social responsibility. Consumers and employees have learnt that some companies are tempted to try to capture the moment by riding the wave of public sentiment by misrepresenting their politics. Famously, Pepsi implied in an ad campaign in 2017 that protesters at a civil rights demonstration offering a police officer a canned drink could change the mood from angry to party. The company misread the backdrop of the #BLM scandal, police violence and unrest, and public sentiment turned against the company for trivialising the issue. Pepsi withdrew the campaign at a substantial cost to the firm.

One might argue that wokewashing does have a form of benefit. In the words of professor Tensie Whelan of the Stern School of Business: "It's extremely useful to get corporations on the record saying they're committing. If they don't carry through, they can be held accountable" [16]. Some might call it providing others with a stick with which to beat you.

Diversity Recruitment: Risk, Reward, and Making Waves

In the absence of a genuine and observable change in leadership mentality, a newly announced D&I policy does not seem to change diversity percentages in the organisation too much; at best, it can be a slow affair. Most managers do not wittingly wish to exclude talented workers from short-lists or be unfair in promotion decisions. There may be a few prejudiced souls, unconscious or otherwise, who staunchly refuse to submit to what they consider "fashionable wokishness" and carry on as before, regardless. However, many will openly acknowledge that ethnic minorities are under-represented in their organisation. Why does this situation persist?

Principally, the answer appears to be twofold. Firstly, companies have a cultural "thumbprint" of bias that impacts attitudes as to what represents a "typical" (hence, low-risk) recruit within the organisation. Secondly, managers experience psychological stress when swimming against the stream of those expectations. In other words, making hires that go against traditional profiles will raise eyebrows and attract the attention of colleagues and management.

Recruitment is never easy, and "what" you hire is rarely exactly what you expected based on the hiring interview. The recruit may be far more productive and creative than you predicted, or perhaps less flexible or willing to go the extra mile than you hoped. Most of the time, we quietly accommodate these differences, and life goes on. However, sometimes we make hires that make waves. Perhaps you recruit a top salesperson from a competitor involving both expensive compensation packages and high expectations. You know your hiring decision attracts the attention of peers and the executive; being in the limelight carries its risks. A good result might bestow more star status on the incoming employee than the person who recruited them; a disappointing result will reflect more on the hiring manager than the failed recruit. A high-profile recruitment comes with high risk and little reward for the recruiter. Suppose you have a choice between two equal candidates, one who fits the standard profile of other employees and another who breaks the mould and attracts more attention than the other. Which would you choose? It would be rational risk-averse behaviour to hire the more "typical" profile of recruit. Also, the less typical candidate from a diverse background, culture or country, is less likely to meet our pre-conditioned perception of merit as traditionally defined in our culture thumbprint.

The risk-averse strategy typically raises the bar of qualifications that the unusual recruitment profile must meet to be considered an equal [17]. For example, McKinsey & Company statistics show that Black women in the USA represent only 5% of entry-level professional recruits, while White women make up 31% of the same category. When I observe that most of my undergraduate management students are women, I immediately sense a gender problem. There is every reason to anticipate an equal representation of men and women recruited to entry-level professional roles instead of the 36% shown in the study. But the picture worsens as we proceed through the corporate pipeline to the level of Vice-President, where Black women only hold 1% of posts (White women 24% and White men 59%). For comparison, we might note that Black male representation amongst Vice-Presidents in the McKinsey study amounts to 2% only (and "Men of Colour", just 12%) [18].

Some organisations have experimented with recruitment algorithms hoping that human bias may be deleted from the equation. Regrettably, this has not proved to be a success. Since algorithms have to be devised and programmed by humans, bias is merely perpetuated in numbers and equations instead. Even self-learning artificial intelligence does not guard against manifest prejudice. It will only register outcomes from decisions that are deemed successful—whilst those definitions favour prevailing wisdom on the definitions of success and do not factor in the external influences on individual performance that can be alleviated. A historical trend of typically minority profile recruits making slower career advances than mainstream candidates will encourage AI to recruit fewer ethnic minority employees. This, irrespective of the fact that (say) Black career progression may be slowed by predominantly mainstream managers' conventional reluctance to promote them [19].

The Inclusive Self . . . or Not

As individuals, we are the sum of our parts. In earlier chapters, we have discussed the many influences on our personalities and character, including the many prejudices, assumptions and biases that have shaped our opinions. We have to conclude that we are not perfect, that we are not always generous and inclusive, and that what seems evident as correct and fair from our perspective, is variable and inconsistent depending on the circumstances [20].

A consequence of the humiliating realisation that we are fallible is that we must always be open to the challenge of other perspectives and be willing to learn and change our behaviours accordingly. In the case of diversity and inclusion, this is certainly not the same as merely bending to a majority view or perceived wisdom. On the contrary, to learn means to evaluate and learn from or reject new ideas, or find a new middle ground based on new knowledge.

Put bluntly, we have to ask ourselves if we are not sometimes too willing to place self-interest ahead of our proclaimed values: too ready to excuse less ethical behaviour if they pay our bills or safeguard our privilege and luxuries. Alternatively, if we feel that our actions as individuals, made on behalf of the organisation, do not have any significant direct negative impact on people we interact with, why should we concern ourselves?

Willful blindness entails being in an opinion "bubble" that quietens our conscience, rationalises our self-serving behaviours, and avoids the discomfort that comes with accepting accountability for our poor personal behaviour. Most people will also baulk at the idea of "giving away" an advantage gained through privilege. Our natural tendency is to look the other way to avoid blame, responsibility or loss; we prefer not to see morally objectionable behaviour which might oblige us to intervene. Willful blindness is an instinct that undermines an organisation's culture of trust, ethics and eventually excellence. Yet, suppose an individual feels powerless to influence outcomes, change the behaviours of others, or fears ridicule for speaking up on an unpopular subject. In that case, willful blindness is what you will get.

5.4   Culture Change: A Human Affair

If only it were as simple as writing a rule. The board could announce that discrimination and prejudice no longer have a place in the organisation. The executive could declare D&I as the new normal, and that performance, career decisions, and recruitment shall be free of prejudice or bias. Would that it were that easy.

Our objective is to promote and create a work environment where discrimination based on race, religion or other forms of diversity are a thing of the past. But, as we have sought to demonstrate, such an environment cannot be assured merely through codes of conduct and rulebooks. Real change requires conviction through hearts and minds—empathy and knowledge. Unfortunately, academic research demonstrates that organisational leadership generally focuses on cultural change only in the absence of alternative courses of action, and when lots of resources and lots of time are available—a rare enough coincidence of circumstances [21]. In the 2020s, however, there is an additional imperative that is mounting in influence every year. The Millennial generation and GenZ are increasingly manifesting their expectations that our institutions, establishments and businesses start delivering a better future than the one currently in prospect for them [7].

There are reasonable concerns if the achievement of a uniform, global corporate culture is at all possible. In a small, single location or regional business, where the executive and senior management are easily visible, approachable and willing to demonstrate the kind of behaviours and attitudes they are asking of their staff, it may well be feasible. But what of the 100,000 employee company present in 30 or more countries? Surely, there comes the point where one size fits all no longer applies, and the focus has to be less on rules and observed leadership behaviours, and more on cultural learning adapted to local conditions and customs. Teaching ethics to a classroom of students all born and raised in Ohio is a very different prospect to winning the hearts and minds of an assembly of business managers gathered together from 25 different cultures. The pedagogical path to gaining their understanding and support of desired outcomes will be different for each culture, and inevitably require ample time and resources. Get it wrong, and there is a high risk of conflict emanating from highlighting different perspectives on morality and religion related to inclusiveness. Confronting cultural differences carries serious risk, and companies are loath to commit the sizable investments required unless absolutely necessary.

Indeed, it is simply not realistic to expect all managers in an organisation to share a single, uniform view of privilege, prejudice and fairness at work. Even less so can we hope that all managers have the necessary communication skills, emotional intelligence and cultural sensitivity required to traverse the treacherously thin ice of race relations. As in many aspects of life, actions speak louder than words. Leaders must be role models, expectations must be clear, and assessments of outcomes and impact objective and transparent. To spread a practice through an organisation is like identifying the source of a river and then capturing the waters to irrigate the land, flowing quietly through the undergrowth, sustaining a natural growth of healthy crops. If the firm does not guide and trust its employees to know what is right or wrong for the company, then it is unrealistic to expect employees to exercise sound judgement on ethical questions such as calling out discriminatory behaviour. The company will need to consider its leadership style as well as its culture.

Walking the Talk

As Divisional Head of International Compliance at Fortis Bank, Belgium, my Head of Division and I discussed what we could do to provide our front-line officers with greater assuredness regarding the ethical standards we wished them to apply to business opportunities. The full board had elected not to establish an ethics committee for the entire group to determine policy concerning dealing with such things as polluting industries, weapons finance, and investments in regimes that did not respect human rights, amongst others. Their preference was to approach these questions with "common sense" and pragmatism. In a homogenous home market in the Benelux, where uniformity is backed by socially driven sentiment, one might argue (and disagree with) that there was a sufficiently common understanding of right and wrong; that our staff would "obviously" know what to do. In the International Division, we did not share that view. We could not allow ourselves to imagine that our front-line officers in Brussels, the Caribbean, Hong Kong, Madrid, New York, Singapore, Sydney and Zurich (to name just a few) would understand the thresholds of tolerance regarding ethical questions in a uniform manner. Consequently, we decided to establish business conduct policies on a range of topics.

The reaction was illuminating in more ways than one. Firstly, the policy discussions themselves engaged the Executive Board of the International Division in an ethical debate that invigorated them; even attracted them to be present and correct for the so-called Business Conduct Committee meeting called at the unearthly hour of 6.30 AM every quarter. The front line business officers of all our various product and service units enjoyed the clarity of expectations endorsed by the executive. They became more efficient in structuring business proposals, and the approval process across the Division became more efficient. Finally, and somewhat to our surprise (and probably of the board), we were approached by the Retail Division, the Private Banking Division and others to help them translate the standards we had defined for international business into their own spheres of business. The International Division's Business Conduct Committee had acted as the source of a stream that grew and ran in tributaries throughout the organisation. The example provided by the initiative provided employees with the courage to speak up for higher ethical standards and say no to transactions that did not match our moral expectations.

The Power of Networks

The equivalent of river tributaries or irrigation systems within an organisation is its social networks. Social Infrastructure Network Theory explains that there are various levels at which networks operate. Such networks exist between colleagues in a single office or diverse colleagues across the organisation when forming an employee resource group. Other networks combine participants in a situational, intermittent and time-limited confederation of interest, such as training events, mentoring or coaching schemes. Such networks can be encouraged and managed—and indeed, in a culture change endeavour, must be. We cannot expect to identify common interests and values before we are, at least, visible to one another.

To prepare the way for an exercise launched to alter the mindset and risk awareness of the injustice and inequality perpetuated by a more privileged majority towards a disadvantaged minority, the manner in which the values and views associated with that change can flow through the organisation must be prepared and nurtured.

- The social networks (also called social capital) of the organisation must be formed and shaped to enable the vast majority of employees both to receive the message on expected behaviours and outcomes, and to observe the behaviour of their superiors.
- The activity directed at the network is not only to clarify what diversity and inclusion outcomes are being aspired to but also to demonstrate the value and creativity that comes from the achievement of those D&I objectives.
- Finally, the workings of the networks must offer safe passage for all those who participate in the dialogue it generates. It must be comfortable to confront past discrimination. It must be safe to speak up about experiences of prejudice. To provide constructive feedback on how we can handle bias better in the future must be free of risks.

It Is a Full-Time Occupation

In this chapter, we have been exploring the question as to why it is that we have not found the universal answer as to how we can successfully implement a diversity and inclusion utopia. The answer is threefold:

(i) Humans are complex, emotional and individual beings who have to be persuaded that overcoming prejudice and embracing diversity will enrich their existence and potential. However, it is neither obvious nor natural to presume that this is the case. Hence, we cannot legislate discrimination and bias away—it requires continuous education.

(ii) The nature of prejudice and bias manifests itself in endless ways. We can exercise empathy and try to understand what our actions and words may mean to a majority or minority group. We have to fine-tune our ability to listen, understand and control our instincts in ways that go counter to our background and cultural upbringing and the conventions from which our prejudice and bias have come.

(iii) Our business education and social definitions of success, especially in the Western industrialised world, includes an expectation of efficiency, effectiveness and rapid results. However, culture change is not a quick fix. Board members and executives who prefer perfunctory evaluations and decisions, followed by delegation and goal-setting, will be frustrated. Indeed, we need to establish the social networks and a dialogue that allows a fluid and changing definition of the social, cultural and ethical values within the organisation; then embed these into the concept of performance evaluations, promotions, and rewards. However, this condition is only the point at which the work of culture management can start—it will never end.

References

1. Chong, E. (2021, May 8). *Your name sounds like the noise you make when you go to the toilet.* BBC 3 at BBC.co.uk.
2. Force, R. A. (2019, October). *Ethos, core values and standards.* Air publication 1, 3rd revision.
3. McEnery, T. (2020, June 5). Jamie Dimon drops into Mt. Kisco Chase branch, takes a knee with staff. *New York Post.*
4. *Business Roundtable redefines the purpose of a corporation to promote 'an economy that serves all Americans'.* Accessed August 19, 2019, from www.businessroundtable.org
5. Flitter, E. (2019, December 14). This is what racism sounds like in the banking industry. *The New York Times.*
6. Jan, T., McGregor, J., Merle, R., & Tiku, N. (2020, June 13). As big corporations say 'black lives matter,' their track records raise skepticism. *Washington Post.*
7. de Chenecey, S. P. (2019). *The post-truth business.* Kogan Page Publishers.
8. Noel, N., Pinder, D., Stewart, S., & Wright, J. (2019, August 19). *The economic impact of closing the racial wealth gap.* McKinsey.
9. Armental, M. (2020, June 23). Microsoft CEO pledges to back racial-justice efforts through promotion, investment initiatives. *Wall Street Journal.*

10. Gallagher, J., Safdar, K., & Terlep, S. (2020, June 8). Workers press Adidas, Estée Lauder, others to act on racism, diversity. *Wall Street Journal*.
11. Nelson, J. C., Adams, G., & Salter, P. S. (2012, December 11). The Marley hypothesis: Denial of racism reflects ignorance of history. *Psychological Science*.
12. (2013, January 15). Claims of 'post-racial' society and other denials of racism may reflect ignorance of history. *ScienceDaily*.
13. Henderson, A., & Kinias, Z. (2020, September 24). *Understanding the origins of White denial*. INSEAD Knowledge.
14. Abdelfatah, R., & Arablouei, R. (2020, October 30). *James Baldwin's shadow*. Throughline podcast, NPR.
15. Smith-Meyer, A. (2018). *Surviving organisational behaviour*. Kindle Publications.
16. Todd, S. (2020, October 22). If everybody hates wokewashing, why do companies still do it? *Quartz*.
17. Caver, K. A., & Livers, A. B. (2002, November). Dear White Boss. *Harvard Business Review*.
18. Noel, N., Pinder, D., Stewart, S., & Wright, J. (2019, August 13). *The economic impact of closing the racial wealth gap*. McKinsey & Company.
19. UN Technology Innovations Lab. *Inclusion & diversity: Tech it or leave it*. Accessed July 10, 2020.
20. Kahneman, D., Sibony, O., & Sunstein, C. (2021). *Noise: A flaw in human judgement*. Little Brown Spark.
21. Crane, A., & Matten, D. (2016). *Business ethics*. Oxford University Press.

Part III

Campaigning for Change

So far in this book, we have explored the nature and impact of diversity in terms of its benefits in the shape of learning and innovation, as well as the harm that results from discrimination and exclusion, even amongst people who consider themselves ethical and just. The intractable dynamics behind our prejudicial behaviours and identities are rooted in legacies, narratives and perceptions of Self that construct formidable obstacles to natural instincts towards enlightenment, inclusion and reconciliation. Hence, there is no unobstructed road to an inclusive society or organisation; instead, there is a thick growth through which a path must be engineered and cut.

An organisation which seeks to achieve diversity and inclusion exclusively through analysis, policies and procedures will fail to reach its objective, as so many do. To go beyond superficial changes of behaviour and open the doors to inclusion and belonging requires empathy and curiosity. The keys to unlocking these opportunities are forged by courageous leadership and a sustainable culture of trust amongst the members of the organisation. These elements provide the roadmap to culture change of a scale and scope few dare to hope to achieve. In Part III, we delve into our toolbox for culture change and discover that, with determination, such hope will not be futile.

#CultureChange: What It Is and How It Works

6

6.1   What Is Organisational Culture?

Organisational culture is nebulous and conceptual. Academics define it in terms of shared values, norms and assumptions that guide members' attitudes and behaviours (Philips & Gully), or taken-for-granted assumptions commonly held by a group that determines how it perceives, thinks about and reacts to a given situation (Kinicki & Fugate). For most laypersons and practitioners, the answer boils down to "the way we do things around here". It is the behaviour and attitudes you observe around you, which you adopt to ensure that you "fit in" with neighbours and colleagues as swiftly and painlessly as possible. The alternative is to risk exclusion. For the most part, when joining a social group of like-minded people, the adjustments asked of the newcomer are minor and straightforward. However, to the individual of a different upbringing and culture, some of the normalised behaviour within the group may seem strange and alien, even wrong [1].

Using our powers of observation, we quickly detect this "way we do things" in the attitudes and behaviours of those around us. The strength of the culture may vary depending on how vigorously group values and worldviews are enacted and communicated. In a very informal setting, culture can be hard to discern, and one might be left wondering what one has to do to be "invited" into some social groupings. However, the stronger the culture, the more pervasive its influence will be.

Most companies have a C-suite which would sincerely condemn unethical conduct, including discrimination. But such things are often taken for granted, leading to a failure to invest time and money in organisational health. Even a prominent, highly respected firm like Mckinsey & Company, who previously prided themselves on their moral sensibilities, are considered in 2021 to have "become very grandiose in their belief in their own success. When they start to get information that challenges this self-belief, the feedback is deemed to be wrong" [2]. Hubris, it seems, can be a symptom of a stagnant narrative.

When Kinicki and Fugate use the term "taken-for-granted" in their definition of organisational culture, it may be correct—but it should not be mistaken as the objective or the characterisation of a strong culture. It implies that culture is just there—take it or leave it. A strong culture is one that is sufficiently robust to live with challenge and debate. If we want a culture that is relevant and meaningful, then this is the benchmark we have to aim for.

The world around us is in constant turmoil. How we behave needs to be continuously questioned and revised with a view to its impact on our corporate purpose, the value of our products, and the effect our behaviours have on our employees, customers, and partners. A culture that includes "taken-for-granted" assumptions is, or is on the way to becoming, a weak and increasingly strategically irrelevant culture.

Levels of Cultural Maturity

If we adapt the various definitions of culture offered by Encyclopaedia Britannica, we can discern four levels of cultural maturity:

1. At the lowest level of definition, it is "the customary beliefs, social forms, and material traits of a racial, religious, or social group; also, the characteristic features of everyday existence shared by people in a place or time". This habit-determined explanation truly reflects the "way we have always done things around here". Behaviour is driven by existing beliefs and customs that are "traits" or hallmarks of the social group in question. It is usually not questioned or open to change.
2. At the second level, it is "the set of shared attitudes, values, goals, and practices that characterises an institution or organisation". At this level, governance has kicked in, and we have a form of institutionalised culture. It is a level where one can seek and find conventions documented in the shape of policies, value statements and codes of conduct. This level is no longer one at which culture has developed haphazardly based on history and tradition. Here, there is an attempt to set a deliberate standard.
3. At the third level, it is "the act of developing the intellectual and moral faculties, especially by education". It goes beyond merely setting a standard to be respected. The organisation can set standards and procedures created to instruct people on how to comply with those standards, yet there can be a lack of understanding of why these standards are important. When the institution aims to develop the employees' awareness of corporate purpose and knowledge of the desired outcome of its values being applied in the business process, it seeks to influence employee mindset and judgement. Employees no longer merely "comply" with the standard set at this level of maturity—they promote it.
4. At the fourth and highest level, we are at a point where "the integrated pattern of human knowledge, belief, and behaviour depends upon the capacity for learning and transmitting knowledge to succeeding generations". We have entered a

virtuous cycle where a culture is self-sustaining, not because "this is the way we have always done things", or even "this is the way we do things around here". It is more than this—it is the gold standard of "this is how we think around here". Culture is a living, self-learning and changing application of our values. Members who understand it can exercise sound judgement in response to decisions and choices that we have to make every day. Values, attitude and behaviour become one and change in line with knowledge gained.

The Power of Culture

Before we consider how culture is created or propagated, let us reflect on why we seek to instil a common culture within our social groupings. We are grappling with the complexity of D&I questions, so developing one culture for all members of an organisation to fit into might seem somewhat "old school". We aim to celebrate diversity and individual creativity. Still, we want to encourage the use of this diversity to the benefit of the group; towards the fulfilment of its purpose. This desire for unity, as well as diversity, is not oppositional; the two are complementary. When applied strategically in support of organisational goals, the whole is worth more than the parts. Group culture promotes certain norms of attitude and behaviour, all serving to:

- *Focus.* By encouraging the attitude and behaviour that is most supportive of organisational purpose, we will help the organisation achieve its objectives and succeed over time. When D&I are part of this focus, it has been shown that creativity, innovation, personal growth and productivity increase.
- *Build Trust.* Humans are social beings, and we thrive on social interaction that conforms to expectations and does not threaten, but builds mutual respect and caring instead. When a group is focused on a common purpose, dealing with cultural barriers to communication and collaboration becomes a secondary, less threatening topic. A shared culture promotes a common objective, raising the target outcome to the level of what is best for the group, not just the individual.
- *Minimise Conflict.* By clearly delineating common standards of behaviour and interaction, the process of resolving conflict or confronting constructive challenge will be ritualised to a point where there is greater confidence and freedom to discuss issues of contention openly. When we perceive ourselves to be on the "same team", our empathy for each other increases. We desire for those working alongside us to thrive for the sake of "the team" and common objectives. In short, mentality switches from a blame culture to one where "your problem is my problem".
- *Shape Identity.* When an individual group member feels at one with the culture clearly associated with the organisation, they will identify with that group. What the organisation stands for, and how society perceives it in general, will be a source of pride and inspiration for the group member who, consequently, will develop a high degree of loyalty: a dedication to the achievement of

organisational purpose. In a military setting, we might refer to "comrades at arms". It no longer matters that we have different backgrounds; we protect one another, and "we are in it together".

The Culture Cycle

Culture exists regardless. If left to its own devices, it shapes itself, with the inherent risk that behaviours will not be those desired. Employees will work out for themselves what is valued by leaders to whom they report.
Sir Anthony Salz
The Salz Review of Barclays Business Practice

The choice appears clear. If a culture exists regardless, we can choose to abide by it unquestioningly or seek to change it. If it is possible to influence it, then it is logical to believe we can manage it. However, like nature and weather, a culture built on emotions and faith cannot easily be instructed to change course. All we can do is use the psychological triggers and drivers of behaviour that we have to hand and hope for the desired reaction to manifest itself. It is important then to understand what the levers of culture and human behaviour are.

The culture cycle describes the process that allows organisational values to influence mindset and behaviours and establish confidence in the veracity of those values, thereby influencing belief, language and attitudes. For the anecdotal new-comer who observes new colleagues adhering to a code of doing things "the way we always do things around here", these habits form expectations of what is considered the everyday ethics of the group.

In a culture change environment, a leadership introducing new values and language sets out to first influence mindset, in turn influencing behaviours. If rigorously implemented and supported by an appropriate rewards and sanctions regime, new habits will form and strengthen belief in the leadership's resolve to uphold the new values.

The culture cycle can be broken and reset to one prioritising diversity and inclusion:

(a) The promotion of specific values, such as respect and care for others, curiosity, continuous learning and a listening mentality, will promote attitudes and per-sonal demeanour that support the inclusion of those who think differently from ourselves. Words and language matter; people hear the nuance in them. Hence, they must be accompanied by role model behaviour by way of example and interpretation.

(b) Attitudes and mindset will alter the perception of expected behaviour. As employees experiment, possibly tentatively at first and with a wary eye on the reaction of supervisors and colleagues around them, new standards of expected behaviours will become apparent and upheld.

Fig. 6.1 The culture cycle

(c) Observed conduct will consolidate or undermine belief in the communicated values. If adherence to the values advocated is rewarded with praise, celebration, kudos and promotion, those who take the first tentative steps will learn that the organisation is serious about its group ethics. Colleagues will take heart from the positive examples set by others and will start to experiment, forming new habits and norms. Of equal importance is the treatment being meted out to those who violate or ignore group values. If transgressors are not held to account, belief in organisational commitment to its values will dissipate.

(d) Finally, as an experience of approval or admonishment amongst employees becomes manifest, the perception that values are genuinely respected will grow. As a result, the role of values within the organisation will strengthen and lead to an even more significant influence on attitudes and, accordingly, personal conduct.

We can understand how a virtuous cycle of cultural influence on behaviour, as depicted in Fig. 6.1, can be created. Indeed, we are entering the universe of quantum management theory, where colleagues act independently, impacting and changing each other through a dynamic exchange of applied ethics and purpose [3].

Suppose the leadership has clarity on organisational expectations where D&I is concerned. In that case, the executive can start to influence a change in mindset or reinforce attitudes by role-modelling target behaviours themselves, supplementing with programmes to educate, reward and enforce the desired standards of conduct.

6.2   On Compliance and Culture

On the subject of racial integration and inclusiveness within the law profession, Tsedale Melaku asks the question: "How can we lean into a table when we are not even in the room?" [4]. We return to the question of what happens when the promotion of D&I is not accompanied by an authentic desire amongst the leadership to faithfully make the changes as advertised.

We have already discussed how you cannot legislate change. Policy, procedures, monitoring and reporting are required, especially when managing a large organisation. Still, effective outcomes relative to D&I objectives will require a genuine conviction that corporate values and an inclusive culture mean something. The establishment of anti-discrimination and inclusiveness controls has its place, but its impact is secondary. It normally serves to capture the errant behaviour of a minority of miscreants who, admittedly, can spoil things for the majority. Its objective should be to provide a strong and clear message that non-compliance with organisational goals will be identified and punished—it should also serve to spot exemplary behaviour that can be rewarded. Above all, it helps prove the quality of organisational justice within the corporation, an essential component in creating a culture of trust that encourages community members to "do the right thing", speak up and experiment with dialogue or other supporting initiatives. Indeed, there is little mention of compliance in the aviation sector, and instead, there is a focus on performance. This emphasis on "performance" relates not to financial goals but to maintaining standards and continuous improvement. Compliance is an outcome, not an approach; the pursuit of values is an aspiration, not a single act [5].

6.3   Defining Strategic Culture

Where we are concerned with our employees' behaviour and the impact their actions have on our external stakeholders, we have to accept that human conduct is consistently motivated by anticipated punishment and reward. Incentives can be in the form of material or physical outcomes, such as the payment of cash bonuses or being fired. But it can also manifest itself in the pride or fear that comes from being recognised for admirable traits leading to Maslow's "love" and popularity, or rejected and despised as someone selfish or duplicitous. For most people, their actions are commonly driven by their desire to be accepted and admired by those around them. The measure by which people consider actions as worthy of esteem or not is determined by the socially accepted values and ethics of the group. The strength of these values and ethics is what institutes culture—hence, culture drives behaviour. Therefore, if we desire our organisation to cultivate diversity and be inclusive of minority groups, we have to approach its culture as a strategic issue.

Consequently, promoting a culture that encourages specific behaviours that serve an organisational objective, such as D&I, becomes a strategic manoeuvre. Institutional values shape culture, but only if they are nurtured, encouraged and supported by the board and its executive. Deciding on the values that promote openness, learning and inclusiveness is not a reactive decision. Intuition and continuing past behaviours deemed successful is a frail basis on which to secure long-term success. Instead, the board should be proactive in understanding the external social and cultural environment, as well as the skewing effect that recruitment policy and profiling has on the employee mix within the organisation.

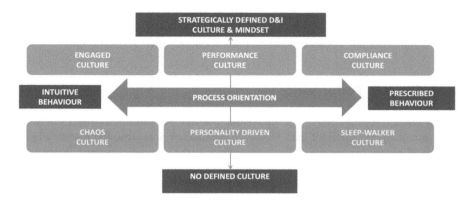

Fig. 6.2 Strategic culture

Every organisation will position itself along a line of low to high process orientation (see Fig. 6.2). Creative, unregulated industries will typically have fewer policies and procedures to act as guardrails for their employees, instead accepting a higher degree of experimentation and imagination to inspire innovation and new product ideas. At the other extreme, certain highly regulated, potentially high-risk activities, such as pharmaceuticals, aerospace and banking, will have a plethora of policies and procedures to prevent uncontrolled experimentation and deviance from the predictable outcomes that hallmark such industries. In the confines of an aircraft cockpit, we want the discipline and thoroughness ensured by tick-box pre-flight checks; in the operating room, we probably prefer the surgeon to use tried and trusted procedures when performing surgery rather than experimenting with an untested, if inspired, idea. Policies and procedures are frequently dismissed as obstacles to getting things done—bureaucratic red tape. However, this is only the case if policies and procedures are not kept up to date and relevant to desired outcomes.

Achieving the right balance of policies and procedures for any single organisation is a matter of judgement and an understanding of employee or membership conduct. In the absence of any strategic behavioural objectives, processes are driven by external regulations governing the sector within which it operates, as well as any identified internal risks and activity that might otherwise disrupt efficiency or effectiveness. A creative arts company may, therefore, not have many externally driven procedures. However, one dealing with potentially dangerous use of sharp objects, chemicals or high temperatures will still introduce practical policies and procedures that protect employees against injury, or the company against liability.

Process orientation, if correctly calibrated, is neither positive nor negative in the context of an organisation. It is a matter of governance and decision frameworks. What does impact how processes contribute to the effectiveness of a policy objective is the organisational culture in which these processes are applied. Is corporate culture evident in its expression of the values it wants its employees to consider when making decisions? Has the leadership been clear as to what outcomes it expects and what stakeholder impact it prioritises? Are such values stale and unquestioned, or is there easy access up and down the hierarchy to discuss and evaluate the choices to be made when espoused values need to be prioritised or impact re-assessed?

From Chaos to Performance

In the context of diversity and inclusion, a strategic culture makes clear that substance is more important than form—that inclusion is an emotional state where a sense of belonging by the outgroup minority is the desired outcome. Without a strategic culture, in a low process-oriented organisation there will be few markers established by the leadership to educate, monitor or control how the ruling majority welcomes or rejects outgroup members. Those recruited from minority or marginalised groups will be treated in line with local, external social attitudes. It is uncontrolled, without direction and might be labelled a "Chaos Culture". Behaviour on the shop-floor will be unaffected by distant key stakeholders or non-existent strategic views. Hot-desking clerks will not feel concerned about or responsible for organisational priorities; employees will not even be aware of them. Even an ad hoc utterances made by the executive during a spate of #BLM protests that prejudicial and discriminatory treatment of Black employees is not to be tolerated within the firm will be dismissed as irrelevant to everyday business. The adage of "actions speak louder than words" will prevail. Unless any deliberate and long-term (i.e. strategic) measures are adopted within the house, past practices and misconduct will continue.

The role of values is crucial in this process of culture management. Barrett maintains that values are a shorthand for describing what is important to us individually or collectively at any given moment in time [6]. By putting values front and centre of the decision-making process, the outcomes of decisions become more predictable and likely to result in the desired impact. Values have to connect and engage with individuals. As a newcomer enters a strategically defined culture, that individual will adopt the values evidenced in the behaviour of their new colleagues. It follows, therefore, that the organisational "old-timers" who are committed to these values become the best ambassadors for them. The objective is to have all members of the organisation acting as role models for each other, not only the leadership [5]. Without a values-led culture, there is only a top-down diktat that will instruct employees as to expected outcomes, but also lead to avoidance and side-stepping when compliance gets in the way of meeting performance goals.

Consider now the executive who acknowledges the need for change and makes the commitment to increase minority group representation amongst board, executive and management ranks. Suppose also that the board ensures appropriate expert advice from diversity and human resource consultants and adopts a plan, including target requirements for hiring and promotion decisions. Such deliberate actions speak louder than words, but neither educate nor engage the existing workforce. Sexual harassment measures introduced years ago do not mean that sexist remarks are not whispered today, nor that offices are not decorated in ways that will make women feel uncomfortable. Overt racist commentary and bullying may decline on the back of new policies and complaint procedures, but it does not mean that the allocation of growth opportunities is distributed without stereotypical prejudgement of ability. Indeed, introducing recruitment targets and zero-tolerance rules on bias-driven behaviours alone can produce resentment or an unthinking application of the rules, potentially leading to a worsening of conditions for socially disadvantaged minorities and marginalised groups [7].

If employees do not understand why rules and procedures have been introduced, they will be followed—but only to avoid sanction and without regard for impact or purpose. We might call this a "Sleepwalker Culture". Employees will go through the motions and tick the boxes required by a process, but will have no concern for the outcome. Hence, situational judgement is lost, procedures are misapplied irrespective of impact, and any evidence of effectiveness ignored.

The Role Model Organisation

There is a middle ground where the company remains without formal policies or values, but informal expectations are still understood to exist. A strong and charismatic executive may take a deep interest in the subject and be determined to stamp out discriminatory behaviour. Subordinates will observe the leader's behaviour and toe the line as instructed. However, without a strategic culture programme, the reasons for the executive prioritisation of D&I within the firm remain uncertain. We hear the diplomatic words, and we observe the reward and sanction decisions taken. Still, we cannot be sure if the interest and commitment are temporary or free of any hidden agenda. This culture is personality-driven and ensures neither monitoring, education or longevity. Once distracted to another issue and the leader changes topic or there is a change of the guard, old prejudices will return, and any improvement be short-lived.

The board and executive who have understood the importance of strategic culture will aim for a culture change programme to guard against all these risks. No matter if the firm has a high or low process orientation, the firm will:

(a) Seek the engagement of its staff
(b) Work to convince them of the importance change has to the success of the corporate venture, and
(c) Educate them as to the justice and fairness of what is being proposed and applied

Rules and procedures introduced will be understood in terms of the spirit of the policy they seek to uphold. For example, in a low-process environment, employees will discover the benefit of diversity and inclusion together and pursue the objective because they see the value it brings. In a high-process context, boxes may be ticked, but if the outcomes of applying these procedures differ from what is clearly explained as desired outcome and impact, they will be questioned, re-evaluated and re-designed. We can move along the process-orientation axis from an

Engagement Culture to a Compliance Culture, but the overall result will be one where we might apply the term "Performance Culture": an effective culture that promotes the behaviours needed to execute the firm's strategies and achieve its goals successfully, be this excellence or D&I [8].

6.4   Culture Change: No Small Task

Much of the demand and justification of making serious of D&I within organisations rests on arguments of social justice and stakeholder expectations. However, as we have seen, studies increasingly show that those companies who lead in the successful implementation of inclusive cultures for women, LGBT+ and ethnic minorities enjoy a likelihood for financial outperformance of a massive 36% compared to those who make no or little D&I effort [9].

Hence, the importance of bringing about an effective culture change within the organisation is difficult to deny. Board directors are now schooled in the discipline of governance, objectives of long-term success, and the strategic importance of culture, including one of D&I. It has become the duty of directors to recruit and empower an executive who shares its conviction and is willing to lead this change personally. The C-suite must:

* Take ownership of the topics of diversity and inclusion.
* Show leadership in being the principal advocates of change.
* Have the courage to face the legacy of corporate history, distant and recent, and, sometimes, the personal challenge of accepting responsibility for the treatment of minorities within the organisation.

The question remains, however, how to go about changing the workplace psychology of potentially thousands, if not tens of thousands of employees. As previously mentioned, leaders must understand and accept that culture is not a task to be delegated and executed. Culture represents the entire value system of the company, and that cannot be left to administrators or technocrats. To advocate a particular cultural mindset means it has to be personified by the company leadership. To change it requires the board and executive to not only be painfully accountable for its success, but also to lead that change by example. Yet even that is only the beginning. In the USA, the Civil Rights Act of 1964 revealed a significant shift in social inclusion and racial policies—it altered the legal test on discrimination cases on racial and other grounds from "intent" to "impact". The burden of proof in discriminatory acts was no longer to be tested against the absence of an intent to do harm; instead, the test was now one that made perpetrators of discriminatory behaviour accountable in terms of harmful impact [10].

The Dismantling of Legacy

#BLM has existed since the acquittal of the killer of Trayvon Martin in 2013. The killing of George Floyd during the reflective days of the COVID-19 Lockdown followed a spate of other shootings involving innocent Black citizens in the USA and has seen the movement come to life in a way that the world has been unwilling to ignore. Thanks to President Trump's 2020 campaign rally in Tulsa, Oklahoma, the world learnt about the 1921 "Tulsa Massacre", when White mobs ran amok on what was then known as "the Black Wall Street", killing upwards of 300 people. We also discovered Juneteenth, the annual celebration of the emancipation of slaves celebrated by Americans everywhere; Black Americans, that is. In the wake of climate protests in 2019, the anxiety caused by COVID-19, the appearance of grotesque videos of illegal and cruel killings of Black Americans, the awareness campaign that is #BLM went both viral and global.

In Europe, Europeans protesting against US injustice and racism started to look at their own histories—now with statues of slave-traders and colonial masters in England, Belgium and France being removed—even a statue of a Norwegian-Danish missionary, Hans Egede, in Greenland and that of the (in)famous favourite privateer of England's Elizabeth I, Sir Francis Drake, came under consideration for removal. People, and that includes employees and consumers, have become painfully aware that there is a shameful legacy that needs confrontation, and a long-standing injustice that needs rectification.

We cannot truly unburden ourselves of our past bias and prejudice if we convince ourselves that "we" are not the problem. Regretfully, for most of us as individuals or corporates ensconced in any society, we have unsavoury legacies that we need to accept ownership of before we can be free of them. Like statues causing offence sufficient to be vandalised or removed, we need to take a fresh look at the symbols and icons of our firm and branding, even the paintings decorating our corridors of power, to see if they are appropriate to an inclusive culture. The headscarfed image of "Aunt Jemima" on the labels of pancake mixture and syrup owned by Quaker Oats had to go. Does the imagery of our company only laud a privileged and exclusive part of society? Such things undermine the message of inclusion and underestimate the hurt and offence they imply. We have to understand the moral imperative for us to act, for such action to be authentic and credible. We have to practice empathy and listening to be able to discern how symbolism can carry meaning beyond our experience, and how society's interpretation of those symbols can be appropriated or altered to highlight negative impacts on minority or disadvantaged communities.

Manifestations of Culture: Ghosts of the Past or Visions of the Future?

What message had generations of boys and girls received as they arrived at this school each day except for the certainty that, to those in power, they did not matter, that whatever was meant by the American Dream, it wasn't meant for them? [11]
  President Barak Obama[1]

In discussing inclusion, the unconscious bias of colleagues or the passive-aggressiveness of certain behaviours immediately come to the surface. Yet, even an empty office building can communicate the history and legacy, proud or otherwise, of the corporation. To the dominant majority who identify with the heritage and feel pride walking in the footsteps of destiny, it can provide confidence. However, to the disadvantaged, discriminated minority, it can bring forth atrocious ghosts of colonialism, slavery, ethnic cleansing and genocide. To be on the wrong side of history is to be excluded from destiny—unless you are willing to turn your back on your own history, eventually culture, family and friends.

Culture, values and behavioural expectations need to be identifiable and accessible. Some of these may result from seeing a culture in action, while others may be deliberately encouraged or highlighted to promote a given culture or legacy. Erecting statues to national heroes is one traditional way to celebrate current notions of success and pride in the values they represent. Through the ages, societies have created narratives and role models for others to follow in this manner.

This nurturing of role models has a flaw, however. In placing our heroes on pedestals, we praise the person rather than the values for which they are recognised. In the UK, wartime prime minister Winston Churchill displayed many qualities that helped keep hope amongst the population and the military alive. His qualities include perseverance, charismatic and emotional leadership, decisiveness and loyalty. However, in different circumstances, he could have been (and was) labelled stubborn, indisciplined and unrealistic [12]. When he has since been identified with negative outcomes, such as the tragedy of the 1943 Bengal famine and racist views that influenced colonial policy, his statements and actions cannot be raised without a denigration of his entire personality and contribution to society [13]. By praising the person and not the values that he is admired for, we are forced to maintain his hero status or shove him from his pedestal. The hero is not allowed to be a fallible human being. For many of my father's generation of WW2 Europeans, he was the leader that gave them the strength to survive the war. For others, he inflicted misery and despair. Is it not better to admire or deplore the values he held rather than hail the man as perfection? Is it impossible to be both an example of heroic leadership in crisis as well as a representative of outdated and callous colonialism? We are all products of our time, and we are all imperfect.

---

[1] President Obama reflecting on his visit to J.V. Martin High School with largely Black pupils during his first presidential campaign.

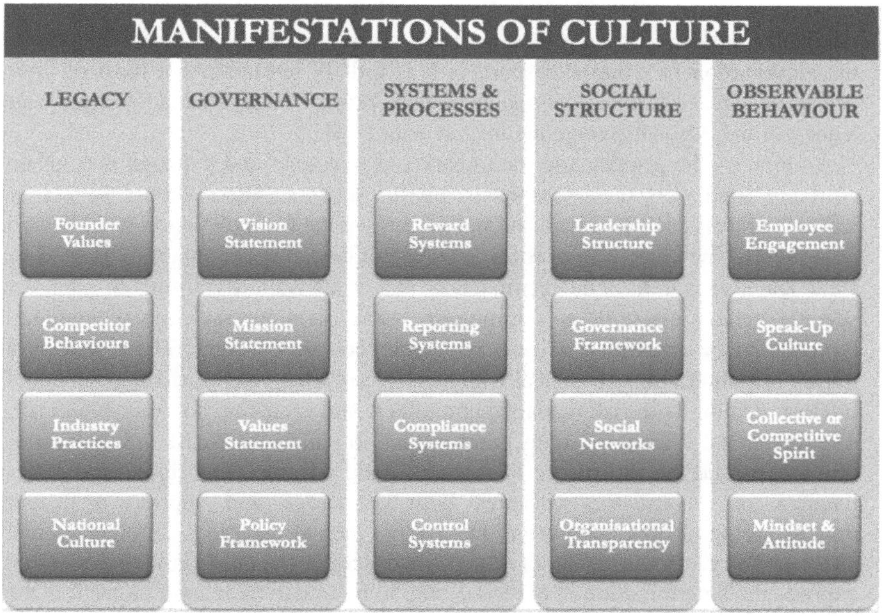

Fig. 6.3 Organisational manifestations of culture

6.5   Pillars of Organisational Culture: The Ground Rules for Change

There are many ways to analyse the cultural condition of an organisation. Often referred to as the pillars of organisational culture, the five crucial aspects of corporate life, depicted in Fig. 6.3, provide clues and evidence as to the nature of its environment.

– *Legacy.* Given that humans have been creating civil societies for tens of thousands of years, the formation of any new social culture will necessarily be marked by antecedents or traditional legacy values in one way or another. We are an innovative species, but one can argue that we cannot invent new things—only learn how to build on already established ideas. Hence, when a founder creates an organisation, he does so with all the luggage of cultural influences from his past. A new company will reflect the founder's values shaped by upbringing, religion, national traditions, etc. Existing attitudes and behaviours prevalent in the industry concerned will also exercise their influence. Within a new venture, the founder will be a role model, a walking example of the culture they enact. The mature corporation may nurture this history, the image and role model, and build a narrative that serves the organisational purpose. The downside of legacy is that the more it celebrates a particular culture or section of society, the more it is likely to exclude others. Consider the Black worker who walks past the bust of a company founder who built the enterprise on the proceeds of the slave trade or the exploitation of colonial resources. It is a daily reminder that most of your colleagues are, consciously or unconsciously, proud of their shared heritage; your legacy of tragedy. Disparage the bust at your peril.

– *Governance*. The governance framework is a construct and a design that, when correctly used, sets the organisation up for success. There should be clarity around subjects such as organisational purpose in the form of Vision and Mission Statements. The allocation of roles, responsibilities and accountability should be clear and transparent. The organisation that is consciously trying to promote specific behaviours will, at a minimum, establish a formal code of conduct, typically to be confirmed as read by employees once a year. There will be a library of policies on how to deal with D&I, alongside matters such as conflicts of interest, dealing with risk management, ethics, and issues such as customer care. The quality of governance reflects the degree to which the board and the executive understand the full nature of organisational purpose. The rigour and effectiveness of governance measures both encourage and support a deeper understanding of how actions and behaviours impact outcomes. In other words: success. The governance charter of the firm describes the procedural protocol that exposes the determination of the leadership to be true to their aspirations: it is the robust skeleton that supports the body and spirit of organisational culture.

– *Systems and Processes*. The organisational design may be formal or informal, determined by such concerns as risk awareness/appetite and the degree to which concerns like D&I influence the activity. Therefore, systems and processes will seek to monitor and impose controls over behaviour, risk, and operational efficiency. The degree to which staff feel subject to supervision and control will impact behaviour and attitudes. If this has a positive or negative effect on employee engagement and trust in the organisation depends more on how supervision and monitoring are imposed than the measures themselves. For example, reward and compensation systems can be precise and transparent or discretionary and obtuse. Promotion and recruitment criteria can ensure fair treatment of employees and equality of opportunity or leave open the door to bias and nepotism.

– *Social Structure*. If governance provides the organisational framework, or the organisation's hardware, the human use of that framework is the software. This framework's ability to deliver a sense of transparency, fairness, equity and trust depends on the diligence and commitment of the leadership and employees in supporting it. Success in this area is determined by the extent to which all employees, irrespective of origin, creed or gender, feel that their organisation treats them fairly. Any sense of favouritism, discrimination, scapegoating or evasion of responsibility by those at the top will be destructive. Leadership behaviours, easy communications and collaboration between colleagues of all backgrounds, and bias-free decision-making: all indicate the nature of the organisation's culture.

– *Observable Behaviour*. The test as to the nature of the existing culture is by simple observation of attitudes and behaviours. Does it evidence trust and mutual respect? Are employees enthusiastic and quick to smile and engage, include and support? Are they motivated and ready to lend a helping hand or make an extra effort to get the right solution? More than any other indicator, the attitude and behaviour of individual members is the greatest one. If you sense this indicator is weak, there is undoubtedly something wrong with the culture supporting (or not) minority group employees.

Some argue that the performance of the organisation relative to its stated objectives is a further manifestation of the quality of its culture. This assertion, however, is to exaggerate the ability of culture to produce positive outcomes. A good culture, combined with a mediocre product or failing markets, will not provide a safety net for poor results. In reverse, it is true that a bad culture can (and does) destroy a good product and can lead to organisational failure. Finding a way to precisely measure the impact of culture on organisations is akin to searching for the Holy Grail. The closest we see are the consistent reports from studies showing superior financial performance over time in "good culture" companies that succeed in achieving high scores in D&I surveys, compared to those who do not.

Evaluating the pillars of culture present in your organisation will provide valuable input in analysing what your infrastructure is communicating in terms of role models, preferences and actual values. Equally, they offer a good starting point for considering how best to convey your aspirations for attitudes and mindset within your organisation in the future.

The Inclusive Culture

Pat Wadors, a Human Resource D&I specialist, describes diversity in terms of uniqueness, and inclusion as respect and fairness. As a starting point for how you want all of your strategic initiatives to impact the organisation, it is pretty reasonable: devise values and encourage behaviours that will celebrate uniqueness, aspire to fairness from every perspective, and guarantee respect between colleagues and stakeholders [14].

However, from the starting blocks to the finishing line is a fair distance. The organisation can start by setting the right conditions for a culture that is equitable in its management of diversity, celebrates uniqueness and embraces inclusion and belonging. To reach the end goal, the leadership can initiate and coach these values and other drivers of behaviour by systematically delivering the message and acting as role-modelling examples. But the quantum path to an inclusive culture relies on the organisation's defined ethics and purpose being kept alive by continuous challenge, shored up by an appropriate governance of incentive and reward systems, as well as close supervision. Making the right corrections and mitigations requires a continuous monitoring and feedback loop from the top to the bottom of the organisation and back again. In this manner, we create the primary tools to ensure our message and values take hold within the organisation. Pat Waldors points to two central factors/drivers:

- Executive mindset. The leadership must be (1) entirely devoted to the pursuit of diversity and inclusion as a path to greater trust, innovation, and employee engagement and (2) willingly and actively taking on the part as authentic role models for their employees. If not, then any attempt to nurture an inclusive, belonging culture will founder.
- Tools and strategies. The most critical virtue of an inclusive culture is its willingness to sit back and listen to the opinions of others and not insist on the established wisdom and assumptions of yesteryear. In doing so, we open the doors to making inclusiveness of all our shades of uniqueness part of the employee experience; an everyday lifestyle at the workplace where we can all feel welcome and enjoy a sense of acceptance of who we are, a sense of belonging. The governance infrastructure established for decision-making, the exchange of knowledge and experience, and the encouragement of inclusive behaviours, provide the guardrails by which we ensure our values produce the culture we are aiming for.

Academic Coat Hooks

Academic theory of organisational behaviour and culture does not provide easy solutions or answers. It does have the virtue of offering coat hooks on which to hang our cloaks of uncertainty regarding the interpretation and analysis of the dilemmas we are confronted with. By understanding the drivers and levers of culture, we can better select the tools suited to achieve the changes we wish to introduce. We can better define what we want as an outcome and impact of our initiatives. We are better able to evaluate the results of our efforts. In practice, no two situations are the same; indeed, as with quantum physics, we have a multitude of possible outcomes co-existing at any one time. All we can hope to do is to formulate a compass by which we can navigate through the complexity of emotions that are fear and hope.

References

1. Smith-Meyer, A. (2018). *Surviving organisational behaviour*. Kindle Publications.
2. Edgecliffe-Johnson, A., Hill, A., & Kuchler, H. (2021, February 23). It needs to change its culture: Is McKinsey losing its mystique? *Financial Times*.
3. Yin, X. (2019, December 19). *Review and prospect of quantum management*. Jinan University School of Management.
4. Melaku, T. (2019, August 7). Why women and people of color in law still hear "You don't look like a lawyer". *Harvard Business Review*.
5. Hodges, C., & Steinholz, R. (2017). *Ethical business practice and regulation*. Hart Publishing.
6. Barrett, R. (2014). *Values driven organisation*. Routledge.

7. Liebig, T. (2021, November17). Diversity policies must avoid benefiting the already privileged. *Financial Times*.
8. Graham, J. R., et al. *Corporate culture: Evidence from the field*. https://papers.ssrn.com
9. Hunt, V., Prince, S., Dixon-Fyle, S., & Dolan, K. (2020, May). *Diversity wins*. Mckinsey.
10. Banks, K. H., & Harvey, R. (2020, June 11). Is your company actually fighting racism, or just talking about it? *Harvard Business Review*.
11. Obama, B. (2020). *A promised land*. Viking.
12. Williams, D. (2015, April 24). *Winston Churchill's terrible leadership failure*. Forbes Leadership Forum.
13. Gopal, P. (2021, March 17). Why can't Britain handle the truth about Winston Churchill. *The Guardian*.
14. Wadors, P. (2019, December 18). *Course "Diversity, inclusion, and belonging"*. LinkedIn Learning.

#OfficePolitics1: How Organisational Dynamics Help or Hinder Change

An Eagle was soaring through the air when suddenly it heard the whizz of an arrow and felt itself wounded to death. Slowly it fluttered down to the earth, with its life-blood pouring out of it. Looking down upon the arrow with which it had been pierced, it found that the shaft of the arrow had been feathered with one of its own plumes. "Alas!" it cried, as it died, "We often give our enemies the means for our own destruction" [1].

The moral of Aesop's Fable is simple and somewhat devasting. "We often give our enemies the means for our own destruction", implying that by not engaging constructively with a conflict, we give it the power to control us instead [2].

As observed, diversity introduces more variety in perspective and outlook, thereby introducing conflict in the shape of discussion or even argument. Left to its own devices, it can be divisive and destructive. However, managed correctly in a trustful and respectful environment, conflict turns to exchange and collaboration. Conflict management, or rather reconciliation processes, consequently has its place amongst inclusive leadership traits and needs to be understood.

7.1 The Nature of Conflict: For Better or Worse

The Oxford English Dictionary definition of conflict reads: "a state of mind in which a person experiences a clash of opposing feelings or needs". A Nobel prize-winning nuclear physicist, Niels Bohr, pointed out that "the opposite of a profound truth may well be another profound truth". His point was that conflict may not be a choice between a "right" outcome over a "wrong" outcome; that there is no single truth, merely perspectives of belief. The implication is that there need not be anything inherently wrong with a conflict; it is only problematic if mishandled. The British playwright, Peter Shaffer, explained it in even more poignant terms when he defined tragedy: "Tragedy, for me, is not a conflict between right and wrong, but between two kinds of right".

A. Smith-Meyer, *Unlocking the Potential of Diversity in Organisations*, Diversity and Inclusion Research, https://doi.org/10.1007/978-3-031-10402-2_7

In the organisational context, where communal effort is the order of the day, we want individuals to collaborate. When we form our twenty-first-century project teams, colleagues overcome potential misunderstandings that result from working in physically distant locations, or when encountering cultures and backgrounds that seem foreign to them. We are ready and even anticipating linguistic and cultural missteps. However, when cultural differences co-exist in the same country or city, it is harder to accept. "These are my people; why do they think differently from me?" Working with people we perceive to be encroaching on our "turf", our privileges and conventions, triggers our fear of losing out that can quickly convert to passive, even actively aggressive, attitudes. In all cases, when we mingle with people whose perspectives we do not identify with, the management of that conflict becomes more complex. If not actively attended to, conflict born of fear or inconvenience will result in dysfunctional behaviour and outcomes, specifically [3]:

- *Miscommunication*. Effective communication requires respect on the part of both the sender and the recipient of a message. The inconsiderate speaker will "bark an order" and not watch for signs of comprehension. The defensive listener, fearing a "trap" or unreasonable demands and conflict, will avoid clarification questions and spend listening time scanning for negative signals rather than ways to improve collaboration.
- *Diminished Coordination*. An unwillingness to collaborate translates to less coordination and an increased tendency to "look out for number one". In organisations, it is common to observe that product areas or differing functions fight for their "share of the group wallet" at budget time. This competition is frequently viewed as a healthy process for the efficient allocation of resources. However, if not tempered by a common understanding of organisational purpose and fair process, interest groups will seek to protect the narrow concerns of their business units at the expense of the collective effort throughout the year. This form of silo thinking leads not only to a lack of will to help, share and support the activities of colleagues of other business units. Less visible, when applied to ethnic groups within the workforce, this desire to retain privilege earned or gained can result in an unwillingness to invite members of other communities to participate or assist with tasks or challenges best resolved through collaboration. Absent trust, we choose to deal with our own problems rather than accept the help or advice of others we view as unreliable.
- *Diminished Performance*. Logically, therefore, poor communication and a reluctance to collaborate will weaken overall performance. This impact goes beyond the "silo effect" problem, where sub-optimally coordinated business units within the organisation pursue goals that are more or less aligned with group-level objectives. Envisage a department where expected skillsets or behaviours are based on stereotypes and prejudice. Then, the quality of communication between these colleagues will be rife with presumptions and misinterpretation, of the negative type. Under such conditions, the ingroup colleagues will likely underestimate their outgroup colleagues, just as minority or outgroup employees who feel

unfairly treated, disregarded or under-valued will not volunteer their assistance and will feel less inclined to be loyal and helpful to the venture.

- *Staff Dissatisfaction.* Disgruntlement is infectious, and unproductive behaviour spreads fast. An unpleasant atmosphere at work is one of the prime drivers of individuals seeking a job change. The unhappy employee is far more likely to move on to a different organisation that promises more potential, openness and inclusivity. As a result, staff turnover will be quick to rise, resulting in the loss of experience and imposing expensive investments in the recruitment and training/ integration of new staff.
- *Workplace Incivility.* As dissatisfaction rises and a culture of conflict dominates, individuals will adopt passive-aggressive behaviours, eventually leading down the path to harassment and bullying. Conflict is not the result of our routine social instinct to work to mutual advantage, but springs from a distrust of co-workers, considering them as competitors and a potential menace. As a result, we adopt hostile behaviours towards those we think may threaten us, even if we perceive this sub-consciously. Once trapped in such a social environment, it needs a firm hand and leadership to restore order.
- *Misconduct.* At the lowest level of respect, and beyond mere disdain for other cultures and colleagues, comes disloyalty—actively acting against the organisation's interests by disregarding and breaching company policies and rules, and engaging in the abuse of company assets, theft of company property and even sabotage.

Functional Conflict and Diversity

It was Father Michael Lapsley who said: "Don't just include us in your community. Instead, come, let's create one together" [4]. If the consequences of unchecked conflict are dysfunctional and harmful, we should actively promote a functional approach to conflict; one where an argument is less about protecting one's corner and more about exploring and connecting to stimulate creativity and find new, optimal solutions. Let us look at how this might work.

- *Constructive Challenge.* If individuals, irrespective of hierarchical level, race, religion or culture, approach each other with respect and in the spirit of problem-solving (as opposed to problem-seeking), we start to understand the nature of a constructive challenge. The word "challenge" may sound aggressive. However, the objective of promoting functional conflict is that difficult questions may be asked and responded to without embarrassment or fear, in pursuit of a common goal. A positive, collaborative and trusting environment will be robust enough to make and take a challenge in the right spirit—without fear and prejudice.
- *Improved Solutions.* Suppose all questions of bias, perceptions and stereotypes can be openly discussed. In that case, there will be a higher degree of transparency and access for "best minds" to gain a deeper understanding of each other. A greater appreciation of one another will enable an improved and unencumbered

capacity to listen to personal observations with empathy and look past prejudice when considering a professional quandary or task.

- *Innovation.* Without collaboration and a free exchange of knowledge and ideas, innovation cannot thrive. Innovation is only really possible where there exists a trust environment. The greater the presence of diverse perspectives in any collaboration, the greater the potential for productive ideas to take shape. We have to trust that our partner in idea creation will explore all possibilities for the common good, that they will not "steal" our ideas, or otherwise act in a manner that is detrimental to the other. Where everyone focuses on the common good, the above process of constructive challenge and solution-seeking will lead to changes—from a bit of tinkering around the edges to radical "out-of-the-box" innovation.
- *Agreement.* To gain the full support of all parties for a proposal, it needs to be fair and equitable; otherwise, it will plant the seed of resentment and future conflict. Again, in an environment where everyone is focused on finding the best collective solution for any given objective, rather than pursuing personal self-interest, reaching fair agreements will happen more rapidly and efficiently.
- *Stronger relationships.* Success in collaborative effort breeds confidence and trust between co-workers. Celebrating joint success and genuine appreciation and recognition of the contribution of each collaborator will make people who would not normally socialise together happy to work or relax together in a group.
- *Learning.* A greater willingness to share one's ideas, hopes and aspirations will lead to more open, curious minds and launch a learning organisation that is more efficient at exploring alternative paths, debating and applying new learning. The inclusion of diversity will lead to better decisions and more innovation.

Conflict between us exists as long as we have differing opinions. Our opinions are formed by our personal history, background and experience. The challenge is how to temper conflict in order to promote the constructive exchange of views and to create learning opportunities from what would otherwise be dysfunctional conflict. The objective is to shape a strategic culture that fosters interaction between colleagues who (1) care enough to concern themselves with those who are isolated, (2) seek out the views and perspective of others, (3) focus on issues and not emotions, and (4) nurture mutual respect and compromise.

7.2   The Trust Antidote: Generating Collaboration Through Dialogue

In confrontation, challenge, and conflict, the fear factor is real. We fear the harm that comes from the confrontation required in dealing with prejudice and discrimination. Apart from having to find the courage to accept that the privilege I enjoy is unfair to others, should I, as (say) a White member of the ingroup, intervene on behalf of my Black colleague being marginalised and risk the anger or disdain of the perpetrator or those I call my "community"? If I am Black and speak up against injustice, bullying or harassment, need I fear possible retaliation or the accusation of being too sensitive or not stoic enough? As a White person interacting with a Black colleague, might my "clever" throw-away comment or use of language inadvertently be perceived as racist where none was consciously intended? I might not even try to overcome my misgivings if I doubt there will be a safe outcome.

There is only one natural remedy to allay these fears, and that is trust. Trust that your message will be received on a presumption of good faith, and confidence that, once delivered, you as the communicator will receive an honest and respectful reply.

There are studies on how to build trust across cultural groupings, a partnering ripe and ready for misunderstandings and unintended conflict. They conclude that treating others respectfully is the most effective way to strengthen bonds between individuals and groups. Respect might seem a rarity in our rapid-fire world of twenty-first-century politics and division. Yet, we all appreciate such behaviour as one that removes suspicion and fear, which helps us engage in a learning conversation with others. Mutual respect makes it easier to listen with empathy and maintain an open and curious mind.

Hitching the Charrette to a Horse Called Purpose

To state the obvious, we cannot start to manage conflict if there is no recognition by all parties concerned that one exists. It may be that where the conflict is profound and obvious to one party, such as a marginalised minority, it is perceived as slight and inconsequential to a majority grouping. Although the distance between the parties entails that the path to resolution may be long and twisted, the fact that there is an objective in sight provides enough of an invitation to start a dialogue, so long as there is a confidence that no retaliation will ensue.

Trust, therefore, remains the principal requirement to allow conflicts and opposing views to be expressed. Recognition of a shared conflict that requires collaborative agreement is the first step towards establishing trust: That all parties have a collective responsibility to ensure each other's well-being. There needs to be an acceptance that the principal objective of all parties is to act as an ensemble in pursuit of common interest or purpose. The process known in town planning circles as Charrette brings communities with apparently opposing interests together to find joint solutions to shared challenges. Charrette works on the premise that the more people interact with each other in the pursuit of innovative solutions, the more they will start to trust one another and cooperate. In this way, dysfunctional conflict will be averted [5].

Placing all co-workers together in an open-plan office is not enough, however. There needs to be a clear projection of common purpose and values. The enforcement of social norms of behaviour around the shared values of honesty, accountability, fairness, respect and caring is necessary to create conditions where contact between colleagues will encourage them to view each other as unique individuals rather than as representatives of a "competing" identity.

7.3   The Politics of Influence and Power

We may understand the main levers of trust and how, in an ideal world, we can lead conflicted parties to the trough of functional resolution of conflict. However, as the proverb says, leading someone to water is more straightforward than making them drink. Within the organisation, there may be an understanding of the power of functional conflict, even a desire to develop it; yet, the presumption remains that if you recruit good managers, the problem will somehow take care of itself. There are forces and interests that prise apart people, or groups of individuals, who believe they have differing interests. The organisation that wants to manage a culture of diversity and inclusion has to understand the dynamics and the politics of its members and the sub-groups that exist within it. Not to do so is to cut corners, leaving rifts and flaws in the cultural construct that will forever remain just below the surface, or be a constant thorn in the side of inclusiveness, ensuring that all attempts at closing the gap between perceived interests will not succeed.

Within any group, there will be sub-groups or individuals who hold more influence and sway over general opinion than others—they may be referred to as opinion-leaders. We have already explained that a culture that does not lead with, and gather members around, a common set of values and purpose will become either a chaos or sleepwalker culture—or a culture ruled by personalities. Such personalities or special interest groups, and their potential to aid or disrupt, will continue to exist even as we promote and embed our strategic culture. We have to understand how influence moves through the corridors of our organisation, who the opinion-leaders are, and how to convince and use them to help change our culture rather than sabotage it.

Studying the nature and source of power of an individual is usually relatively straightforward. It falls into categories like physical strength, superior intellect, courage, or even willingness to inflict pain on others. However, the most prevalent form of power we are all subject to is of a higher order entirely. We have institutions and organisations that help us function as a society and wield colossal levels of influence over our behaviour. Yet, in a well-ordered society, we rarely think of the nature of their power unless we fall foul of them, and we rarely question their exercise of power when that power is enforced on others. It was US President Lincoln who said: "We all declare for liberty; but in using the same word we do not all mean the same thing. With some the word liberty may mean for each man to do as he pleases . . . while with others the same word may mean for some men to do as they please with other men" [6]. Only when those in authority appear to go beyond some vaguely defined limit, or when they are perceived to be undeniably abusing their power, might there be a reaction.

Institutions control their constituents and direct their behaviour through rewards and punishments. Their function is to provide us with a stability that provides confidence in the future. Viewed in this manner, we understand institutional power to be at the service of the people—subject to changing perceptions of what is fair and equitable in line with the collective interests of the group.

A more cynical view is that institutional power can be directed to serve the interests of a privileged few; that it may no longer be empowered by the collective will of the people. Instead, it can be the tool of an elite to inflict punishment on opponents and reward those loyal to their interests.

7.4   The Management of Influence and Power: The Alignment of Objectives

Politics gets a bad name. It is associated with Machiavellianism, back-stabbing and selfish obsession with personal success. Some academics support this perception by defining organisational politics as "intentional acts of influence to enhance or protect the self-interests of individuals or groups that are not endorsed by the organisation" [7]. Playwrights and authors have forever drawn on the drama of intrigue and deception in their storytelling. It is a popular refrain that we hold no trust in politicians. Yet, once we have chosen our "political" champion, we do trust them; we trust that their actions are driven by the intent of creating a better future—for society, not themselves.

We might instead consider the alternative definition of a political organisation as a "perspective which holds that an organisation is made up of groups that have separate interest, goals and values, and in which power and influence are needed in order to reach decisions" [8]. This definition does not prejudice office politics as either good or bad, but it refers to the importance of influencing ability to conjure up a common position. Let us consider that we are speaking of politics in organisations. It becomes clear that we are concerned with managing relationships between colleagues in the pursuit of a common policy objective, or shared organisational purpose. It is, after all, normal that we hold different opinions as to what our priorities may be, or vary in our interpretation of success or mission.

Hence, we have a board of directors to consider the organisation's vision, values and purpose and an executive charged with devising an appropriate strategy for its achievement. We have already argued that autocratic, top-down instruction or delegation is inappropriate in the realm of culture and emotions; that culture change is not a simple matter of writing well-intentioned policies and procedures. Just as in government politics, the message must be:

– Convincing in its logic and context. The audience must be able to believe in the authenticity of the message and the viability and value of the desired impact.
– Authentic and sincere at its source. The leadership advocating change must be visibly committed and determined to achieve the objective set out as the vision of success.
– Inclusive and show concern for those asked to comply or even sacrifice a piece of themselves. Any change is scary and sometimes tough. The political leader has to persuade their followers that their interests are part of the equation; that no one will be left behind.

Influencing Networks

Let us suppose that the leadership cannot successfully implement its vision by top-down instruction. In that case, even a powerful executive and board will have to approach culture change as an exercise in indirect power. Like irrigation canals, goals, ambitions and vision must flow uniformly through the organisation and cover all necessary terrain.

This architecture will make use of formal hierarchical lines of communication, but also informal power and influencing networks within the organisation. The traditional hierarchical line is arguably easier to manage. Clearly identified managers will need to be educated and convinced (or replaced) to ensure an orderly distribution of the message and effective communication of expectations regarding altered behaviours and attitudes. The hierarchical line will also monitor adherence to the new ethical standards of expected behaviour, rewarding or sanctioning individuals as appropriate.

Alongside the hierarchical networks of managerial authority, there is a powerful influence exercised by opinion-leaders throughout the organisation. Their influencing power is based on the grass and roots of other employees. This informal network of individuals is far more subtle than the organisation chart. Opinion-leaders can be individuals held in esteem by colleagues due to their history, achievements, reliability or expertise, even in some cases charisma or their accessibility to and control of information. These are the go-to people in the organisation who are willing to form and voice their opinions. To those who wish to disseminate a message or mood in the organisation, opinion-leaders may be viewed as either a threat or an opportunity.

In marketing terms, these individuals would be termed "influencers", and they are particularly potent in defining what we might call organisational culture or enacted group ethics and mindset. Indeed, due to the informal nature of their influencing power, a message or opinion received from an influencer is accepted as authentic far faster than a remote executive who may simply be "repeating the party line"; or demanding change that eventually will turn out to be against "my" best interests. Therefore, opinion-leaders must be identified ahead of a formal campaign launch and be convinced to join the team and buy in to the merits of the targeted culture change. We can name them influencers, ambassadors or allies, but the objective is the same: we must seek to attract and engage them as willing spokespersons for the cause. To do so, the arguments must overcome any element of scepticism. The influencer's greatest asset is their credibility and integrity—they will not sacrifice this to benefit a cause they do not share.

The vision and goals of the change management initiative must be:

– Clear and transparent
– There must be evidence of adequate resourcing to ensure success.
– The request for their support must come from executives that the influencer respects, and who are willing to be held accountable for their assurances.

In other words, there must be integrity around a viable plan to carry out what is a political campaign of persuading the diverse members of an organisation to adopt the new behavioural and ethical standards being established.

7.5 It Is Not What You Say, It Is How You Say It

The integrity of a persuasive message must be of high quality. Consequently, its content must be carefully crafted. As discussed, any demand for change will meet resistance for two principal reasons.

1. It is uncomfortable: Change is de-stabilising, alters definitions of merit and success and might be challenged by peer pressure and cultural traditions.
2. It generates fear: Those asked to change are being asked to face the unknown. Employees will fear what might happen to their status and job identity that they have worked on for years. They will fear failure to meet new demands, not to mention the fear of personality conflicts.

Change management is problematic when there is no immediate recognition of any benefit. Consider an airline passenger who is told there is no seat available for their ticket. The immediate reaction is disbelief, anxiety, and outrage, before potentially descending into a state of anger. Resistance is usually in plentiful evidence. However, for all but the most churlish, resistance dissipates when the attendant offers an upgrade from economy to first class. In like manner, imposed change in the workplace will result in delusion and disengagement at best, or active resistance at worst, unless mitigated by interesting alternatives. Leadership needs to communicate change with empathy, good timing, and its necessity explained and legitimised.

To craft a persuasive change message, all the concerns of those impacted need to be addressed. The starting point is to identify as many pockets of potential resistance amongst different stakeholder groups as possible. Next, stakeholders can be categorised by how they perceive the changes will affect them. The advocate of change must view the demands being made on stakeholders with empathy. Culture change is an exercise in persuasion, not diktat. Once evaluated, an appropriate level of care and attention must be paid to each stakeholder class based on the impact your actions will have on them. Finally, the change advocate must consider either what knowledge or provision can be provided to calm any lingering fear; or, eventually, determine what actions you are willing to take in the event their fears cannot be addressed.

Preparing the Campaign

Undertaking a culture change management programme is akin to rolling out a political campaign. We are seeking the attention of the congregation and trying to win their support and conviction. We might therefore compare the exercise with an

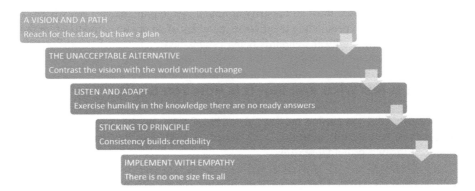

Fig. 7.1 Developing support for the D&I vision

analysis of the re-election campaign of President Obama in the USA in 2012, which identified five critical success factors (Fig. 7.1) [9].

1. *It is not just the vision*

In launching an initiative, it is expedient, if not essential, to have a lofty vision. In the words of the German footballer, Thomas Muller: "If you raise your gaze, you don't see the boundaries anymore". Add to this the additional quote of the marketing guru, Leo Burnett: "When you reach for the stars you may not quite get one, but you won't come up with a handful of mud either", and you have the arguments at hand.

What is important for politicians and business leaders alike is not to mistake goals for plans, or ambitions for mechanisms and logistics. Idealistic aspiration must also be believable objectives. The path to reaching the stars must be identifiable. The leader will not get support for being a dreamer, but because followers find them credible.

2. *Define the alternative*

Intuitively, if we believe strongly enough in our aspiration and vision, it should be a simple matter to accept that in "reaching for the stars", you have to forgo some options. Nor is it a leap of faith to understand that for followers of that vision to fully accept and engage with your aspiration, it helps to depict how impoverished the world will be, should your ambition fail to materialise. In business, some decisions are costly or may not bring obvious benefits within a "normal" time frame.

Many ethics and compliance functions struggle to accomplish their mission for lack of resources and funds. The phrase "the business simply cannot afford it" is a common refrain, and many executives believe that a higher tolerance of ethical risk is manageable. In truth, many executives believe that "just enough" is a good enough policy to get through their turn at the helm.

This is a flawed strategy that allows for the existence of a sizeable uncontrolled risk akin to gambling; "I may risk losing everything, but I may also win everything".

In governance terms, this is simply a betrayal of the director's duty to work for the long-term success of the company. In compliance terms, an infraction of the law may result in the payment of a fine, the loss of a contract or an out-of-court settlement. Only in rare cases do businesses fail, get acquired by a competitor or lose their licence to operate. Although such things do happen, it is generally classified in the category "it won't happen to me", otherwise known as invincibility bias.

The executive and board must be clear, therefore, on what benefits we expect to reap by making the strenuous reach for the stars, but also clear on what life in the mud looks like. People are willing to go to extreme lengths to pursue an ideal, but they are even more committed when they understand that the alternative is unattractive and unacceptable.

3. *Adapt*

Leading a campaign for a new ideal is typically associated with articulating a persuasive message with good content and delivery. If you are lucky, you may get it sufficiently right at the first attempt to gain a second hearing. However, just as we know the risks of one-sided dialogue and what happens when we do not listen to the response or reaction, so it is with public speaking and listening. Public listening is the discipline of showing humility in the face of your audience; looking for, learning from and adapting to the feedback that they give you.

Being reactive to the audience's response is essential irrespective of whether the message is delivered from the podium or at close quarters. On the one hand, it enables the speaker to better evaluate if their message is receiving support or not. It also directly engages with the audience and builds a relationship with them, increasing their engagement and potentially their alignment with your ideas. By adapting the message, you acknowledge the audience as worthy of your attention and respect; you reward their engagement by responding to their direct concerns. In short, you build a relationship and generate trust between you. And finally, you will discover that your delivery of the message improves.

4. *Consistency matters*

The manner of delivering your message can continually be improved: the dynamics of a changing audience demand it. However, the substance of the message must be unwavering. Allowing exceptions or agreeing to compromise on principles will only weaken the conviction behind your aspiration. On the subject of diversity and inclusion, a "just enough" mentality is not possible. The cost of one case of discrimination, one betrayal of trust, one Twitter storm of outrage that tells of racial injustice or tolerance of prejudicial behaviour equates to the loss of the inclusive culture you have been trying to establish. It is, in fact, no different to the maintenance of the elusive ethical culture that we (generally speaking) all pursue. Just as everyone understands what constitutes ethical behaviour, everyone observes how ethical and unethical behaviour is rewarded, punished, or simply tolerated by those in charge who look the other way in exchange for pragmatic gain. The result is that everyone pretends to uphold the firm's values and advertised ethics, yet no one dares to speak up when they observe wrongdoing; nobody trusts that their actions will be appreciated by their colleagues or that sticking their head above the parapet is worth the risk. On the topic of diversity and inclusiveness, it is harder to discard the evidence of exclusion and discrimination. News of one incident not dealt with appropriately will spread through the organisation like wildfire and, potentially, years of confidence and trust-building—like reputation—lost in an instant.

There is no halfway house on ethics, but we have become rather good at concealing "less serious" unethical acts and learning to live within the norms of the unspoken group ethics. On D&I, there can be no tipping point of "acceptability" or tolerance. Although members of the more privileged majority frequently lay claim that they are themselves non-discriminatory and inclusive, the minority (along with their majority group allies who advocate social justice and equity) will rarely delude themselves to believe that "a little discrimination" is fair and acceptable. Anything less than wholehearted commitment is a fiction because the people impacted by discrimination are our colleagues. Their anger, frustration or distress are present next to us in the office, the canteen or the board-room. There is nowhere to hide the uncomfortable truth.

5. *A united coalition*

It is part of the definition of inclusiveness that we recognise everyone as unique. It is a dichotomy of the promotion of a culture supported by one vision and global values that we know it will be interpreted in as many different ways as we encourage uniqueness in the organisation. It was Professor Geert Hofstede himself, the pioneer of cross-cultural organisational theory, who said: "Culture is more often a source of conflict than of synergy". How diversity, inclusiveness, discrimination, and exclusion are interpreted and expressed will vary between Beijing, Copenhagen, Lagos, New Dehli, San Francisco and Sao Paulo. Therefore, what is required is not an insistence on the views and practices of the dominant culture at head office, but rather the direction of travel and the fair and respectful outcomes derived from differing interpretations of D&I objectives. There must be universal comprehension of the D&I challenge and common agreement on the desired consequences of our behaviours and actions. We have to overcome the variances of our many perceptions to join together in a coalition for the cause. To realise our aspirations, we must unite the many various communities and individuals in our community.

7.6   Know the Terrain: Choosing Messengers Wisely

Once the leadership is ready with its D&I campaign strategy, it is time to take the measure of who may act as your allies and where you might find pockets of strong resistance. It is necessary to create a Power Map [10].

Although essential, it is not enough for organisational leadership to walk the talk and act as a role model. For your ideas on inclusion to permeate the organisation, you

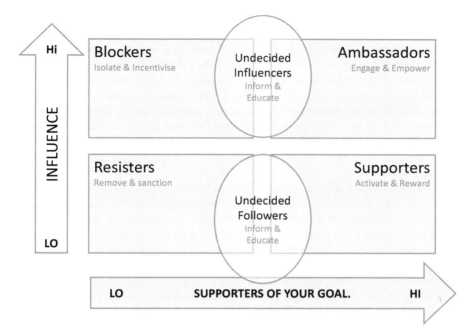

Fig. 7.2 Culture change power map of influencers

must engage the grassroots and the opinion-leaders in the firm. Those individuals who are most entrenched in "the old ways" need to be identified and either persuaded to align with your objectives or, regrettably, moved out of any position where they can disrupt or undermine your efforts.

Specific individuals will have influence over the opinions and attitudes of others as a result of their "legitimate" power resulting from their function or title. Many of these have an impact derived from a hierarchical role in the organisation that bestows the direct ability to reward or sanction an extensive range of employees. These would include members of the executive board, heads of divisions, and some strategic functions depending on the organisation's governance framework. In addition, the leaders of human resources, ethics and compliance, risk management, or similar roles may (or may not) be influential depending on the firm's governance arrangements. Then we have the opinion-leaders who exert "expert" or "charismatic" power. These are individuals who have no direct reward or legitimate authority, but who are held in high esteem by colleagues and who, on the basis of reciprocity, can exercise significant influence over the opinions of employees—even to the point of subverting the direct influence of hierarchical superiors.

Having identified and categorised these individuals in terms of their high or low influence, the second step is to compare your objective, in this case to promote D&I within the firm, with the self-interest or views of your "influencers". These individuals will typically fall into three categories as shown in Fig. 7.2: Allies or Ambassadors for your cause, Blockers or Resistors to change, and Undecided.

In a third step, these individuals may be approached based on their classification.

- *Ambassadors or Allies*: These individuals will support your objectives and be willing to speak up for them. Their task is to either influence and activate the grassroots of the organisation to help the endeavour. Depending on their type of influence and network, they may also be recruited to persuade Blockers or Resistors to either change their views or at least stand down. They need to feel connected to your campaign and encouraged to play an active part in its execution. Their opinion should be listened to, and they should be made to feel part of the process, that they "own" the objectives alongside you as a partner; a valued ally.
- *Blockers*: Sceptics who hold significant influence or hierarchical power are a serious threat to your culture change efforts. Blockers can use their network to evidence a disunity in leadership determination to complete the transformation. Their negativism will encourage and fuel those who fear the change or are simply prejudiced against it. Some Blockers simply see no value in the proposition and think it a waste of time and resources. These can either be persuaded to align themselves with the programme by either enlightening them on the indirect benefits of the change or by offering specific incentives in exchange for their collaboration. In the event a Blocker is ideologically opposed to the proposition, then the hard options are:
  - To cloister the individual through peer pressure. If it is clear to the opinion-leader that they cannot swim against mainstream sentiment, they are less likely to oppose the endeavour, as to do so would erode their influence within the same network that provides them with their influencing power.
  - To ensure that the individual is quarantined from their influencing power base by way of re-assignment or change of function.
  - To remove the person from the equation by a negotiated parting of the ways. An outright dismissal is unadvised as this, in itself, may be seen as a non-inclusive act and undermine the authenticity of your intentions or even create a "martyr" to others who resist the change.
  N.B. The handling of employees who stand in the way of corporate objectives is a disagreeable subject rife with legal and reputation risks. Decisions relating to this group of employees must be handled with tact, fairness and compliance with local labour laws. Unempathetic or unfair treatment of opponents to a policy advocating greater inclusiveness is likely to detract from the objective in itself. In such cases, it is better to "grab the rose by its thorns" than to hope the problem will go away, only to reappear as a constructive dismissal lawsuit.
- *The Undecided Influencers*: For various reasons, there will always be a group of people with influence who neither identify with the cause nor have strong views against it. They may even engage with the moral rectitude of the objective, but not consider it relevant to their personal situation. Indeed, suppose the culture change includes the potential of uncomfortable conversations. In that case, they may prefer to shirk from the effort and take a "wait and see" attitude, letting Ambassadors and Allies lead the change instead. These individuals need to be

informed of the why and how of the programme and educated on its benefits. The undecided will tend to ally themselves with organisational objectives, or at the very least be supportive of the leadership, by being shown the benefits to the organisation in terms of long-term success. Even more compelling is the knowledge that they themselves may benefit from increased influence and responsibility, not least by experiencing respect and esteem by being engaged in the discussion.

- *Supporters*: These employees are aligned with the moral and intellectual intent of the change. They will be listening to the words and watching the actions of the Ambassadors and Allies to the cause, as they will to any Blockers present. These are the people who individually have little power, but collectively represent the grassroots of the change being cultivated. They must be:
  - Informed to ensure they understand why the changes are necessary
  - Comforted that the change will hold benefits to their environment and futures as opposed to threats
  - Rewarded for "doing the right thing"

  Such rewards may be delivered in the shape of performance incentives, but equally and perhaps more effectively, through participation. The individual who is encouraged to view themselves as a positive force in resolving the "problem" is more likely to help the process by acting appropriately and discussing the change positively.

- *Resisters.* Employees who perhaps see themselves as part of the problem that needs solving will deny the seriousness or even the existence of "the problem". They will tend to reject the need for change, as to do so is to acknowledge themselves as being in the wrong [11]. Their attitudes will prevent any change of behaviour or mindset. Misconduct or passive-aggressive behaviour and language amongst this group must be dealt with swiftly and fairly. Not to do so is to undermine the authenticity of the culture change programme. If they do not respect the organisation's values and ethics, they cannot be seen to "get away with it".

- *Undecided Followers:* These employees have little ability to influence the opinion of others, but they can still impact the perception of the success of the venture. Easily overlooked as harmless, in the context of D&I, their unintended exercise of unconscious bias will create discord or even harm their personal reputation by being associated with Resisters-like behaviour. The undecided follower needs to be informed and educated on both the need for change and how to avoid the pitfalls of missteps. This group must be pushed or cajoled into the category of Supporters; if not, the likelihood is that, confused and discouraged by what they perceive to be unfair condemnation, they will seek comfort in the ranks of Resisters. Undecided followers must be invited into the fold of supporters and persuaded that it is both a safe environment, and the right one for them.

References

1. *The eagle and the arrow*. Aesop's fable as quoted by Eliot/Jacobs. Accessed November 23, 2021, from fablesofaesop.com
2. Rodriguez, T. *Dealing with conflict: The problem is the problem*. Accessed November 19, 2012, from conorneill.com
3. Smith-Meyer, A. (2018). *Surviving organisational behaviour*. Kindle Publications.
4. Lapsley, F. M., & Karakashian, S. (2012). *Redeeming the past: My journey from freedom fighter to healer*. Orbis Books.
5. The film: "The best of enemies", (release 2018) as directed by Robin Bissell depicts the Charrette process as applied to a 1971 school integration dispute in North Carolina. Based on a book by the same name by Osha Gray, 2007.
6. Lincoln, A. (1864, April 18). *Address at Sanitary Fair, Baltimore, Maryland*.
7. Kinicki, A., & Fugate, M. (2012). *Organizational berhaviour*. McGraw-Hill Irwin.
8. Huczynski, A. A., & Buchanan, D. A. (2007). *Organisational behaviour*. Prentice Hall.
9. Galunic, C. (2012, November 10). Lessons from Obama's campaign victory. *INSEAD Knowledge*.
10. Jap, A. (2020, June 11). To navigate office politics, map out your friends and foes. *INSEAD Knowledge*.
11. Nelson, J. C., Adams, G., & Salter, P. S. (2012, December 11). The Marley Hypothesis: Denial of racism reflects ignorance of history. *Psychological Science*.

#OfficePolitics2: Marketing the Change

8

8.1 The Tools of Persuasion

The objective of organisational persuasion is not to court the darker sides of Machiavellianism. Manipulation, bullying, coercion or the abusive use of (real or fake) information is counterproductive to establishing trust. Our objective is to convince those willing through respect, fairness and transparency, consistency, effective communication, and the kind of support that allows members of the organisation to open their minds to the uncertainty of change [1].

Observing the rules of fairness, authenticity and integrity, the change leader can influence opinion by stimulating neurological triggers. People are busy, and unless the prompt to engage with change is exciting, fresh and attractive, it will garner little support. Receiving an impersonal memorandum explaining a new emphasis on D&I outlining the anticipated benefits to be gained will likely generate a skimmed read at most before returning to more pressing daily tasks. If we are to request our rational selves to digest and weigh new written information, our emotional interest needs to be awakened. Scientifically, we need to connect with our neurological systems to stimulate interest and prepare the mind for persuasive arguments to follow. Known as neuromarketing, it is a method borrowed from the marketing world. It sets out to capture the target audience's attention and get them both excited and rationally engaged with the objective. A new set of values or priorities, a different culture or perspective; these are ideas that need to be sold, attract attention and arouse enthusiasm. It makes sense, therefore, to work on the neurological trigger points that lead to persuasion. Morin and Renvoise identify six such levers [2]:

- *Personal*: The message must attract the individual's attention in as much that it concerns them personally. At the early stages of raising awareness, empathy without affinity is only a passing emotion, not a sustainable trigger.
- *Contrastable*: We deal better with choices than concepts. Hence, we need to present the audience with a radical and straightforward choice between two or three options, of which one is plainly more exciting (yet still achievable) than the

other(s). Once a particular objective or improvement goal is accepted, the human, primal brain generates far more enthusiasm for a revolutionary choice.

- *Tangible*: Complexity and obvious obstacles will discourage the listener. The message must be simple, its goal well-defined, and the proposed path to success easy. If an objective is attractive, it must also be a viable one.
- *Memorable*: In marketing, the experts tell us that a product name must be mentioned seven times before it becomes memorable. A message with a striking opening paragraph and a conclusion that echoes the opening sentences is more potent than one that does not. Our brain attaches greater importance to a tagline than elegant prose. Telling stories that the listener can identify with is more effective than lists of facts.
- *The Visual*: One of the most intuitive and effective senses with which to get attention and a rapid reaction from our primal brain.
- *Emotional*: Once the intuitive mind is ready to digest education and rational explanations of strategy, enthusiasm needs to be maintained through the power of empathy and group unity. We all want to be part of the community. Hence, efforts have to be sustained to ensure that a team spirit and joint celebration of effort continue during and after the campaign.

Incentives and Disincentives

To encourage acceptance of change, we need to persuade individuals to feel good and secure about the consequences. The outcomes must make them feel virtuous or successful on the one hand and secure in the belief that the change will benefit rather than harm them on the other. Sparking our intrinsic craving to build our self-esteem, or even the esteem of others towards us, provides us with a motivation to change. In terms of organisational change, we would like to convince our blockers and resisters to become ambassadors and supporters on the merits of our arguments. However, realistically, some people will not shift their opinions and behaviours without an additional nudge in the form of extrinsic rewards; call them incentives.

In their book "The Persuasion Code", Morin and Renvoise argue that there are three types of impact that can move an individual to determine their interest in the consequences of change. If the leadership that promotes change neglects to consider these extrinsic drivers of the mind, the uphill struggle becomes steeper and less predictable. They identify three types of value that will influence and possibly derail the acceptance of a change programme. Adopting their marketing language to cultural change, we might describe them as follows:

- Financial value: the direct creation of measurable wealth, either by revenue increases, another form of cash, or highly likely future benefit.
- Strategic value: the presence of an indirect tangible benefit to the business, which reflects on the individual's outwardly-perceived success story. Actions or behaviours that prove praiseworthy in performance evaluations that open doors to career opportunities, or enhance perceptions of the individual as a leader within

the organisation, can prove particularly attractive in the pursuit of long-term ambition.

- Personal value: the influence of change on psychological or physical benefits such as stress levels, working hours, workplace relations and environment, self-esteem and recognition—one might refer to a general sense of well-being.

Each of these buckets can result in a perception of value creation or value loss. An individual that feels "left behind"—that doors of opportunity are closing—or otherwise perceives that change offers no benefit to them, will resist the proposed changes and, in certain situations, might even resort to sabotaging attempts at its implementation.

Therefore, it is essential that the change leadership runs a campaign geared to successful communication and persuasion and consider the value matrix that determines individual calculations of direct and indirect gain or cost to them personally.

It is not enough to make bold claims and present utopic aspirations that the target population feels are unfounded or unrealistic. To all but the most idealistic, we need to present tangible evidence that the cost and sacrifice of stability and comfort that change implies will have a positive outcome. The form of proof may range from cold, hard numbers to our emotional experience and reaction to what we see and hear. Morin and Renvoise argue that there are four potential sources of proof that can convince the individual that the proposed change will positively or negatively impact financial, strategic or personal value. They list these by order of importance, as follows:

1. *Social Proof*: Counter-intuitively perhaps, but individuals are more affected by the testimony of others than documented facts. We prefer to listen to the advice of friends and family on the merits of a particular restaurant rather than read an impersonal review in the food column of the local newspaper; we act on the directions of a stranger in the street rather than study a map. The instinct of reciprocity or social contract that "what goes around, comes around" implies that it is in our common interest to be truthful to one another. The more consistent the social proof that the proposed change has proved beneficial to others, the more likely we are to be persuaded. The more we already associate with or respect the provider of social proof, the more we trust them. This relationship is the power of the opinion-leader.

2. *Observable Proof*: Seeing is believing. If social proof relies on the credibility of what we hear, then visual proof relies on our sight, whether as a bystander to events in our immediate surroundings or how we observe the tangible impact of similar changes elsewhere. In a world of alternative truths, fake news, manipulated videos and cloned voices, being sure that we can believe everything we see, read, or hear, is becoming a moot point. The advantage of, or need for, change will be more readily accepted if we observe those who adopt change being lauded as positive influencers or leaders. Equally, if we read that competitors who have adopted the change are experiencing superior performance, boards might sit up and take more notice.

3. *Analytical Proof*: This is an aspect that advocates of cultural change will find challenging to make use of. The introduction of new machines or working practices, for example, will be able to point to reductions in processing time by (say) 10 min, or an increased quality of output by (say) 7.62% as measured by practical experiment. A culture change might generate some data points, but they will typically be less precise. Comparative statistics from employee surveys might confirm employee satisfaction higher by a certain percentage, that sentiments of well-being have changed, or internal trust levels improved or deteriorated. Over the long term, an improved culture and work environment might be expected to reduce staff turnover and complaints. The introduction of performance assessment scores rewarding or punishing those who are working for or against the direction of change ("team spirit" or "flexibility" scores, for example) might generate short-term indicators of behaviour also. It remains that qualitative data has to be supported by quantitative data, however.

4. *Aspirational Proof*: Within the field of D&I, we often refer to studies evidencing correlations between increased levels of trust, innovation and profitability. This form of evidence is aspirational; they require an element of faith in statistics on behalf of the audience. Such studies may often be potent for those who want to receive confirmation of what they already believe as correct, energising effort towards achieving the objective. However, the sceptical employee whose predisposition renders the aspiration undesirable will most likely wait for more conclusive forms of proof to manifest themselves before committing to change.

A Bird in the Hand Is Better Than Two in the Bush

The tools of persuasion deployed in the change management campaign will probably reference various sources of proof that address the three forms of value creation that catch the audience's attention. Strategically, completing a Value Matrix (as shown in Fig. 8.1) to include options on how best to reinforce proof of the benefits and identify the costs of change would be a good start. Have we used our available sources of

VALUE ↓ PROOF ➡	SOCIAL	OBSERVABLE	ANALYTICAL	ASPIRATIONAL
Financial	Leader statements on strategic content & positive financial impact.	Promotions, bonuses & awards based on inclusive behaviours.	Non-financial reporting evidencing a D&I dividend encoded in the budget process.	Market leader status. First mover advantage.
Strategic	Ranking of "Best places to work" or similar.	Expertise and skills imported to the enterprise from diversified hiring.	Training and education on the benefits of D&I.	Vision, Mission & Value statements incl. D&I goals.
Personal	Better work culture, relationships & recognition of individual worth.	Improved sense of wellness at work. Opportunity to express oneself without fear.	Recognition of D&I behaviours and performance in reward decisions	Sensations of optimism and hope for career, growth and personal growth.

Fig. 8.1 Examples of types of proof of the benefits of D&I changes

evidence to best effect? Can we introduce new measures to emphasise perceived gain? Do we understand the perceived negative expectations of change based on fear of change or stressful confrontations between old and new?

We are unlikely to complete all of the boxes covering the social, observable, analytical and aspirational proof of gain for all three of the values sought by individuals. But the simple understanding that social proof has a greater influence on personal choice and behaviour than statistics accentuates the need to ensure that change is not launched as a top-down instruction. Instead, we realise that we must accompany change with transparency, candour and opportunities to interact. Employees need to hear of the experiences, frustrations, hopes and aspirations of their peers; subordinates must be able to raise their concerns and discuss the change experience freely with their superiors without fear of retaliation. In preparing our change campaign, we must plan for the availability of proof of concept and respond to the challenge of overcoming psychological barriers such as bias and prejudice.

8.2 Social Networks for Change

Once we understand the optimal manner in which to shape our message, we need to consider how best to spread the message throughout the organisation. In a subject area of equity, diversity and inclusion—even belonging—the balance of proof based on the value matrix is more likely to rely heavily on the side of social and observable evidence rather than the analytical (of which much is academic or indirect proxy metrics) or the aspirational (which best serves to bolster pre-existing desires or opinions). Focus and investment in efficient and effective social platforms and networks that enable the sharing of knowledge, experience, cultural and emotional observations, are the primary pathways to communicating the benefits and progress that can be achieved through diversity.

Any social platform, discussion forum, alumni organisation—indeed, any initiative that allows individuals to mingle in a safe environment to share and exchange views and experiences—serves one of three essential network types (Fig. 8.2).

1. *Bonding Networks* consist of closely-knit groups of individuals with strong historical, ethnic or other background connections, shared interests, fears and aspirations. They have a similar life perspective, and opinions are largely held in common. The advantage of such networks is that they are fluid and can operate successfully in an informal manner outside an institutional setting. The disadvantage is that these are bonds that often reinforce stereotypical views, myths and biases. Platforms such as Facebook have come under considerable criticism for how their algorithms direct new information to users based on their previous "likes", tracked interests and opinions. The bonding network finds comfort in imagining a community where attitudes are shared and unchallenged. Diversity has no home in such networks.
2. *Bridging Networks* connect diverse communities, or "worlds"; individuals from different social or organisational backgrounds and influences. This network is the

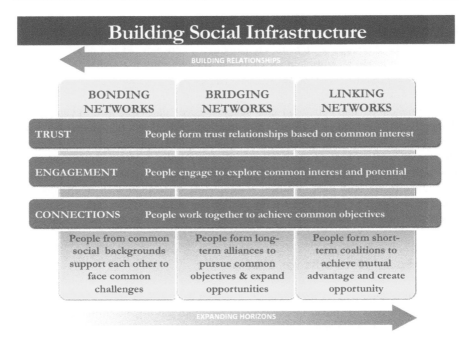

Fig. 8.2 Social infrastructure and linking networks

primary form of network required to promote diversity and produce the benefits to be advertised by way of social proof. Such networks rarely occur spontaneously. Rather, we create organisations for the express purpose of encouraging exposure to a world of diverse views and stories. For example, a Chamber of Commerce in London, Paris or Singapore introduces international business people to the local community. It helps them reach out or build bridges to potential local business partners. For an organisation, a bridging network includes any initiative to bridge the communication and cultural gap that might otherwise exist between offices in Hong Kong, London or New York; or even between employees of diverse ethnic backgrounds in the same city or building. At its core, it enables individuals to meet, exchange viewpoints, and connect with fellow employees facing challenges similar to themselves. It is the path to interculturalism and pluralism. A word of warning, however: a bridging network may easily tend to include those interested in exploring other cultures and diversity and exclude those who see no benefit in doing so. The greatest danger of a bridging network is that of "preaching to the converted", mirroring the same tendency as bonding networks.

3. *Linking Networks* are the loosest form of network based on a situational, intermittent and time-limited confederation of interest. The relationship between an employee and an executive may be hierarchical, and their concerns may not overlap daily. However, knowing who does what, who holds certain opinions,

who has an interest that might generate support or mutual effort, obviously has value. The executive may know specific individuals with whom they have formed a linking network that they know they can trust to get a sounding as to what is happening on the shop floor. An executive might also be happy to respond to a request for advice on a professional or career matter from a junior they know. Often cited in the context of private or non-government organisations seeking connections within local authorities or government institutions, these networks try to establish a problem-solving network to be used as and when needs arise. The alumni books of business schools, listing individuals who graduated from the same school, are in part established to enable graduates who do not know each other to reach out and ask for advice relative to creating opportunities for business or personal careers.

In the D&I context, each of the above forms of social capital networks plays their role and requires management.

The Chains That Bind Us

Legacy bonding networks need to be recognised and worked on as potential blockers or resisters. They may consist of social groupings belonging to those who see change and diversity as a threat to the very privileges of bias they enjoy and that the organisation is trying to counter. Equally, groups of systematically disadvantaged minorities may have established viewpoints and behaviours designed to protect them from exposure to prejudice and discrimination and fear what might happen if they are dismantled. Both extremes will likely consider change with suspicion and need to be engaged and persuaded to support the venture. Bonded networks based on what their members are against must be flipped to be willing to commit to being for something instead. Black and other minority employees who say, "More of the same. We've had focus group after focus group in the past who have achieved nothing" have to be persuaded that, this time, the leadership is sincere and able in its efforts to introduce inclusiveness [3]. The corps of employees who fear the loss of advantage and privilege, or who simply do not want to relinquish their notions of superiority, need to understand that the leadership will not tolerate dissent on D&I; that if they are not willing to explore the potential of change, it may be time to go separate ways.

Bridging the Divide

We should, here, distinguish between zero-tolerance and active culture management. Members must be allowed to experiment, discuss and learn from experience in good faith. If we are to be inclusive, we must encourage a learning culture to evolve—one where mistakes and failure are allowed as long as it is acknowledged and represents a lesson learnt.

If we want mindsets to alter, we need to establish, nourish and facilitate a bridging network. This engineering of social capital has to be managed to ensure that interaction within the network remains "safe" and free of the interference of the older mindsets that might prevail in legacy bonded networks as they are brought together on this new platform. The rules of engagement and code of conduct must be determined, communicated, and enforced by facilitators trained in mediation and debate. It is not a process that runs itself. The aim is to allow members to understand our conflicting biases and emotions. We need to understand the impact that current or previous attitudes have on those who experience them as tools of suppression. Our aim must be to develop a genuine curiosity of what other perspectives bring to the table and have to offer in terms of achieving organisational objectives.

Linking Potential

The linking network should create a framework that allows external sources, such as educational establishments or NGOs expert in D&I, to assist in our endeavour. It should encourage contact between senior managers and junior staff that might not "naturally" ally themselves with one another. Expanding links between peers can contribute to a mutual interest by way of intermittent dialogue or collaboration. We can think of time-limited mentor or reverse-mentor programmes. Network participants who would not typically join together can discover how to work on culture change with colleagues on a more or less daily basis, teaming up to discuss solutions to workplace situations at a more distanced level.

How we interact and nurture relationships with family (bonded networks), brothers-at-arms (bridging networks), and pragmatic alliances (linking networks) differ and offer varied benefits. If social proof is derived from such networks, we must ensure that we facilitate and manage them to benefit our shared objective. If we are to create positive associations with our end-objectives, then central to your communications strategy should be:

– Establishing an overview of the presence of such networks within the organisation
– Identifying the influence they hold on group ethics and opinion
– Facilitating constructive exchanges across and between the networks

8.3   Spheres of Influence: Empowering the Messengers

Once the firm understands the networks within the organisation and the opinion-leaders who influence them, it is time to prepare and assist your ambassadors and supporters with the tools and words needed to help them start the ripples you hope will become waves. Ideas and behaviours spread from these opinion-leaders, influencing their friends and colleagues, in turn communicating ideas to their friends and colleagues that the influencer does not even know, and—so studies show—to people within the network three times removed from the source opinion. If the sphere of influence of the right ambassadors is so extensive, then creating a wave of social proof via word of mouth is a powerful tool in driving culture change [4]. The power of this viral transmission of opinion is the result of our human socialisation instincts. As long as the shift in mindset and culture is not too distant from an individual's core values, the person who seeks acceptance within the group will look to those they admire, their friends and role models for signals as to what attracts approval and respect and mimic them. Eventually, they will appropriate, repeat and propagate those views as their own, continuing the chain of influence. The phenomenon will only meet barriers where these new ideas run counter to the audience's core beliefs—in this context—those who are determined to maintain the superiority of the dominant class or who hold deep fears of the consequences of diversity to them personally.

Tooling Up the Ambassadors

Surely, most of us have felt sympathetic to a cause or idea without actually having the proper arguments to make our case or put forward a persuasive justification. Potential ambassadors for D&I will be predisposed to promoting diversity as a straightforward matter of organisational or social justice, or they will be sympathetic to being persuaded on the subject. In either case, the provision of information on the benefits of diversity and the harm caused by discrimination needs to be placed in their hands so that they can better make their arguments and broadcast a message of tolerance and openness. The life of an ambassador should neither be difficult nor precarious. Active executive support for the message they espouse is a sure way to ease the pressure on ambassadors and supporters speaking in its favour. Are your ambassadors able to speak with authority to the entirety of the social network with the confidence that comes from knowing they have hierarchical backing?

Three essential tools make us feel enabled and confident when stepping forward to enter a debate.

A. *Information.* Opinion-leaders do not last long if their opinions are shown to be based on bluster, alternative truths and bluffs. Durable opinion-leaders have earned the respect of those around them by exhibiting expertise grounded in serious reflection and research—they are right more often than wrong. They have credibility in the eyes of their social networks. An influencer who does not have a sufficient grounding in the facts and figures of a topic may be willing to agree with basic principles and express sympathetic support for a cause. Still, it is rare that they will actively promote it unless—as previously explained—(1) it fits with direct personal interest or values, (2) represents an indirect strategic support to ideas and causes that they are directly concerned with, or (3) offers a financial benefit to themselves or their other activities (such as their business unit). Therefore, information that provides analytical and political support to the views you hope to propagate is the first tool that ambassadors need to bolster their conviction with credible arguments. Educational programmes that focus on understanding (rather than training on procedures and processes) need to be rolled out, and ambassadors encouraged to volunteer to take an active part as participants or even as facilitators.

B. *Platform.* As already discussed, the sphere of influence of opinion-leaders typically extends to three social steps removed from them. However, we can enlarge this reach by providing the opinion-leader access to platforms that promote focus and debate on the topics that concern us. Organising bottom-up and top-down discourse between colleagues and peers has the potential to attract new allies and fan the flames of interest around the subject of D&I. The design of social platforms will enable our ambassadors to project the sparks of their message on issues such as the rights and wrongs of behaviour and the benefits and harm caused by inclusion and exclusion farther afield to larger audiences. Most people in any given social group accept the status quo as the norm; they rarely question where these norms come from or why they are thought to be "good" or beneficial. Until we are confronted by our prejudicial assumptions of stereotype and natural privilege, we tend to be oblivious to the injustice or harm they cause others. The creation of employee exchange platforms can educate us on the benefits of diversity and the unintentional injury we have been imparting on disadvantaged groups. These platforms can be both the source and the communicator of the social proof we need to reach tradition-bound bonded networks; networks that potentially were not even aware that their presumptions and attitudes were at the heart of inequity and injustice within the firm.

C. *Empowerment.* The informed ambassador or supporter of D&I will observe behaviours that suppress diversity and discriminate based on colour, creed, gender or sexual identity. They will either feel empowered to intervene and speak up or merely cringe at the injustice of inappropriate or ignorant behaviours of colleagues. Because the ambassador and supporter of your cause will, by definition, be sensitive to harmful behaviours, they will be motivated to ensure such observations will not be repeated. The question is, do they feel entitled to raise the issue or even intervene while it is happening? Have they been trained in what an acceptable form of challenge to abusive behaviour looks like? Are they emboldened by the knowledge that the hierarchy will celebrate their courage? Are those subject to discrimination grateful for the allyship offered, or do they fear some form of subsequent retribution? All of these aspects demand clear values and objectives that are actively promoted and enacted by the executive and the board. Leaders must walk the talk, and talk while walking.

Gaining the Support of the Crowd

The ambassador is an individual predisposed to carrying the banner of justice and change. By virtue of their grassroots status, they often have more credibility even than the more distant executive or board member. Through their endeavours and the power of social proof, other peers and colleagues will be encouraged to feel accountable for the behaviour and outcomes conducted by themselves or others. If role models are loud and clear on expectations, changes in rewards or sanctions related to behaviour apparent, and facts in the form of statistics and psychological studies support the call for change, then the job of persuasion is almost done.

The final "nail in the coffin" to any remaining blocking attitudes or resistance will be to win the aspirational argument. Involving sceptics, detractors and potential resisters in the project by including them in working groups is a tried and tested method of achieving "buy-in" by the reticent, or at least avoiding the "not-invented-here" syndrome of rejection. Using platforms for social discourse within the organisation to debate and win support for renewed core values and agreement on the shared norms that shall govern future behaviour turns the traditional top-down instruction into a bottom-up collaboration [5].

Asking individuals to change their behaviour in a given setting is not all that difficult. It only requires clarity as to what is expected, fairness in applying the rules and observable justice being meted out to those who follow the rules and those who break them. However, convincing people to accept that their past behaviours were harmful and that new, better behaviours need to be adopted to be deemed ethical is far more complex. Once social norms of conduct have been established, observed and explained, we have won the minds of people. Still, in a matter as sensitive as group prejudice, stereotyping and discrimination, minds are not enough. Actions must be accompanied with empathy, with authenticity, with a desire to include strangers in your midst—we must win over hearts as well as minds.

The strategic value of the D&I Ambassador is particularly high in large companies with several sub-cultures born of location, market practices and education, amongst others. Being part of the local sub-culture, the ambassador connects with their community in a way that "Head Office" cannot. Research on the broader but related topic of ethical cultures emphasises the value of the local ambassador. "The creation of a shared and consistent ethical culture is mentioned more frequently by companies with ethics ambassadors" and "companies which have established a network of ethics ambassadors tend to put in place a more comprehensive ethics programme than those who have not" [6]. The impact of ambassadors, be they for ethical, moral or behavioural issues, improves both interactions with the organisation's grassroots and facilitates the communication of bottom-up expectations and needs to the executive—if they are listening.

8.4 Appointing the D&I Change Agent . . . or Not?

Once the demands and requirements of culture transformation are apparent, it is time to consider who to appoint as the "face" of change. There are many variations of the title that can be bestowed upon this person. Those boards which focus on a narrow subject like the fight against corruption may nominate a Head of Compliance or Ethics; if the task is to stop discriminatory practices, the board may create the dedicated function of a Head of D&I. If we wish to empower the role, the title conferred may elevate the person to the C-suite. If the board has a more general cultural overhaul in mind, the search might be on for a Chief Transformation Officer instead.

Some argue that the establishment of such a function can be counter-productive. If you wish to have an authentic cultural change—the argument goes—it is dangerous to categorise and box in such a vital and strategic initiative. A dedicated function with a necessarily limited mandate "cannot ensure the holistic approach required to change attitudes throughout the firm". D&I objectives—to continue the argument—are the responsibility of all employees and should be left to each individual business unit to deal with. These arguments betray a lack of understanding of the challenge posed by culture management.

It should be clear by now that organising and managing a change programme that reaches for the stellar goals of altering the attitudes of, potentially, thousands, or tens of thousands of people, is a highly complex and sophisticated operation. Hence, responsibility for the execution of culture change should rest with the board or the CEO, or at the very least with the Director or Head of Human Resources. It takes expertise, time and resources to [7]:

  (i) Identify the existence of discriminatory practices, their drivers and origins throughout the organisation.
 (ii) Assessing the drivers and origins of bias within the firm, its expression and impact on all stakeholders, internal and external.
(iii) Develop training, coaching and advisory processes to educate and help business units and the various communities impacted confront their non-inclusive behaviours.
(iv) Formulate policies and processes to guarantee a safe environment for conflict resolution and reconciliation. Review existing policy frameworks (such as compensation, promotion and reward systems) and align these to stated D&I objectives.
 (v) Create effective strategies for the long-term struggle against bias and discrimination for the approval of the board—followed by the execution of same.
(vi) Permanently monitor (a) the evolution of internal and external exclusion risks in line with the holistic assessment made [in (ii) above] and (b) compliance throughout the organisation with corporate policy and processes [defined in (iv) above].
(vii) Gather and report on the evolution of exclusion risks, stakeholder attitudes, strategy implementation progress and bottle-necks, and newly identified risks and remedies.

The achievement of the above demands placed on a function that is to be held accountable for successful transformation to inclusion cannot be done through high-level diktat. It cannot be achieved by wishful thinking or some form of amorphic osmosis resulting from the "ethical thinking and standing" of the board or the executive. Nor can a Head of Human Resources or Compliance be expected to "magic" all of the above to happen in the routine of the working day. Instead, the designated department would themselves have to appoint a change manager—a person with the competencies to plan and execute all of the elements covered in this book, so far, and the chapters to follow.

Indeed, the visibility rendered to the culture change project is an essential part of the credibility of the venture. It is apparent to every observer that activities and functions actually considered to be of strategic importance have a seat at the top table. For the D&I function to be a sub-department of HR is to communicate that it is of sub-strategic significance—no matter what the leadership says. This visibility is more subtle than merely having an individual with the title of Chief Diversity and Inclusion Officer, frequently (and wrongly) shortened to CDO rather than CDIO. The organisation's members must experience and understand that the CDIO has the ear of the most important individual impacting their everyday: the CEO. When the CDIO speaks, there is no alternative channel to appeal to. The CDIO must be seen to be at one with the Executive, and the Executive known to have complete confidence in the person who fills that role.

Choosing the Face of Diversity and Inclusion

"No prophet is acceptable in their own land". These words of Jesus, as reported by Luke, imply that an individual who preaches change from within the world in which they live will have a tougher time convincing brethren than an outsider carrying the same message [8]. The Contemporary English Bible puts it more bluntly "no prophets are liked by the people of their own hometown". Naturally, there are reams of theological debate to explain what these words mean, but an old story lies at its core. It is harder to be seen as credible when speaking in the village that raised you or considered neutral and unconflicted compared to an educated, apparently qualified outsider who does not carry the luggage of familiarity or vested interest. It is not unusual for companies to hire large consultancy firms to deliver a message that is already advocated internally, because they are seen as "more qualified" or neutral.

If the board wishes to be serious about changing its culture towards less discrimination and more inclusiveness, one of the strategically most important decisions it has to take is to select the individual to carry the mantle of responsibility for its implementation. It is far from uncommon to witness companies appoint a member of the hitherto excluded community to head the programme for change and inclusivity. The temptation of an executive that reflects the dominant social grouping (let us presume White and male) is to focus on finding a Black female candidate. This choice may be the right decision; the question is with the procedure (or lack of) that preceded it. A failure to consider the support and credibility that will be afforded the candidate by virtue of their ethnicity, background, gender or sexuality can easily result in a fading impact of the programme over time. To presume that the Person of Colour in the room is the most knowledgeable about the race question and, therefore, the obvious choice for the role of Chief Diversity & Inclusion Officer, is to vastly oversimplify the task.

The candidate to any position that relies on the genuine intent of the organisation's leadership for the success of their mandate ignores this reality at their peril.

Donna Johnson, the first Chief Diversity Officer of Mastercard, advises caution and care in making the right choice when she says: "Look for an individual who can speak to the business with passion and intelligence and with knowledge. Do they have that executive presence, and could they talk to peers in the business or at another company about how to partner a D&I drive?" [9]. She estimates that half of the recruits to executive diversity roles resulting from the #BLM focus of 2020 will be struggling by 2022. The other 50% she expects to experience success in their role will have probably asked three questions of their employer before accepting the position.

1. How important is diversity to the company in terms of its mission, vision, and bottom line? If the initiative for diversity and inclusion is an emotional one alone, it will not endure. There must be a conviction that diversity is part of the formula for future prosperity and a critical business success factor.
2. What kind of funding is the company willing to put into the D&I initiative? How ready is it to invest in the time and capital needed to build a strong diversity initiative? The D&I programme must control its own resources and be viewed as an essential evolution that transcends temporary cost-cutting measures and hiring freezes. To achieve cultural change, there needs to be consistency and no hint that change is less critical than quarterly results.
3. How does the company view D&I in the firm over the long term? What changes are they expecting, aiming for, and what are the key performance indicators they wish to improve over time? There has to be clarity around the definition of success for there to be meaningful tracking and reporting, adjustments and debate.

Avoiding the Glass Cliff of D&I

Previously, we have spoken of the dangers associated with the good intentions of corporate and political leaders who have been quick to express what they stand against rather than detailing what they are in favour of doing about the problem. In choosing the Chief Diversity & Inclusion Officer, or equivalent, it is natural for the leadership to choose a figurehead who symbolises the culture change campaign. As indicated by Donna Johnson, that person has to be empowered, provided with appropriate resources, and supported by a mission, vision and business strategy that demands inclusion as part of the success story. Too often, this perfect wave on which to surf to inclusive success is rare, and often the waters are choppy and the weather intemperate. Appointing a Black CDIO to "fix" a problem of White employees being less than inclusive can result in a perception of discrimination as a "Black person's problem". Consequently, White colleagues may see themselves as relieved of any duty to be proactive in seeking change; they may perceive themselves as labelled the "guilty" dominant group that cannot be trusted to be part of the solution to rebalancing D&I within the firm.

In some circumstances, the appointment of an acknowledged leader from the "majority" employee grouping who is authentically motivated to make change happen will have greater chances of success in persuading the "powers that be" of necessary actions. The "establishment" candidate's challenge may then be to win the trust of cynics amongst "minority" group employees. The danger in this scenario is that outgroup employees may suspect that the appointed CDIO cannot conceive what it is to suffer marginalisation and lacks the cultural understanding to properly empathise with the minority group's experience of exclusion. The White CDIO may be viewed as an ally, authentic and well-meaning, but still not gain the confidence of minority employees that effective change will ensue. Without this trust, code-switching and "safe-harbour" behaviours will continue and weigh down on efforts to promote inclusivity. Therefore, the essential requirement is that the team responsible for implementation have the capacity to identify with the potential harm experienced by disadvantaged groups such as Blacks, Asians or other minority communities. The mandate to take effective action on D&I must come with influencing power amongst decision-takers and involve a team with credibility in both camps of the prejudiced majority and the suppressed minority [3].

The Diversity Cocktail

Minority employees cannot fight systemic racism, nor should they be expected to. That is the job of leadership. The board and the executive need to appoint a CDIO, of minority origins or not, who can competently manage the governance and managerial task of running a culture change programme. The candidate must be charismatic, insightful, empathetic and capable of assembling a diverse team of programme managers who will meet the expectations of the excluded groups within the organisation while being a recognised and influential executive within the leadership itself. Those who, until now, found themselves bonded by a privilege that they may fear losing must be made to feel that their interests are being cared for and that the change in prospect also carries opportunity. The hitherto disadvantaged need a leadership they trust will accomplish the diversity inclusion agenda. More critical than who is appointed as the figurehead of change is a board and executive that "walks the talk and talks while walking", all the while evidencing that [10]:

- The firm is genuine and committed to advancing the development of a racial inclusion agenda.
- The efforts and programme being rolled out is not a tick box exercise.
- Those targeted for inclusion are valued as employees, and there is a recognition that their inclusion will allow that value to better manifest itself within the firm.
- The disadvantaged minority are not blamed for their exclusion. On the contrary, they have the support and allyship of the advantaged majority to rise in the organisation.

- The leadership sees itself as accountable for addressing the concerns around equality. Those experiencing exclusion and discrimination are not by default experts in D&I who can change workplace culture by their singular efforts.

Finally, all employee groupings, more or less privileged or disadvantaged, must be convinced that the organisation as a whole is willing and enabling open and respectful dialogue. Only with employees conveying how they feel throughout the change process, will a community built on a sense of belonging be created.

References

1. Smith-Meyer, A. (2018). *Surviving organisational behaviour*. Kindle Publications.
2. Morin, C., & Renvoise, P. (2018). *The Persuasion code*. Wiley.
3. Banks, K., & Harvey, R. (2020, June). Is your company actually fighting racism, or just talking about it? *Harvard Business Review*.
4. Brands, R., & Rattan, A. (2020, July 13). Use your social network as a tool for social justice. *Harvard Business Review*.
5. Hodges, C., & Steinholz, R. (2017). *Ethical business practice and regulation*. Hart Publishing.
6. Business Ethics Briefing. (2017, April 6). *Ethics ambassadors: Promoting ethics on the front line*. Institute of Business Ethics.
7. ESMA, the European Securities and Markets Authority. (2012, September). *Drawn from the "guidelines on certain aspects of the MiFID compliance function"*. Ref: ESMA/2012/388.
8. The Gospel of Luke 4:24, English standard version.
9. Johnson, D. (2020, December 3). *Race at work: Lessons in diversity and culture from Mastercard*. HBR IdeaCast featuring Donna Johnson, Chief Diversity Officer at Mastercard.
10. Morris, C. (2020, July 23). Racial inclusion: What your Black employees really need you to know. *Forbes*.

#ImperativeConditionsOfChange: What Are the Critical Success Factors?

President Barack Obama settled into the Oval Office as the first African-American president in the history of the USA. On taking office, he felt a particular obligation to ensure that the White House would be an inclusive workplace. The President was determined to role-play the part of the inclusive leader, and he was known for practising Management by Walking Around. He believed that "small stuff mattered" as he wandered through the West Wing checking in on his co-workers, high or low. His administration had appointed the most diverse cabinet in history, and his office was replete with "talented, experienced African Americans, Latinos, Asian Americans, and women". He had recruited a diverse team, and he led by inclusive example. Yet, he made the error of presuming that when the leadership demonstrates inclusive values, this would be sufficient to establish an inclusive culture. What he discovered to be the reality eventually taught him that an inclusive culture requires more than a good example—it requires a trust environment that empowers all who might otherwise be marginalised to speak up and the opportunity for them to do so. He learnt that to alter the mindset and behaviours of all actors, be they from more or less privileged backgrounds, required candour and a willingness to listen, exchange and learn that does not come naturally to us. Leadership in and of itself is not enough [1].

So far, in this book we have looked at the causes and drivers of exclusive behaviours and why it influences our treatment of others in discriminatory ways. We considered the harm that bias and prejudice cause us as individuals, employees and, more broadly, as members of society. We have examined the enormity of the challenge facing us as we try to temper our treatment of minorities, be they based on gender, race, culture, sexual orientation and more. We conclude that altering the mindset and culture within an organisation requires dedicated leadership and is a change project like no other.

In this chapter, we shall identify the critical and necessary conditions required before we dare believe that culture and mindset change is possible. There is no single, step-by-step solution to eliminating prejudice and discrimination; it requires a multi-faceted, holistic approach. Like seeds scattered on infertile soil, none of these

A. Smith-Meyer, *Unlocking the Potential of Diversity in Organisations*, Diversity and Inclusion Research, https://doi.org/10.1007/978-3-031-10402-2_9

will succeed if the base conditions for culture change are absent. We can raise awareness of the topic or educate people on new behaviours to adopt, but they will fail unless combined with a commitment to fairness, transparency and respect.

Implement D&I initiatives under the wrong circumstances, and our endeavours will be ineffective and fail to motivate any genuine desire to foster change. The exercise merely becomes a blind application of well-meaning policies and procedures applied by managers who do not share the same conviction as those who initiated or designed the programme. As discussed in our last chapter, too often, a token representative of the discriminated minority will be tasked with the "culture change project". Appointing the victim to solve the crime is the worst form of delegation [2]. Race discrimination is no more a "problem" to be solved amid marginalised communities than the harassment of women is an issue to be left to women to resolve. Solutions to these problems are to be found in altering the perpetrators' mindset, no matter how much they may believe that they "are not the problem" Asking the victim to rectify an injustice only invites those who enable the perpetrator to consider their responsibility to be at an end.

9.1   Of Leadership and Culture: The Path to Inclusiveness

The pitfalls into which most culture change initiatives drop appear self-evident when observed. The grumblings of employees are usually many: perceived injustice, the pursuit of political advantage, management by exception and fading leadership interest are amongst the most common. Many business leaders have promised to find and repair racial disparities within their organisations. It is a commitment not to make lightly. The path to inclusiveness will be uncomfortable, and the leadership has to prepare and equip their staff for the journey.

Genuine acceptance of diversity and inclusion is a personal decision, not a technical process. The board and executive can introduce numerical diversity, but the pursuit of inclusion requires an emotional admission that allowing diversity to play its full and equal role is to recognise that their mission and organisational purpose will be enriched and outcomes improved as a result. It must be personal because it requires vulnerability and humility to understand that in opening hearts and minds to a greater variety of perspectives and accepted beliefs, their lives will be richer, and their interactions with work colleagues or friends more inspiring and fascinating. It must be personal beyond the boardroom or the C-suite: it has to be personal to all members of the organisation, whatever their predisposition or previous assumptions as to what is "normal" or accepted practice. D&I aims to nurture a culture of acceptance that allows those previously excluded to feel a part of the team emotionally; it is not a mere policy or goal. Inclusiveness is about showing respect for the person, considering the different viewpoints expressed and fairness in deliberation, reward and sanction [3]. It is challenging because inclusion is not the pursuit of sameness; it is the celebration of differences.

Five Steps to Inclusivity

Many recipes are put forward for advancing culture change or behavioural change based on ethical and moral values. An ethics management textbook might offer four or more approaches to the design of a culture change programme. They range from those intended to protect the firm and its leadership from reputation loss or blame in the event of failure, to an external orientation that tries to identify and address the ethical expectations of stakeholders. Alternatively, some advocate a compliance orientation that emphasises detection and prevention of conduct that risks breaking the law or other regulations imposed on the firm [4]. None of these will succeed in bringing about authentic changes of behaviour that will allow a trust culture to develop, employees of diverse backgrounds to bond, or allow benefits, ideas and innovation to thrive. In a 2020 report, McKinsey identified those firms that harvested the most significant rewards from D&I programmes, heralding them as "Diversity Winners". McKinsey concluded on five "bold and often innovative actions that diversity winners are taking to embed inclusive culture, mindsets and behaviour in their organisations" [5]. As with many other approaches espoused and written about, these encompass the concepts of leadership, trust culture, and dialogue within the organisation.

Leadership

- *Strengthen leadership accountability and capability for diversity and inclusion.* Core business leaders and managers have to be willing and want to take an active role as agents for equitable and inclusive behaviour. Objective-setting and remuneration decisions must be designed as either facilitating diversity or as a driver of inclusiveness. To fulfil this requirement, managers need to be both effective in their role and possess adequate levels of emotional intelligence to enable balanced debate and collaboration in the presence of varying, and sometimes opposing, perspectives.
- *Ensure representation of diverse talent throughout the organisation*—horizontally across functions and hierarchically, starting at the top of the organisation. It requires a revision of traditional recruitment and promotion paths and the redefinition of required profiles for individual roles and team compositions. In essence, diversity must be seen to be the norm, not the exception.

Trust Cultures

- *Enable equality of opportunity through fairness and transparency.* Equality is probably the most crucial aspect of McKinsey's observations as it points to a necessary, practical outcome of an effective diversity and inclusiveness programme. Employees will be quick to observe, then to either praise or condemn promotions and job opportunity decisions. An inclusive culture needs a high degree of trust amongst members of the organisation that equality is a cornerstone of executive decisions to the detriment of favouritism or discrimination.

- *Promote openness and tackle discrimination.* This requirement goes beyond any "open door" policy. It implies proactivity and demands the capability of managers and employees to identify, surface and openly discuss any indication of excluding behaviours or mindsets, including micro-aggressions, unconscious bias or misunderstandings.

Open dialogue

- *Foster belonging through unequivocal support for multivariate diversity.* McKinsey's study concluded that the biggest diversity winners were innovative in their ability to look at their various diversity talents and seek to highlight and promote their use. Inviting diversity and ensuring it has its equal "place at the table" is good, but if it stops there, it is passive. It is insufficient to rely on the diversity representatives themselves to find the opportunity and courage to bring their fresh perspectives to the discussion; they must be invited to do so. Redefining roles and team compositions to create space for diversity and encouragement for employees of all backgrounds to express themselves is a form of social engineering necessary to make D&I succeed.

9.2   The Three Imperatives

Qualities such as leadership, trust and dialogue have stand-alone virtues, all of which will promote the cause of integrity, ethics, inclusiveness and more. Yet, each on their own will know only short-term success. Decisive leadership must establish the foundations of integrity and trust. The charismatic leader can inspire behavioural change through role modelling and being clear on behavioural expectations. By facilitating and negotiating concord between the various factions, the leader can police an inclusive environment for as long as they are present and actively promoting the subject. A trust culture will allow community members to learn from and support each other, but in the absence of determined leadership cannot protect against unconscious bias or a gradual deterioration of trust in the face of conflicting interests. A living dialogue is achieved by continuously managing conflicting perceptions using open discussion and feedback loops that encourage learning and collaboration. Such a conversation cannot exist in the absence of a trust culture that builds confidence against the fear of retaliation; the dialogue will not be maintained as a living and continuous debate without the discipline imposed by solid leadership.

Once this trio seen in Fig. 9.1 is in position, the multivariate diversity of talent can be recruited and brought into the community as equal partners, exchange learning across bridging networks, develop mutual respect and a support mindset for turning potential conflict into creative solutions instead. This trinity of imperatives forms a base for culture change, without which any programme will not be sustainable over the medium or long term.

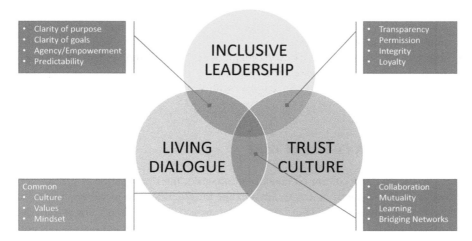

Fig. 9.1   The three imperatives of culture change

Imperative #1: Inclusive Leadership

The imperative need for executive ownership and leadership on a culture change project is demonstrated by the plethora of failed efforts evidenced by culture scandals, such as Wells Fargo and Barclays, or the widespread fraudulent behaviour seen in Worldcom, Volkswagen and, more recently, Boeing and Wirecard [6, 7]. Experience and studies show that corporate executives consistently fail to transmit their advocated ethical and moral values to the shop floor [8]. Once the lofty words in speeches are delivered and replicated in the rarified language of corporate policy, most employees return to the performance criteria upon which they are judged or most often tested. Moral issues fade to be replaced by simple financial indicators, irrespective of any impact on "softer" objectives. Weak ethical leadership reflects itself more in middle management and junior levels of the organisation where goals tend to be more performance than behavioural-based. The difference in the severity of racial and gender bias between senior and lower levels can vary by a factor as much as 44–70% [9]. It is essential that the leader not only walks the talk, but also talks while walking if the chances for success are to be optimised.

To be a leader of culture change requires determination, courage and, not least, integrity. Studies show that there are four organisational factors linked with employees' strong sense of inclusion. All of them are unlocked at the initiative of their leadership.

- Diverse, inclusive leadership evidencing openness to a presence of gender, race and LGBT+ minorities at senior levels within the organisation, and a managerial culture that empowers employees and builds team cohesion.

- Definitions of competence and performance that increase fairness and deliver consistent performance evaluation procedures and transparent, non-discriminatory outcomes.
- The presence of in-house sponsors, mentors or coaches who support individuals from historically marginalised communities.
- Access to senior leaders who engage with employees and are supportive of individual growth.

Imperative #2: A Culture of Trust

Once leadership and culture ownership are assured, the organisation is primed for effective D&I measures. A key to any change programme is to avoid any risk of a "them and us" discussion. "They" must not be seen as "the problem", just as "us" do not have all of the answers. The precursor to any honest engagement, education, or reconciliation is the existence of a culture of mutual respect; an environment where:

- Those in a position of privilege empathise with minority colleagues who, all too often, are subjected to, often unintended, micro-aggression.
- Everyone feels free to speak up on "sensitive" subjects.
- The fear of retaliation or abuse is absent [10].

The development of such a trust environment is essential to any thriving, inclusive culture. The marginalised employee must feel sufficiently safe and secure to express themselves, be themselves, and intervene as the individuals they are. The dominant group employee must see their culturally diverse, gay or disabled colleague in terms of their uniqueness, competencies, and contribution; "who" they are rather than "what" they are. In creating a trust ecosystem, many concurrent paths have to be trodden, principally paved with values of mutual respect, empathy and transparency. The concept of organisational justice encompasses all of these elements, whereby equal consideration and respect shown to employees based on behaviour and performance is unquestionably the norm. As with an ethical culture, or a learning and innovation culture, honesty and trust between colleagues are the bedrock of team spirit, inclusion, open discourse and innovation.

Imperative #3: A Living Dialogue

As with any ethical debate, there are two significant obstacles to a meaningful discussion about discriminatory behaviours: (1) individual interpretation and (2) fear of confrontation [11]. Alongside authentic leadership and the conditions for trust, the final building block essential for an inclusive culture is to find the courage to push for a continuous "living" dialogue amongst all parties involved. As much as with ethical behaviour in general, inclusiveness is not to be promoted simply by promulgating specific beliefs and principles, but through facilitating personal moral engagement, dialogue and choice [4]. This living dialogue must be explicitly centred around:

- A shared understanding of the objective
- Clear definition of supportive values and expected behaviours
- A culture of mutual respect, care and empathy
- A governance and social framework that facilitates and encourages frank and honest debate
- The courage to stand by the conclusions and consequences derived from the dialogue

The objectives of this dialogue are to:

1. Raise awareness of the nature and impact of prejudice on minority groups. We must trigger the curiosity of majority group individuals to explore the realities of minority group life and experience. Those in the majority must be educated to empathise with, rather than rationalise away, the different work and life experiences of the excluded. Members of minority groups must be encouraged and recognised for consenting to, and engaging in, difficult conversations and for speaking up in a spirit of collaboration and coaching. Finally, stereotyping must be discouraged and a common understanding of organisational equity, fairness and justice established.
2. Explore, discover and understand the causes of alienating experiences, prejudice and behaviours to reduce bias and welcome new perspectives.
3. Replace prejudicial stereotypes with an appreciation of the value of the uniqueness of individuals and what they bring [12].
4. Concentrate minds on shared purpose and values; to bond colleagues in the pursuit of what they share, rather than what separates them.

By creating informal workshops, research groups and other platforms, we can demonstrate the value and benefits of a diversity of perspectives in a joint endeavour, and we can shine a light on behaviours that create division and mistrust. The product of this dialogue will be action points that can be implemented to face down dysfunctional attitudes and micro-aggressive behaviours and build a more inclusive workplace.

There is one finishing touch required for success: the monitoring of outcomes and the transparent communication of results. When a group identifies an issue, it must be seen to be internalised and acted on by decision-takers. If not, the whole dialogue process will be undermined and disregarded. Questions raised and initiatives started must be revisited and reported on and, if necessary, modified to ensure the intended outcomes are indeed achieved. Like the burden of Sisyphus, the task of maintaining a culture that forever renews itself is a never-ending task.

The Trinity of Imperatives

What we are describing is not that different from change management theories of continuous improvement; only we are not speaking of procedures and process, but of emotions and mindset.

The essential ingredients are:

1. Clarity of expectations to be provided by the leadership
2. Observable compensation and promotion systems that reward desired behaviours and do not tolerate misconduct
3. Feedback and information sharing platforms that encourage exchange and mutual learning with the objective of improvement, followed by
4. Reinforcement of new learning derived from experience—successful or otherwise

Targeting continuous improvement, sharing and learning from failure as well as success, requires a culture of mutual respect. Just as a stool cannot stand on two legs, culture cannot be achieved without the three pillars of leadership, trust and dialogue.

References

1. Obama, B. (2020). *A promised land*. Viking.
2. Roberts, L. M., & Washington, E. (2020, June). US business must take meaningful action against racism. *Harvard Business Review*.
3. Wadors, P. (2019, December 18). Course "diversity, inclusion, and belonging". *LinkedIn Learning*.
4. Crane, A., & Matten, D. (2016). *Business ethics*. Oxford University Press.
5. Hunt, V., Prince, S., Dixon-Fyle, S., & Dolan, K. (2020, May). *Diversity wins*. Mckinsey & Company.
6. Committee on Transportation & Infrastructure, Majority Staff. (2020). Final committee report: The design, development & certification of the Boeing 737 MAX.
7. McCrum, D. (2020, June 25). Wirecard: The rise and fall of a German tech icon. *Financial Times*. https://www.ft.com/content/284fb1ad-ddc0-45df-a075-0709b36868db
8. Caver, K. A., & Livers, A. B. (2002, November). Dear white boss . . . . *Harvard Business Review*.
9. Bailinson, P., Decherd, W., Ellsworth, D., & Guttman, M. (2020, June). *Understanding organisational barriers to a more inclusive workplace*. McKinsey & Company.
10. Smith-Meyer, A. (2018). *Surviving organisational behaviour*. Kindle Publishing.
11. Smith-Meyer, A. (2015, December). Ethical culture: Much ado about nothing? *Journal of Business Compliance*, (6) Baltzer Science Publishers.
12. Prime, J., & Salib, E. (2014, May). *Inclusive leadership: The view from six countries*. Catalyst.org

#InclusiveLeadership: The Imperative Inclusive Leadership Traits

10.1 The Effective Leader

Effective leaders get the job done; how they achieve their objective has generally been viewed by boards and shareholders as secondary. However, the advent of corporate responsibility and stakeholder management theory highlights the importance of role model behaviours and "tone at the top". In academia, we start exploring the comparative conduct of leaders by defining them in terms of people- or task-orientation, reflecting the findings of the Ohio State Studies [1]:

- People-oriented leadership is based on the leader's concern for subordinates and behaviours that are supportive of and conducive to creating trust relationships. Acting to encourage meaningful interaction between superiors and associates, the people-oriented manager will de-emphasise the hierarchical structure and promote equality between team members. In addition, this empathetic manager will work for the personal well-being of group members and be visible and accessible to all.
- Task-oriented leaders focus on process and the procedural structuring of subordinate behaviours to best achieve the immediate delivery of a desired outcome. The leader's behaviour will be marked by a disciplined approach to target setting, managing expectations, quality control issues, organisation and project management.

The Ohio State Studies placed leadership style on a scale that tips from one extreme to the other. In reality, any one leader will have a style that lies between the black and white of these behaviours, and the exact tint of grey is probably subject to contextual/situational influences. Neither type is deemed to be more effective than the other. Leadership effectiveness, it is generally acknowledged, is a function of a style matching the situation.

These studies made the valuable point that leadership can be executed in different ways. We can either encourage employees to complete their tasks based on

© The Author(s), under exclusive license to Springer Nature Switzerland AG 2022
A. Smith-Meyer, *Unlocking the Potential of Diversity in Organisations*, Diversity and Inclusion Research, https://doi.org/10.1007/978-3-031-10402-2_10

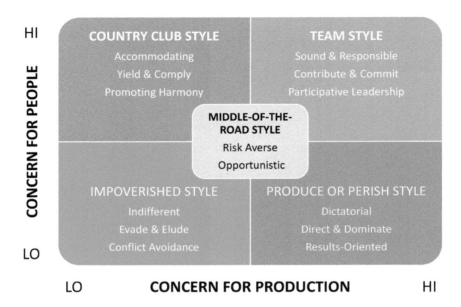

Fig. 10.1 Adopted from Blake & Mouton's Managerial Grid

motivational drivers, or through instruction, process and procedure that ensure that the specified job gets done and that all boxes are ticked. Subsequent theory explored how these orientations express themselves in leadership behaviour and traits. Blake and Mouton's Managerial Grid Theory refined the consideration of orientation to one of caring; either concern for people or concern for production (see Fig. 10.1) [2]. The overly people-concerned manager might become ineffective due to a greater desire to please subordinates than to complete a task (the Country Club or Accommodating style). The manager who is excessively concerned about production might adopt uncomfortably dominating controlling behaviours that result in high performance in the short term, but disaffection and declining productivity over time as staff become disengaged, or even seek employment elsewhere (the Produce-or-Perish, or Dictatorial style).

10.2   Identifying Inclusive Leadership

When trying to define inclusiveness, there is always a tension between:

(a) The recognition and celebration of the value of differences by being inclusive of the uniqueness of talents, experiences and identities that individuals bring to our endeavour—a process of inclusion—and
(b) Encouraging integration, teamwork, harmony and formulating a tactical path to successfully completing a task

To welcome diversity is to enable each individual to contribute their uniqueness to the group. To work towards a defined end result requires the uniqueness of each to blend into one coordinated team effort. A people-orientation may serve both these objectives, but the challenge for the inclusive leader is to create the right conditions for diversity to find its full expression in an inclusive, harmonious environment.

Therefore, it falls to the inclusive leader to go beyond the narrow people-concerned traits of Ohio and Blake and Mouton and, instead, emphasise the entire team's collective well-being, including a sense of purpose. It is no longer sufficient to ensure each employee is engaged and happy. The modern-day demand is to ensure that all team members feel valued as individuals while also enjoying a sense of belonging [3].

Catalyst identified this challenge in a cross-cultural study, albeit with varying emphasis [4]. The need to identify as unique while also being a part of a common culture was evidenced in all countries studied, including such diverse countries as China, Germany, Mexico, and the USA. Their further research into which leadership traits were most likely to qualify as inclusive highlighted the following behaviours:

- Empowerment—Enabling direct reports to develop and excel
- Humility—Admitting mistakes, learning from criticism and different points of view, and acknowledging and seeking the contributions of others to overcome one's limitations
- Courage—Putting personal interests aside to achieve what needs to be done. Acting on convictions and principles even when it requires personal risk-taking.
- Accountability—Demonstrating confidence in direct reports by making them responsible only for a performance they can control

Catalyst termed this Altruistic Leadership a concept strongly linked to Servant Leadership. These leadership qualities were identified as being most likely to result in the unique employee identifying themself as a "citizen" of the team community and consequently helping to boost innovation in the execution of their joint mission.

Returning to management theory, the altruistic or servant leader appears to lean strongly towards the people-oriented manager; the one who has a sincere concern for ensuring subordinates are satisfied in their role. It is not problematic to envisage that a happy employee is a productive employee. Indeed, studies show time and time again that there is a strong link between employee engagement and productivity, innovation and profit growth.

An Iron Fist in a Silk Glove

We might conclude that the inclusive board should immediately evaluate or recruit its executive to ensure that qualities of delegation ability, courage, humility and accountability are all present. At the same time, in the absence of a strong sense of purpose and objective, these qualities might flounder and result in unproductive outcomes. Governance elements such as vision and mission and a clear

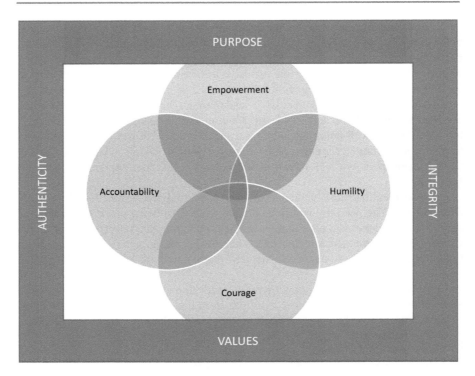

Fig. 10.2   The parameters of inclusive leadership

understanding of purpose, value creation and achievable performance metrics are necessary to channel the positive energy generated. The inclusive leader may need to exhibit the traits of the Altruistic leader, but to lead effectively, they also need to symbolise clear purpose, determination and discipline.

Altruism, an unconflicted and selfless concern for the well-being of others is, therefore, a misleading label. The implication is that the leader will do everything possible for the members of the team to achieve their growth and personal goals leading to their individual well-being—this cannot be true of an effective leader in pursuit of a greater objective. If we are to reach for the stars, there must be some commonality as to which constellation we are aiming at. The inclusive leader must indeed adopt a coaching style of management with respect to the growth and development of each of their subordinates. Still, as depicted in Fig. 10.2, it must be with an eye to a common purpose and shared values that ensure each team member identifies as part of the community rather than a lone wolf.

If we are to pursue long-term outcomes, such as a sustainably diverse and inclusive culture, it is not sufficient merely to embody people-oriented traits. To persuade a group of individuals to set aside some of their personal objectives and behavioural preferences for the achievement of a common purpose, no matter how noble, they have to be convinced of the resilience and durability of the endeavour.

For this, the inclusive leader has to enjoy the credibility born of trust: Clarity of expectations, integrity in all matters and authenticity in conviction and behaviour.

Motivation and Leadership

In line with the positive psychology movement, the transformational manager is people-oriented and looks to a future beyond the immediate task. The transformational leader is convinced that employee engagement, long-term loyalty, and trust relationships will yield superior performance over time. The transformational manager will also highlight the importance of role and task, but will place greater emphasis on job fit and the continuous development of their staff, fulfilling McClelland's three elements of motivational need for one's subordinates [5]:

- The need for achievement, whereby the individual gets satisfaction from overcoming obstacles and accomplishing something difficult (uniqueness)
- The need for affiliation, or the desire to be loved and valued as a group member (belonging)
- The need for power, where exercising influence over others through teaching, coaching, encouraging or facilitating others to grow and finding purpose in our lives is a prime motivator (equality of opportunity and equitable recognition).

In transformational leadership, the manager seeks to trigger the motivational power of our inner needs over time, with a lesser emphasis on monetary or task-based incentives. Do we believe that it is in the power of managers to enhance or awaken these needs in a manner that will stoke the fire of motivation amongst their workers? On balance, we probably do. But do we believe that it is easy? Probably not.

10.3 Leadership by Example and Conviction: Transformational Leadership

Placing the transformational manager in the context of enhancing diversity and inclusiveness in the organisation, we can see how the leader's behavioural traits gain in importance. The situational context is, as previously expressed, on the one hand where the excluded or disadvantaged minority must be encouraged to trust that their uniqueness will not be viewed as a disqualifying or unwelcome contribution and, on the other, where the dominant majority do not feel threatened by the discomfort of the challenge of alternative perspectives or fear the loss of privileged esteem. The strength of equality of opportunity and organisational justice within the community is paramount to creating an environment that allows diversity to flourish and produce benefits. In the context of the D&I challenge, it is easy to understand how the Altruistic Leader (as defined above) can pave the way for inclusive mindsets.

Richard Barrett, in his book "The Values-Driven Organisation", showed that the average annualised return (AAR) of the companies identified as the "Top 40 Best Companies to Work For" in the USA, between 2002 and 2012, was 16.4% compared to the average equivalent of the S&P 500 which was 4.1%. In the same book, the author showed that the performance of 18 "Firms of Endearment" focused on leadership, culture, stakeholder integration, and a "higher purpose" supported by core values achieved an AAR of 13.1% compared to the S&P 500 over the same period [6].

In a Harvard Business Review article in 2015, KRW revealed research that linked financial performance to employee perceptions of four traits of their CEO. The higher the perception that the CEO was a "virtuoso" leader in the fields of integrity, responsibility, forgiveness and compassion, in contrast to "self-focused" CEOs, the better the companies fared financially. The study concluded that virtuoso-led companies exhibited an average return on assets over 2 years of 9.35%, compared to those led by self-focused CEOs, which achieved 1.93% [7].

Other studies consistently evidence part of the reason for these differences; engaged employees are stronger on customer service and quicker to recommend their employers than disengaged staff. The same can be said for the number of "sick days" and costs of operational mistakes in the production process.

Evidence shows that an individual who feels an alliance of personal self-interest with that of their supervisor will be far more attentive to helping that supervisor achieve their objectives. Conversely, an individual who only sees a contractual or near-term interest in doing whatever task has been set, and does not anticipate any benefit from a future relationship with that supervisor, will do no more than what is specified contractually as the expected outcome. Consequently, organisations that look to fulfil long-term ideals that include fairness, equity, diversity and inclusion will view relationship-based transformational leadership as more productive over time than transactional leadership. Therefore, an inclusive leadership style allows both the minority and the majority employee groups to see their long-term interests as being symbiotic with the leadership.

Inclusive leadership builds on the definition of the transformational in its intention to deliberately encompass diversity into the team and optimise long-term team relationship building, rather than primarily focus on individual engagement levels.

Conviction, Consistency and Outcome

Without conviction and leadership by example, the D&I objectives will remain noble words in a policy document. It may be that (e.g.) recruiting managers feel their "higher-than-normal-profile" female or Black recruit is now less risky as "there are quotas to fill". However, it is insufficient to change the environment and prejudice encountered by these new or promoted employees. Indeed, the environment can quickly turn more hostile as "quota" recruits or promotions are viewed as having obtained "special treatment"—oblivious to the fact that it is the previously detrimental treatment of minorities that is being addressed. An organisation where it is viewed as politically, rather than morally, correct to appear positive towards minorities will lead to conflict-avoiding attitudes, strategic colour blindness, or unremedied unconscious bias. As a result, constructive feedback and serious development discussions with the outgroup minority will be withheld [8]. Indeed, a mindset of non-engagement will allow prejudice and stereotypical views of minorities to develop or remain institutionalised.

Escaping stereotypes and what is sometimes termed "White (or male) blindness" to the potential of minorities is seemingly tough. Under the illusion that the majority ethic or convention is the unquestioned norm, managers forget that the minority deserve equal respect. Unless rewarded for the initiative, only the courageous few will dare to challenge themselves by considering how the uniqueness of those who are different might bring new dimensions, knowledge and talents to our monochrome group attitudes. At best, those viewed as "different" risk being considered as lesser versions of the existing majority population. At worst, they will be regarded as a threat to the status quo and, ultimately, to the "hard-earned" privileges of the established elite.

In the absence of credible conviction by all concerned that diversity and inclusion are necessary, beneficial, and an authentic goal, those perceived as hitherto more privileged will be tempted to engage in risk-averse, conflict-avoidance behaviour. Dominant group members will likely not wish to be viewed as politically incorrect by being thought hostile to the leadership's anti-racist initiatives. Those believed to be benefitting from "positive discrimination" initiatives will continue to suffer embarrassment, perpetuating issues of low esteem. The underlying problems of racism or minority discrimination will remain uncorrected, irrespective of any changes in KPIs.

The inclusive leader is swimming against the current of human instinct. It is said that tradition is merely the opinions of the past imposed upon the present. In the absence of challenge, this has some truth in it. Simply perpetuating behaviours and procedures because "that is how we have always done things around here" suppresses learning and innovation. Equally, the idea of what we consider to be meritorious or praiseworthy is generally based on past definitions of success as defined by the dominant social ethic [9]. It is an attitude born of hubris that needs to be adjusted through dialogue and deeper cultural understanding.

If we are to be open to the influence of diversity and be inclusive in accepting those new perspectives, humility is required. Inclusive leadership success depends on sufficient confidence on the part of the dominant ethic to acknowledge that those in power do not have all the answers: they have to be vulnerable and humble enough to learn new truths.

10.4   Proactive Inclusion: Walking the Tightrope of Vulnerability

The inclusive leader has a deep concern for people, high regard for organisational justice, is clear and determined in their pursuit of the common purpose, and consistently exhibits a willingness to embrace new perspectives. However, until we have completed our culture transformation to one that is perfectly inclusive of all diverse elements in our global society (arguably a utopic and unachievable objective), the inclusive leader has to have the courage to spearhead changing attitudes and to be openly, publicly vulnerable. The leader has a point of view, but they must accept that they have no monopoly on perfection. The inclusive leader must desire challenge because it is the only way to learn from different perspectives and unleash the potential of the uniqueness of team members.

Inconveniently, inclusive leadership is closely related to transformational management and so-called "servant leadership", which in turn is all too often associated with weak or indecisive management. It is, therefore, useful to briefly explain how far from the truth this label is [10].

Inclusive and servant leadership is not about:

- Abdicating responsibility. By delegating a task or problem to solve, the manager gives agency to their subordinates to use their unique perspective and experience to approach the matter at hand from a different angle. The responsibility for ensuring the task is done, and accountability for its performance, remains with the manager. The servant manager is always available to ensure the subordinate has the information, resources and tools to tackle the issue. The manager is also responsible for reviewing the work and proposed solution, using their own experience and skill to improve on a solution when and if required. The servant manager acts as a coach and teacher and thereby increases the subordinate's willingness and confidence to experiment and express their creativity in a way that only they know how.
- Losing objectivity. The inclusive servant leader needs to be approachable, observant of their subordinates' mood and confidence levels, but this does not mean that they are "best friends" with team members. Informality may encourage higher levels of trust and openness, but the manager remains accountable to the firm regarding outcomes and results. Being people-oriented or "concerned with people" does not imply compromising on mission, quality or rigour. The inclusive leader is the one person who provides direction for the team, focusing on the "cause" which everyone is working towards: the purpose and values of the company.
- Being a martyr. Retaining responsibility for performance and accountability for outcome does not imply that if all else fails, the inclusive manager will finish the job themselves. Indeed, giving up on the belief that the team is capable of completing a task themselves is to fail as a servant manager. Empowerment of, and support/concern for, people is to trust that with your facilitation and advice, the team will provide the required solution.

Fig. 10.3 Leadership style
and employee engagement

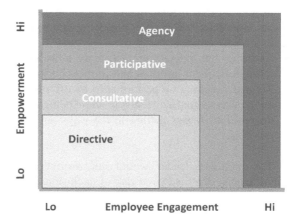

The leadership style, therefore, invites subordinates to participate beyond mere consultation as depicted in Fig. 10.3. The inclusive leader will maintain the role of affirming the agenda and facilitating the debate. Still, for diversity to flourish and ensure that all ideas are free to influence our determination of the best answer to the question we pose, the leader has to be proactive in empowering subordinates and encouraging them to use that autonomy as a team.

10.5   Baby Steps to Empowerment: Participative Leadership

All leaders get better responses when they possess credibility and have the trust of their colleagues. Without it, opening the doors to diversity is to embark on a futile and eventually humiliating venture. Subordinates, irrespective of privilege, have to believe that their opinions are actually and authentically welcome. The socially excluded worker, in particular, has to feel that their views are genuinely accepted and that their opinion is not only tolerated, but that they are part of the everyday discourse: that they belong. In the words of one financial worker: "I feel as though I am in a constant battle of censoring/watering down my views, thoughts, and personality for the possibility of being looked at differently than a nonblack man or woman in the workplace if they exhibited the same behaviour. It's exhausting navigating an all-White workplace" [11].

The leader, irrespective of background or leaning, must demonstrate their active pursuit of inclusion by continuously expressing their curiosity and thirst for different opinions. The inclusive leader must support, cajole and motivate those colleagues, under-represented or not, who might otherwise adopt a low profile and engage in extensive "code-switching". Indeed, the Path-Goal Leadership Theory of Professor Robert House can be applied explicitly to the process of helping disenfranchised individuals take their place at the table by:

- Improving transparency, consistency and clarity on what is expected in terms of personal contributions and providing alternatives to maintaining a "low profile" in job performance.
- Ensuring they possess the necessary tools and resources to achieve their goals through frequent informal and formal check-ins and support.
- Regular coaching on performance by offering motivating feedback and rewards on the way to goal achievement while being aware of the possibility of one's own unconscious biases getting in the way—and developing techniques to mitigate this bias.

The inclusive leader would not restrict such encouragement for outgroup subordinates identified as at risk of exclusion on the presumption that the ingroup colleagues do not need such support. The inclusive manager needs to identify all workers who face challenges in enabling their best selves to emerge.

Forms of Empowerment

Historic expectations of leaders encourage an image of strong leaders who think on their feet, are resolute and quick to take command. Consequently, by some measures, 98% of executives are described as extroverts and only 2% as introverts. However, introverts are more readily identified with humbleness than their extrovert colleagues, and therefore more likely to provide space for all employees to thrive [12].

The traditional view of leadership does not naturally tend towards the empowerment of subordinates, but rather to directive power as exercised by the autocratic leader. Their hierarchy is strict and vertical. There is no doubt who is in command and who is to obey. Decisions are centralised, deliberated by the leader and imposed on subordinates. This form of power is frequently linked with directive leadership.

Where a degree of empowerment is present, the leadership will encourage the participation of subordinates in decision-making. Empowerment can vary in degree, and we can explain this best by defining three of them as depicted in Fig. 10.3:

1. A consultative leadership style is to ask for and take the opinions of subordinates into account. The extent of deliberation and discussion with subordinate group members can vary, but in the end, it remains a consultation. As associates feel they have at least had the opportunity to voice their concerns and suggestions, resistance to change is reduced. The leader's authority is not questioned, although they may still be termed a supportive leader.
2. Participative leadership is the progressive stage of this consultative process. It is frequently seen in collective cultures such as in the Nordic countries, where flat organisations are common, and subordinates participate in making decisions. The leader no longer "pulls rank" on the rest of the group. Instead, agreement and buy-in on a consensus basis are generally sought. The decision is made with

everyone (in- and outgroup employees) sharing responsibility for its quality and the outcome's success.

3. Power Distribution or Agency is the definitive level of empowerment. Power is now decentralised and delegated. The leader trusts the ability of the subordinate (s) to take command of the task and to own it, to evaluate and decide on the best course of action. The team only reports back to the leader with the results of their deliberation and on the progress of the project towards its objective. It speaks to McLelland's need for power and Maslow's need for self-actualisation. Naturally, the now autonomous individual still needs the assurance that they are not abandoned. The empowering manager has to remain a servant manager, ensure that the team culture is as it should be, check in regularly, and provide necessary resources or clarification of objective. The common cause remains more important than individual achievement.

Inclusion and Empowerment

In any culture change situation, the inclusive manager will need to ensure that the members concerned respect the new parameters of behaviour being introduced. Therefore, the manager will need to be viewed as someone of authority. They also have to possess strong facilitation skills to ensure that the established dominant grouping does not exclude newcomers when forming the team. The extent to which the organisation can introduce employee empowerment will be situational and depends on where you are in the maturity curve of culture change. The deciding factor will be the degree to which the leadership believes that group members are comfortable with fairness, diversity and inclusiveness principles and are persuaded that accepting new perspectives is beneficial to the team effort. The lower the engagement amongst organisational members regarding the benefits of diversity and the meaning of inclusion, the more people will look to the leader to indicate a direction of play, waiting for them to speak up first. However, there are other times when employees need frequent reminders of expectations and objectives. Arguably, therefore, the second level of "participative power-sharing" is more likely to be the better choice in change management situations when reducing prejudice and encouraging diversity of contributions are required and not yet customary.

10.6 Moral Leadership

The courage to drive change needs to be sourced from the conviction that change is necessary, especially if those around them are not convinced of the merits of the change management exercise being pursued. Inclusive leadership is many things, but one element that genuinely must be present is the belief that diversity and inclusiveness are desirable and achievable. According to Kotter, leadership is about coping with change, setting direction and vision, motivating and inspiring people, and facilitating learning [13]. Leadership is a moral role, and the leader has to have the courage to speak truth to power as well as to subordinates. It is about defending what is right, challenging resistance and championing those who—in the context of D&I—are subject to prejudice or peer pressures to code-switch and conform to non-diversified behaviours. The determination of the inclusive leader has to be authentic to be believable. It is their personification of the new ethic that will inspire imitation and provide subordinates with the courage to:

(i)   Adopt new behaviours
(ii) Step up to the challenge
(iii) Release their creativity through a willingness to experiment without fear of being ridiculed or belittled

Stoic Leadership

To be a change leader is to seek continuous improvement. Many organisations work to the rhythm of instigating and completing a change, then settling into a period of stability where new routines become embedded, habitual and more efficient. This is never the case for the inclusive or coaching style leader. If we wish to reap the benefits of diversity, we must forever be inviting challenges and ensure that all perspectives are encouraged and welcomed. Inclusive leaders cannot allow themselves to be complacent in the belief that the job is done. D&I is a continuous process of renewal and expansion. It is hard work, and the human preference to be satisfied with "good enough" is ever-present.

In fine, the role of the inclusive leader is to encourage and school staff to engage with the subject of diversity, to empower them to rationalise and experience how working life is enriched by the embracing of uniqueness and the choice of equity and fairness, and to force the pace of change. The D&I leader's task is to both spark change and to cope with the consequences, not to dictate change.

Working hard for something we don't care about is called stress; working hard for something we love is called passion.

A team is not a group of people that work together. A team is a group of people that trust each other.

Simon Sinek

References

1. Stogdill, R. M., & Coons, A. E. (Eds.). (1957). *Leadership behavior: Its description and measurement*. Ohio State University.
2. Blake, R., & Mouton, J. (1964). *The managerial grid: The key to leadership excellence*. Gulf Publishing.

3. Randal, A. E., Galvin, B. M., Ehrhart, K. H., Chung, B. G., Dean, M. A., & Kedharnath, U. (2018). Inclusive leadership: Realizing positive outcomes through belongingness and being valued for uniqueness. *Human Resource Management Review*.

4. Prime, J., & Salib, E. R. (2014). Inclusive leadership: The view from six countries. *Catalysts*.

5. Van Nostrand, D., & McClelland, D. C. (1961). *The achieving society*.

6. Barrett, R. (2017). *The values-driven organisation*. Routledge.

7. Kiel, F. (2015). Measuring the return on character: The real reason leaders and their companies win. *Harvard Business Review*.

8. Roberts, L. M., & Mayo, A. J. (2019, November). Advancing black leaders. *Harvard Business Review*.

9. Sandel, M. (2020). *The Tyranny of merit*. Farrar, Strauss and Giroux.

10. Kalhorn, R. (2021, January 5). What servant leadership is not. *INSEAD Knowledge*.

11. McCluney, C. L., Robotham, K., Lee, S., Smith, R., & Durkee, M. (2019, November 15). The costs of code-switching. *Harvard Business Review*.

12. (2021, January 11). *The power of quiet leadership* video by Dr. Jacqueline Baxter of the Open University. BBC Reel.

13. Kotter, J. P. (2001, December). What leaders really do. *Harvard Business Review*.

#ClearingTheAttic: The Imperative Condition of a Trust Culture

11

There can be no leadership without followers. In our discussion of leadership styles, we have indirectly considered the nature of a leader's influence over their followers. Is it a question of legitimate, hierarchical authority, as when an officer orders their soldiers to execute an order—or is it one of moral authority? These forms of authority, and more, are all expressions of power. Circumstances dictate the most effective expression of the sway exercised by a manager in any given situation [1].

11.1 Leadership and Culture

The exercise of power can take many forms. We have argued that the promotion of D&I requires the active participation of those who follow the lead of their role models. We have also stressed that to embed new behaviours and mindsets within an organisation, we need consistency and a sustainable belief that the leadership is authentic and determined to see the changes through. If not, power is exercised behind a veneer of pretence and bravado, and like in the Wizard of Oz, credibility may be brought crashing to earth the moment someone dares to look behind the curtain.

In Chap. 6, we considered the impact of the lone CEO crusader in what we described as the "Role Model" organisation. Without an ingrained D&I governance strategy, culture change becomes too closely identified with one person who, once no longer performing their role model task, allows the objective to fade alongside them. Leaders will leave, or even stumble and lose credibility, with a knock-on effect on the culture they have stood for. If we want permanent change, the culture we create must be more robust than they themselves are—it must be institutional, not personality-driven. The organisation as an over-arching body must be seen to be committed to ideals of ethics, integrity, fairness and justice, and the governance framework strong enough to withstand the departure or weakness of one person.

To be a leader of culture change and the inclusion of diversity, we have argued, requires determination, courage and, not least, integrity. Studies reveal four predominant organisational factors linked with employees' experiencing a strong sense of inclusion [2]:

- Inclusive leadership evidencing openness to diversity of gender, race and sexual orientation at senior levels within the organisation, and a managerial culture that empowers employees and builds team cohesion
- Broad-based meritocracy and measures that increase fairness in consistent performance evaluation procedures, and transparent non-discriminatory outcomes
- The presence of in-house sponsors, mentors or coaches who advocate for inclusion and equity and support any individuals potentially challenged or intimidated by any non-inclusive tendencies
- Access to senior leaders who engage with employees and support individual growth

For these conditions to be feasible, employees must view them as permanent and a given in all situations. Staff have to believe that these factors form the bedrock of the institutional framework and that these facets of organisational behaviours are enforced and trustworthy.

11.2   A Culture of Trust: Its Purpose and Character

In any community or organisation, the leadership's ability to influence depends on its members having faith that what is said is accurate, complete, and respectful of each other's concerns. Mutual trust is not to be confused with the absence of conflict. It is only through experiencing conflict that we discover both (1) the need to build trust as a conflict handling mechanism and (2) those issues and topics that demand careful and respectful handling. If we are to find common ground upon which to build our collaboration and inclusive relationships, these dialogues are essential.

Once leadership and ownership of the pursuit of diversity and inclusion are assured, the organisation is primed for effective D&I measures. The key to any change programme is to avoid any risk of a "them and us" discussion. The precursor to any honest engagement, education or reconciliation is the existence of a culture of mutual respect; an environment where:

- Members of the dominant grouping empathise with minority colleagues who, all too often, have experienced unfair treatment and discrimination. That they are willing to show humility and the authentic will to understand and alter any prejudicial behaviours.
- Those who have been misunderstood, or feel subject to past discrimination and injustice, are willing to trust, engage and experience the pain of forgiveness in the face of remorse.
- Everyone feels free to speak up on "sensitive" subjects.
- The fear of retaliation or abuse is absent.

We have argued that there are many ways to use influencing tactics to promote one's ideas or further an agenda, but that success over time depends on a reputation for authenticity and trustworthiness. Therefore, building a trust relationship is essential if we wish others to join us in longer-term initiatives or to invest in our ideas and proposals. As with all aspects of psychology, trust is derived from the observed behaviours and beliefs of the individuals involved.

Trust: The Foundation of Lasting Change

There are six accepted building blocks of trust that can be applied to creating inclusion-inducing trust within the organisation (see Fig. 11.1). Once we have become aware of them, each will seem obvious; however, each trust factor must be gauged and steps taken to improve or safeguard them if acceptance of diversity and genuine inclusive mindsets are to prevail [3]:

- Respect—Mutual respect in the form of empathy, understanding and concern for one another lies at the heart of any trust relationship. By its nature, diversity introduces alternative expectations, norms and priorities into our working relationships. By the standards of one culture, an individual may be considered unreliable due to a lack of punctuality. Yet, in their own culture, this individual may think it more disrespectful to abruptly cut off a meaningful discussion with another colleague merely to rush off to another, seemingly more important meeting. Who in this scenario is unreliable? The individual can still be considered trustworthy in their conduct and intentions, even if not adept at meeting at an appointed time. Respecting and showing empathy to alternative views on

Fig. 11.1 The building blocks of trust

priorities and solutions will allow the protagonists to appreciate the good intentions of behaviour, rather than jump to negative judgement or defensiveness when challenged. Alternatively, someone who is dismissive or disrespectful to you—who leaves you convinced that they have no interest in your welfare, will become someone to avoid and distrust.

- Fairness—Being treated equitably is probably one of the most potent emotional drivers of trust. If we consider trust to be a belief that others will consider your interests alongside their own, then any betrayal of that faith will result in a strong emotional reaction. In the organisational context, if we want a culture that encourages knowledge sharing and a willingness to help one another when required, there has to be a belief that doing so will not result in any disadvantage to yourself. For example, someone taking credit for your work; a lack of reciprocity when asking a colleague for help or information; a lack of recognition or gratitude; or being denied opportunity in favour of the ingroup. Such breaches of unspoken trust diminish the willingness of the individual to engage with, share or help others in future.

- Predictability—This factor strongly aligns with the concept of reliability. No one likes nasty surprises; or a failure to keep promises, agreed to deadlines or support. When others are counting on you to behave in a specific manner, failure to meet expectations makes it easy for others to believe that you either do not respect them or are acting in a way that is inconsiderate of their interests. Showing consistency in behaviour is, therefore, a valuable trait in any culture. However, expectations should not mean that "failure" is not allowed. Fear of criticism, or even "loss of face", should not prevent colleagues from experimentation or dealing with sensitive topics, including performance delays. The key is that any experiments that fail to meet their aspirations are communicated with candour and in a timely fashion.

- Competence—It is not helpful if, in a desire to please or for fear of appearing incompetent, we agree to do/promise things that we cannot deliver. Nor does it inspire confidence, loyalty or trust if colleagues make presumptions on ability based on stereotype, positive or negative, rather than authentic evaluation. In the case of unsubstantiated positive attributes, we find ourselves potentially burdened with unreasonable expectations and a path to failure. In the case of negative attributes, we find ourselves denied the opportunity to make a full contribution and the chance to show our value. Indeed, as discussed above, wrongful assumptions about competence challenge other trust factors such as predictability or fairness. Ensuring competence is correctly applied, investing in technical skills and showing good judgement in "negotiating" the level of performance asked, is integral to building trust. "Fake it till you make it" is about non-transparency and pretence concerning abilities you do not possess today. Pigeon-holing individuals into stereotypes restricts their learning and growth opportunities.

- Communication—Transparency and openness generate trust. The absence of hidden agendas, the sharing of purpose and honest discussion of the challenges faced, personal or professional. All invite others around them to share in the mission and contribute to the solution. Communication is at the base of participative leadership. However, it applies equally amongst peers. The adage "information is power" runs counter to this principle of transparency and openness. If ever this adage is true, it is in situations where precisely trust is not present, where we fear that others will use information against us or somehow disadvantage us. In a trust culture, we believe in the idea of karma, that what "goes around, comes around"; that at the end of the day, we will all achieve more and grow closer by working together. If there is no communication, there can by definition be no engagement or common purpose, and there is no basis for trust.

- Support—Having a supportive mindset is to be willing to help others and respond or volunteer to help those in need, even to mentor or coach someone trying to understand better the uniqueness of others who are different to them. From the above, we can appreciate that a trust culture makes it easier for the individual to work with others towards the greater good. Equally, if there are individuals who are not team players and are not willing to do what they can to help others meet their objectives, then we have discovered the proverbial "rotten apple" in the barrel.

The development of such a trust culture is a subject worthy of an entirely different book, yet it is essential to any thriving, inclusive culture. The minority employee must feel sufficiently safe and secure to express themselves, be themselves, and intervene as the individuals they are. The dominant group employee must see their colleagues who are of different ethnicity, nationality or heritage, sexual orientation, gender or ability, in terms of their uniqueness (based on multiple, not single, identities), competencies, and contribution; "who" rather than "what" they are.

In creating a trust environment, many concurrent paths have to be trodden, principally paved with values of mutual respect, empathy and transparency. The notion of organisational justice encompasses all of these elements. The belief that management evaluates behaviour and work contributions in an even-handed way, and that rewards and punishments are applied equally across hierarchy and high- or low-performing colleagues, is the strongest foundation on which to create trust in the organisation. In other words, fairness is the closest proxy to the five parameters of trust: Respect, predictability, competence, communication and supportive behaviours. Honesty and trust between colleagues supported by a resilient governance framework that guarantees organisational justice is the bedrock of team spirit, inclusion, open discourse, innovation and ethics.

11.3 Organisational Justice

Justice is very much a matter of perception, so transparency and communication of decisions, especially in cases of punishment and reward, are essential. There are three measures by which a member of an organisation evaluates and concludes if the workplace is fair and which, as a result, are crucial ingredients for a universal culture of trust [1]:

- Distributive Justice concerns how promotions, bonus awards, recognition or sanctions, even responsibilities for leading a task force, are distributed. Are decisions based on merit, in which case whose definition of merit? Is there any apparent favouritism, nepotism or other forms of discrimination (positive or negative) interfering with the allocation of reward or sanction? Are senior managers or top salespeople excused from sanction? Is blame passed down the line or attributed to individuals based on a bias of expectations? Do managers accept responsibility, and are they held accountable?
- Procedural Justice relates to the transparency of process. For example, are decisions on reward or sanction subject to transparent decision processes, or are they variable and not always explained? Is the workload evenly shared in accordance with actual ability and capacity, or is there a presumption based on cultures, accents or social groupings that some are less valuable, even capable, than others? Is there clarity regarding expected performance? Good governance and transparency around such decisions will generate confidence in fair process, whereas its absence will make decisions vulnerable to conscious, or even unconscious, bias or destructive gossip.
- Interactional Justice has to do with how rewards, benefits or sanctions are delivered. An award may be equal to another, but if one is given with smiles and celebration, and another is in the form of a memo with no mention of appreciation—the entire quality of the prize may be denigrated. Someone may face an equal sanction for a similar breach of procedure or mistake, but if one receives a slap on the wrist behind closed doors while another receives public admonishment, the impact may be seen as quite different.

We revert to the same building blocks of trust mentioned above. In the context of organisational justice, we can see how each parameter of trust operates and how, individually, each can be destructive if not correctly applied. The outcome is again the extent to which a culture of trust can exist within the organisation, which in turn influences how we relate to and treat one another. In effect, organisational justice sets the scene for the manner in which we experience and manage our relationships with colleagues at work.

The Assumption of Trust

We can easily envisage how a trust relationship can enter into a downward spiral or build on itself to create a virtuous cycle. After all, that is how we make friends or enemies. There is usually a starting position that creates an expectation of things to come. Do we approach the arrival of a new colleague determined to tame and cow the newcomer, demonstrating to them that code-switching to accepted behaviours is the safest option? Or do we greet the latest addition to the team with openness and the presumption that their uniqueness will enrich our interaction and debate?

The human species has a suspicious mind, but once we engage with someone, there is an implicit expectation of trust. The more naïve we are, depending on our life experiences and the amount of "street" wisdom we possess, we may trust others easier than someone with a more sceptical mind. However, much of this expectancy of trust is dictated by the circumstances in which we find ourselves. We trust the friend of a friend faster than a stranger. We impart goodwill assumptions to those of a similar background.

Thus, generally speaking, we are quite apt at judging the circumstances in which we meet people. If the environment in which we find ourselves is known and familiar, such as at the school we know well, we are prone to assumptions of trust. At the workplace, we greet a new employee positively in the knowledge that HR and the bosses have selected them based on the qualities they bring to the workplace.

A newcomer to a social group or workplace will quickly evaluate "how things are done around here"—if people are solitary and distrustful, or open, sharing, support-ive and respectful. Such institutional cues will influence trust assumptions and quickly set the individual off on a cycle of virtue or a downward spiral. What then, are the cues that welcome the newcomer into their new environment?

11.4   The Cultural Legacy of Prejudice

The #BLM protests of 2020 produced some surprising moments of truth for White society. In the 1950s and as late as the 1980s, the confederate flag was a fashionable symbol of heritage amongst youth in the USA and further afield. It became a symbol of youthful rebellion, regional pride and rock music. There was widespread igno-rance amongst Western democracies of its darker symbolism. Outside the USA, the flag that featured on T-shirts was considered "cool", with little thought to its tragic association with lynchings, slavery and racism. A 2019 survey by YouGov revealed that Americans aged 65 and over are more likely than younger Americans to say that the Confederate flag represents heritage more than racism. Among Americans aged under 45, the association is clearly with slavery and White supremacy [4].

In Bristol, most people did not know that the statue they did not even notice when passing was of a city benefactor called Edward Colston, let alone that Mr. Colston had been a renowned slave trader. This association only became apparent once pictures of his statue being dragged from its pilon and tipped into the harbour's cold waters were shown on the news. It has led to further questions about the role of colonialism in the accumulation of European wealth, but such reflections are often uncomfortable ... and generations distant. Nevertheless, these statues, palaces, stately homes and not a few traditional celebrations are all tributes to a time and worldview that is outdated yet thoughtlessly glorified as heritage [5]. They provide a colourful backdrop to national pride in history and achievements. Traditional school books only reflect history from the victors' point of view—those who are the advantaged and more privileged in society or who feel pride by association.

For some of the advantaged, the #BLM demonstrations gave rise to the unwel-come realisation that a number of these proud symbols of national heritage are founded on the suppression or exploitation of others; glory that translates to shame. The Confederate flag is a frightening reminder of how far the US South was willing to go to keep slavery in place. What was a proclamation of regional pride and Southern gallantry for its White population has come to symbolise the determination of White Supremacists to maintain their superiority. In 2021, the Confederate flag evokes memories of organisations like the Ku Klux Klan and legislation such as the Black suppression Jim Crow laws introduced after the US Civil War. Words such as "woke", meaning awareness of social issues, have been borrowed from African American English and brought into general usage. We have become aware that the same notions, symbols and words that evoke pride in one social group can generate anger, a sense of injustice and oppression in another. This wokeness makes us more aware of the potential of our words and symbols to hurt others, but it does not necessarily enable us to identify associations and question them. To do this, we must examine our surroundings, our legacy, our history. Instead, many defend their preferred versions of history, giving birth to the notion of "cancel culture" [6].

Unburdening the Past

We cannot truly unburden ourselves of our past bias and prejudice if we believe that "we" are not the problem; that if those who take offence are merely overly sensitive and have chips on their shoulders that have long since lost relevance. Regretfully, most societies have unsavoury legacies that we need to accept ownership of before we can be free of them. In its colonial context, the UK pub chain, Greene King, denounced the slave-owning origins of its founder (1799) in 2020 and committed to invest "to benefit the BAME community and support our race diversity in the business". Similar commitments and denouncements have been made by the insurance group, Lloyd's of London, which insured slave ships during the slave trading era [7]. Like statues causing enough offence to be vandalised or removed, we need to take a fresh look at the symbols and icons of our firm and branding, even the paintings decorating our corridors of power, to see if they are appropriate to an inclusive culture. Such things undermine the message of inclusion. We have to understand the moral imperative for us to act, and for such action to be authentic and credible.

It is part of the manifestation of culture and values to surround ourselves with symbols of past achievements. Who are our corporate heroes? Are our halls decorated with portraits of White men in colonial dress? How does this impact the self-esteem of a female Black manager? If, like Greene King, Lloyds of London, or any other organisation which has profited from the exploitation of others or what we now consider criminal or immoral sources, the culture change organisation has to be willing to be "woke" about its history, legacy and responsibilities.

An organisation that is not aware or accepting of its past misdeeds or suppressive attitudes and refuses to consider how it can adapt its activities by engaging with its past history in terms of current and emerging ethical principles can never succeed in the inclusion of diversity today. To the descendant of people wronged by history, it will be impossible to gain a sense of belonging, no matter how welcoming the organisation tries to be. The firm that works towards a future that involves alignment with social justice and equality and is openly apologetic for its past behaviours, on the other hand, will provide a cleaner slate for workers from historically marginalised groups to join, engage with and contribute to as an equal, respected colleague.

The Fallacy of "Cancel Culture"

For many, the most straightforward and least disturbing way to deal with skeletons in the cupboard is to pretend they are not there. For some who cannot ignore their existence, it may feel acceptable to turn their back on history, to denounce and walk away from any association with the past and seek to erase any vestiges of shame or guilt by association. For a company that is merely seeking to "clean up" their brand image, this form of cancel culture may be sufficient—on the other hand, it may also backfire. For the organisation seeking to embrace minority cultures that have been negatively impacted by its past actions, the mere shunning of artefacts related to that painful past is surely insufficient. Once the image of the headscarfed Aunt Jemima was linked to its association with Black slaves cutting sugar canes in the field or cooking meals for their White slave-owners, then the removal of the offending image was inevitable and necessary. However, if Quaker Oats is to retain the trust of Black consumers and workers, then the company has to be seen to reflect on and learn from the re-reading of their history. The company needs to become particularly woke on social issues surrounding people subjected to the impact of colonialism or other forms of annexation, such as fighting discriminatory practices and promoting equality of opportunity in the community as well as within the firm itself.

11.5   The Creation of Open Cultures

In a trust culture, transparency, candour and institutional fairness must be present. In an inclusive culture, or one moving in its direction, particular attention must be paid to the inclusive values embedded in the mindset of the leadership and its members; it must be part of group ethics.

Hodges and Steinholz speak to the necessary foundations of an ethical organisation. If those ethics include openness to diversity and equality of opportunity for all who are part of the organisation, these principles can be equally applied in this context [8]:

- Clarity and observable evidence that equality, diversity and inclusion represent the expected norm and is everyone's responsibility.
- Executive and leadership behaviours and language that emphasise commitment to adopted values, transparency and openness, equity, diversity and inclusion.
- An articulated and inspirational purpose that embraces diversity and inclusion and provides a common goal around which collaboration can flourish.

- Thoughtfully defined core ethical values (1) that encompass equality, diversity and inclusion, (2) whose meanings are clear to all employees, and (3) which are continuously communicated and taught to all (including the executive and the board).
- Dedication to fairness in all aspects of the business and relationships. Professional and commercial networks should be free of any form of discrimination and offer equal opportunities for previously excluded counterparties or individuals to engage with the firm.
- A conscious commitment to continuous learning and improvement through listening and feedback platforms that allow discourse and dialogue on matters of equality of opportunity, diversity and inclusion topics without fear of ridicule or reprisal.

These foundations for ethically diverse cultures ensure that adopted values are constantly applied and embedded in the organisation's working culture. In this way, adherence becomes the norm, and any deviations from them may be called out as a learning experience or for sanction. To support this, the governance framework must integrate values in the firm's decision-making process, performance evaluation criteria and compensation policies.

Before its demise in 2009, when Fortis Bank AG was acquired and absorbed into the BNP Paribas Group in the wake of the financial crisis, the bank had developed a behavioural performance evaluation framework called the Fortiomas. It was considered rather complex and intricate by many, and there was scepticism about whether the executive truly supported behavioural goals ahead of financial targets. However, the framework and the idea was well-intentioned and sincerely applied by some management in their annual appraisal meetings. The system introduced a mandatory discussion between manager and subordinate as to the manner in which financial and other goals had been achieved.

Behavioural Assessment and Compensation

Throughout my career, I have observed individuals who have climbed the hierarchical ladder, been lauded as success stories, and rewarded according to the governing definition of merit. Some have been friends or people that I have admired. Unfortunately, rather too many of them have been distant, not relationship-oriented, self-serving individuals whose only merit has been "hitting the numbers" combined with effective communication of same. I have often had mentees complaining about unsupportive superiors and peers who take more than they give to the team; people who have used both jobs and colleagues as steppingstones in the pursuit of the aura of success. Indeed, most studies on psychopathy (individuals who lack empathy or a conscience, but know how to influence and manipulate others) indicate a significant presence of such people in the executive ranks of business. Whereas the threshold definitions of degrees of psychopathy may differ between studies, it is estimated that the executive positions of the business world are 3.5× more likely to boast psychopaths than the average working population [9].

Poor collegial conduct, therefore, is arguably no hindrance to career success. Indeed, it may be that those who have less caring instincts for their colleagues are willing to claim credit for the work of others, and who relentlessly promote themselves before others, benefit from the existing parameters of defined merit. Such behaviour, however, is an obstacle to the establishment of a trust culture within the organisation.

For most of my career (1979–2004), the annual goal-setting and performance review consisted of listing tasks for completion, enunciating number targets to reach, and occasionally setting a personal development goal of attending a course or acquiring a technical skill. During this period, personal conduct or attitude objectives were never discussed or openly considered. Indeed, the only time I heard of behaviour being a discussion point was after it was too late, the damage of misconduct already apparent, and the offender dismissed. Good behaviour, integrity, team spirit and openness were assumed until proof indicated otherwise. When surveys of employees suggest that 60–75% of the worst aspect of their job is their immediate supervisor, then this optimistic assumption appears questionable at best [10].

The Fortiomas Behavioural Targets

In 2005, Fortis Bank introduced the Fortiomas: 14 behavioural targets from which a limited number could be selected to serve each job description and which would feature as a mandatory and significant element in the annual appraisal. However, it was not always fully implemented. There was insufficient training provided to supervising managers on how to approach the unavoidably contentious topic. The higher up the senior and executive hierarchy one went, the weaker the discipline of evaluating performance was. Personally, I implemented the measures and made clear to my direct reports that the Fortiomas would influence promotion and bonus decisions. What resulted was, in my experience, a constructive reflection on behavioural aspects of collegiality and working styles that steered attitudes and behaviours in the desired direction: And this merely by elevating the importance of such questions. Targets still had to be met. Yet, the manner in which these were achieved was just as important. Few people perceive their behaviours in the same light as others. Having someone to pick up the mirror for you to see your reflection can be illuminating, if not always comfortable. When asked how they had experienced the evaluation discussion, one subordinate replied: "Tough, but fair". Rightly or wrongly, I took that as an indicator of success.

Including behavioural targets in annual objective-setting and performance criteria is a practically achievable amendment to most supervisor-employee evaluations. It does, however, require that:

- Everyone in the organisation, up to the level of the CEO, supports its implementation.

- Supervisors need to be trained in handling sensitive discussions and communicating "hard-to-take" truths.
- Senior and executive evaluation must include targets that relate to employee perceptions of the trust environment and the inclusive attitudes of management.
- When an employee appears to be failing in adhering to a behavioural objective, feedback should be delivered at the time of observation; not several months later at the annual evaluation meeting.

The Fortiomas addressed four aspects of the corporate workplace: productivity, personal growth, mindset and collegiality. Of the latter category, collegiality, the behaviours targeted included:

- *Team spirit* aiming at achieving the full potential of the team through inclusive behaviours, fair facilitation and organisation.
- *Act as One* by breaking down barriers, expanding networks, encouraging innovation and learning, and stimulating collaboration.
- *Communicate the Story* by being clear on vision, mission and expectations; in short, providing employees with a clear sense of common purpose.
- *Encourage Diversity* by recognising individuals as unique, confronting prejudiced behaviour, and actively hiring people from backgrounds different from the norm or majority group.

Already, accentuating the importance of just these behaviours would be a boon to organisational efforts to enhance equity, diversity and inclusiveness within its walls. Yet, amongst the ten other Fortiomas listed under the remaining three categories, we could highlight many as highly relevant to the achievement of a more just, trusting and open workplace:

- *Stimulate Entrepreneurship* by stimulating innovation and making room for mistakes
- *Give the Example* by inspiring others and keeping your promises
- *Develop* yourself and others by identifying needs, coaching and creating opportunities
- *Show Courage* in addressing difficult issues, standing firm and stimulating others to "do the right thing"

Each behavioural Fortioma is sufficiently agile to be adopted to the rank and position of the employee concerned:

- For the executive or senior management, behavioural objectives that drive inclusive leadership, integrity and elevate ethical concerns to the same level as financial objectives should, and could, be highlighted.
- For the middle manager, objectives will naturally look to promote communication, networks, sharing, coaching and opportunity creation.

- For the employee, standing firm on the right thing to do, showing openness to colleagues and enabling a sense of belonging for all members of a diverse team are behaviours that can be observed and commented on. Indeed, such conduct readily identifies as a mere broadening adaptation of what is already established as desired behaviours, only previously applied to a narrower population.

The Fortiomas are not here presented as a ready solution for formulating the behavioural targets that best support D&I. However, they are a proven example that personal conduct goals can be integrated into objective setting and performance evaluation if the organisation so chooses. Each organisation, each dominant culture, will be different in the challenges of prejudice they face. For example, Netflix relies on a feedback culture, including regular feedback-on-demand meetings and a concept referred to as a 360-dinner. It seems terrifying to imagine a dinner with your team where each, in turn, provides their opinion on your qualities as a colleague—but it appears to have general support [11].

The correct definition of targets and expectations associated with those targets will be specific to the organisation. However, unless all recruitment, promotion and reward decisions are based on clear parameters of behaviour, as well as merit, the integrity of any group D&I objective will remain questionable.

11.6   You Can Lead a Horse to Water, But You Cannot Make It Drink

In the context of compensation policies and performance evaluation procedures, it is crucial to remember that any temptation to rely on such governance arrangements alone will fail to achieve a significant and lasting cultural change. The temptation to issue a top-down diktat without the reinforcement of (1) a values-led, inclusive leadership, (2) clear and evidenced enforcement of the new, expected behaviours, and (3) an open, learning environment that facilitates discussion and resolutions of complex social topics, will only lead to avoidance of the problem and a side-stepping of the rules. Over time, the lack of engagement on the topics and a failure to alter the real ethical expectations placed on all organisation members will result in eventual reversion to the unresolved issues that remain simmering beneath the surface.

Most employees will seek to avoid an uncomfortable confrontation or discussion of previously held prejudices. The inclusion of behavioural objectives in the performance appraisal process is a useful stop-gap measure to ensure that there comes the point when the evaluated employee has to take on the challenge and reflect on their conduct relative to expectations. It renders it impossible to avoid feedback from their supervisor regarding the perception they and others have of their conformity with the new group ethic.

The importance of inclusive leadership, including all the necessary traits of walking the talk, and talking while walking, courage, providing transformational and equitable growth opportunities for all employees irrespective of gender, creed, colour or sexual orientation, has been emphasised several times in this book. For the inclusive society to be consistent and sustainable, the leadership must be supported by a governance framework of rules and policies that clarify expectations on conduct, judicious processes that guarantee fairness in the evaluation of behaviours, backed by a fair and consequent distribution of rewards and sanctions.

But good intentions, systems, processes and procedures are still not enough. Those who have lived in privilege have been blind to the fact. We experience the world around us in purely relative terms. We are, perhaps, a rather ungrateful species. We take it for granted that things that come easy to us are basic, acquired rights. We do not consider that what comes easy to some may be unobtainable for others. We do not appreciate our freedoms until they are taken away from us. In Europe, most citizens take the universal welfare system (for which they pay taxes) for granted and complain when they do not receive timely treatment for even minor complaints. They are only thankful for that safety net when confronted by the cost of medical insurance when travelling abroad, or glance with horror at the limited allowances for paid vacation guaranteed elsewhere. The fairness that the privileged experience as a member of the dominant social group is accepted as the natural state of things. Those who protest otherwise, it is surmised, are assuredly only at fault themselves for their deprivation—a result of their own actions—thereby falling into the traps of stereotyping minorities and exercising blinkered, prejudiced minds.

In the author's foreword to this book, we identified five categories of people of which dominant culture individuals might mostly be described as oblivious, complacent or deniers. Some of these, faced with exposure to personalised accounts of marginalised colleagues and the history of their peoples, will start to realise that the narrative and conventions they have been taught are incomplete. If they are strong enough, they will be open to a voyage of discovery that they may find disturbing and disruptive. Others may seek seclusion in the company of deniers, unable to re-write their understanding of the legacy upon which they have based their identity.

Indeed, the historian Dr. George Makari identifies two sources of xenophobia (the fear or loathing of strangers). One is merely a human suspicion of the unknown—he describes it as "other anxiety"—a sentiment and prejudice that can be dispersed by contact and dialogue. A second is a xenophobia born of institutionalised prejudice. It is grounded in the laws and institutions born of history that make up the national narrative. It is enshrined in a victory or colonial view of the world where the conqueror casts itself as the benevolent civiliser of less developed and ignorant peoples. Again, a closer inspection of all sides of the story can result in intellectual enlightenment where the near propaganda-like narrative is revealed for what it is. The third is a far more threatening projection of an internal psychological desire to find self-esteem in the denigration of others. This condition exists where there is a need to look down on others in order to elevate personal self-esteem. Habituation and exposure have no effect. To let go of one's prejudicial sense of superiority is too destructive to one's perception of Self [12]. Reconciliation with "others" is simply not an option.

If we are to achieve an inclusive culture, we cannot have xenophobic or "them and us" differences in the interpretation of reality. Inclusiveness demands a high degree of self-awareness by the dominant population as to how the life experience of the disadvantaged through time compares to their own. The marginalised, who have had to endure harsh discrimination through generations, have suffered from an impact far worse than the mental contortion associated with the revision of an individual's sense of identity; they might be tempted to offer little sympathy. However, all less privileged individuals who wish to work towards an inclusive society have to be willing to provide that contact and dialogue, to share and explain their frustration. It requires the personal courage and trust of all parties. The privileged have to allow their worldview to be eroded. The less privileged have to stake their claim to equality with patience, forgiveness and the courage to risk bringing their uniqueness to the table. Just as certain individuals of the dominant group will be unable to re-evaluate themselves, some individuals of marginalised groups will be unable to find forgiveness for the ages of struggles for equity and injustices endured.

In short, inclusive leadership can do much to create the necessary conditions for a trust culture to exist. To achieve it, they must advocate and facilitate an ongoing conversation between those who have previously (consciously or unconsciously) excluded minority groups, and the excluded groups themselves—if they are willing to do so.

References

1. Smith-Meyer, A. (2018). *Surviving organisational behaviour*. Kindle Publishing.
2. Roberts, L. M., & Washington, E. (2020, June). *US business must take meaningful action against racism*. Harvard Business School.
3. Kinicke, A. J., & Fugate, M. (2012). *Organisational behavior* (5th ed.). Mgraw-Hill/Irwin.
4. Sanders, L. (2020, January 13). *What the Confederate flag means in America today*. Yougov.com
5. Huxtable, S. A., Fowler, C., Kefalas, C., & Slocombe, E. (2020, September). *Interim report on the connections between colonialism and properties now in the care of the National Trust*. National Trust.
6. Savage, M. (2021, May 9). UK government's heritage culture war is stifling museums, say trustees. *The Guardian*.
7. BBC. (2020, June 18). *Pub chain and insurance hub 'sorry' for slave links*. https://www.bbc.com/news/business-53087790
8. Hodges, C., & Steinholz, R. (2017). *Ethical business practice and regulation*. Hart Publishing.
9. Boddy, C. (2015, October 19). Psychopathic leadership: A case study of a corporate psychopath CEO. *Journal of Business Ethics*.
10. Hogan, R., Raskin, R., & Fazzini, D. (1990). Reflections on the dark side. *APA PsycNet*.
11. Meyer, E., & Hastings, R. (2020, September 8). *No rules rule*. Penguin Random House.
12. Makari, G. (2021). *Of fear and strangers: A history of xenophobia*. Yale University Press. In addition, we recommend George Makari's interview with Zia Haider Rahman on youtube https://www.youtube.com/watch?v=PUAs7IzkGkQ, Accessed December 6, 2021.

#LivingDialogue1: The Imperative Condition of a Living Conversation— Sowing the Seeds

12

12.1 Of Headwinds and Tailwinds: The Dynamics of Privilege

Cycling to the neighbouring town one weekend, my son was delighted with his performance regarding speed and fitness. It was only on the return trip that he had to somewhat dejectedly admit that what was now a strong headwind may have provided him with a helpful tailwind on his outward journey.

Conversation Partners

Those who have grown up and achieved success within the dominant social grouping inherently "understand" that success is based on personal merit. At our first level of consciousness, we do not comprehend that we may have enjoyed privileged access to the components of worth as defined by our privileged parents and mentors [1]. To be accused by a member of a disadvantaged social group of having benefitted from a position of privilege is to be accused of having achieved success through unfair means; that the rules of the game have been skewed in their favour guaranteeing relatively easier success. An assertion that we have benefitted from privilege denied to others is a direct attack on our self-esteem and our sense of integrity. It is in our nature to defend ourselves against accusations of "cheating" and our claim to honest achievement.

For those denied privileges, such differences are painfully obvious. As mentioned, we often only become aware of our freedoms and benefits when they are denied us. Racism and discrimination are a reality in every society. In the Western world, gentile White society is guilty of suppressing Black communities, amongst others, and treating them dreadfully. The slave trade and colonialism in Africa and Asia, like medieval pogroms and the holocaust persecution against Jews in the last century, are just the most evident examples. Is it any wonder that the oppressed feel just anger about being denied what others appear to obtain so easily merely due to their differences? We have previously described how a community under attack,

© The Author(s), under exclusive license to Springer Nature Switzerland AG 2022
A. Smith-Meyer, *Unlocking the Potential of Diversity in Organisations*, Diversity and Inclusion Research, https://doi.org/10.1007/978-3-031-10402-2_12

ethnic or religious to mention just a couple, seeks comfort and protection by bonding more closely with others, including ingroup allies, who share their sense of frustration and injustice. Together, they face the establishment classes or communities and do their utmost to protect themselves from the consequences of prejudice and discrimination; together, they adopt defensive strategies, at times finding expression in anger and aggression.

In a divisive society, it is easy to see how these two groups of a dominating majority and an oppressed minority might view each other with suspicion and hostility. The culture we seek is that where justice and fairness prevails, where the two parties find common objection and antipathy to injustice and discrimination. Hence, the final imperative to the achievement of an inclusive organisation is to bring these two parties together; not to argue about who is right or wrong, but to listen to the different perspectives and experiences of each group and to learn from them; not to debate, but to have a conversation on how to interpret those different life experiences and provide space for empathy and respect between all involved. Suppose the organisation genuinely seeks to promote inclusion and address social inequality. In that case, leaders of the majority culture, in particular, must begin by understanding why a segment of their workforce believes that they cannot authentically be themselves in the office, or indeed, why they do not wish to be [2]. Equally, leaders of minority origins must lead by example also, encouraging minority employees deliberately maintaining a low profile while simultaneously avoiding the accusation of favouritism. To remove racism from the workplace, we need to embark on a continuous loop of dialogue and feedback on how it expresses itself, what drives it and how to counter it.

Natural Selection; and Deselection

Organisations differ from broader society. In Utopia, we can imagine a democracy shaped around an idealistically altruistic community. A world where everyone is born into a world of equal opportunity, free of divisive conflicts of interests, where effort has just outcomes and esteem is bestowed by a community of peers. We might dream of a society where those who suffer obstacles and setbacks are cared for generously and respectfully. Actual society is far messier than our Utopic vision. Yet within the confines of an organisation, the board of directors can define a shared vision for the company, a well-articulated purpose driving the mission of its members, and appoint capable, inclusive leaders. It is possible to determine the values and behaviours that will guide recruitment, promotion and other acts of reward and sanction within the firm.

In doing so, the firm will, somewhat ironically, be selective as to who may join this micro-community, excluding would-be blockers and resisters of D&I. Purists may be morally correct to argue that true inclusion would not de-select those with the "wrong" mindset. Instead, they would demand that everyone be informed and persuaded to voluntarily "convert" to an all-inclusive perspective. Practitioners, however, are likely to consider this a step too far. The inclusive organisation may invite all who would be ambassadors, allies or supporters of its D&I vision, mission and values to join their purpose. Still, it cannot allow those who counter notions of D&I the opportunity to block or sour the values that support the culture the organisation is seeking to strengthen or maintain. To be inclusive, we have to be exclusive. This is an avenue available to company directors, not to parliamentary politicians.

12.2   The Foundations of Dialogue: Communication

If we are to create a meaningful communications loop between the parties concerned, we have to consider the nature of the exchange of information between two potentially conflicted parties. If we have managed to select participants to the dialogue who are supportive of consensus and identify common solutions, then the barrier created by opposing interests has already been reduced, if not removed altogether. Therefore, we consider that we have individuals participating who are keen to impart their points of view and share their experiences—an interpretation of communication frequently put forward. In general, this is not difficult to achieve— most people are keen to explain what they see as evident to those who appear (to them) ignorant of the facts. The challenge of dialogue is that communication does not start with articulating a message; it begins with the ability to listen to the question and the assumptions behind opinions voiced or avoided.

At the core of communication, therefore, is the act of listening. It is true that if no one is communicating, there can be no listening. However, it is even more true that if no one is listening, then there is no communication no matter how much you try; there is no successful conveying of ideas or meaning. To date, communications in the twenty-first century appear dictated by the disruptive chaos of undocumented opinion spread through unregulated social media in the guise of fact. Individuals hold strong opinions and trumpet them largely unchallenged across the internet. Anyone who disagrees with their worldview is called a "Troll" or a peddler of "Fake News". Whatever your political leanings—can anyone earnestly contend that any meaningful debate or communication takes place when people only defend their original position and shut their eyes and ears to any evidence that might go against their precious "point of view"? The political climate has undermined the exploration of detail and consideration of alternative solutions. No wonder the average person follows the lead of their political champions and rigidly insists on their "truth", all the time rejecting all contrary voices without regard for consequences. Suppose this is the natural state of dialogue within society. In that case, it is clear that to enable an honest conversation between equals pursuing mutual advantage and a common objective to take place, we require a deeper understanding of what it means to listen.

Theory U and the Four Levels of Listening

The persistent challenge of dialogue is the misinterpretation of another's intended message. As a result, we apply selective listening and focus on anticipated rather than actual feedback. In the words of Alan Greenspan, the Chair of the US Federal Reserve between 1987 and 2006: "I know you think you understand what you thought I said, but I'm not sure you realise that what you heard is not what I meant".

Professor Otto Scharmer of MIT has developed a concept for change management that encourages the transformation from a current state to a desired state. His thesis is known as Theory U. Within this theory, listening to others and being sensitive to the dynamics of the realities surrounding you are essential. He explains listening on four levels (see Fig. 12.1). Each level faces, or overcomes, barriers to listening and enables learning and the realisation of potential and ambition [3].

1. Downloading
   It is unfortunate that we listen at a very superficial level much of the time. In line with our tendency of succumbing to confirmation bias in support of our social prejudices and stereotyping, we listen with a filter in our mind that sorts the "convenient facts and truths" from the less digestible "inconvenient" ones. We pay attention to, and capture, information that supports our existing opinions and judgements. As a result, the alternative viewpoint normally fails to get past our bias and prejudice.

2. Factual—Open Mind
   When encountering and assessing new contacts and acquaintances, open-mind listening is the approach that we most frequently apply. We pay attention to

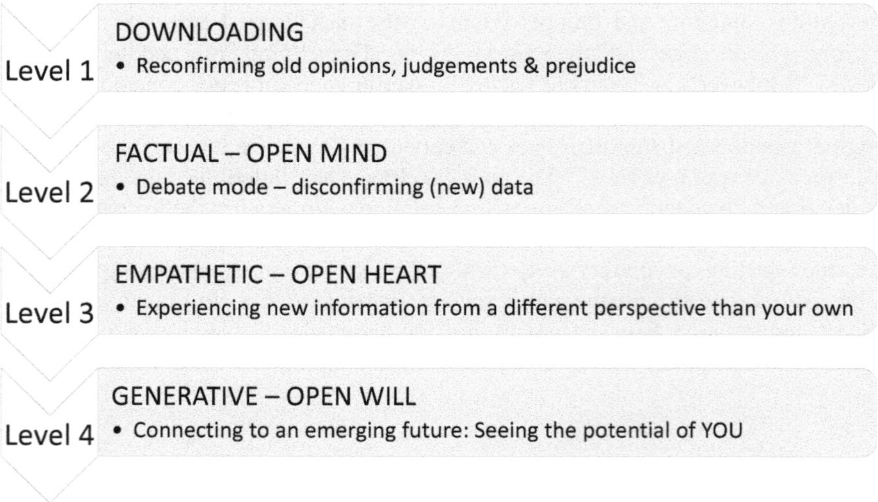

DOWNLOADING
Level 1 • Reconfirming old opinions, judgements & prejudice

FACTUAL – OPEN MIND
Level 2 • Debate mode – disconfirming (new) data

EMPATHETIC – OPEN HEART
Level 3 • Experiencing new information from a different perspective than your own

GENERATIVE – OPEN WILL
Level 4 • Connecting to an emerging future: Seeing the potential of YOU

Fig. 12.1 Listening concepts sourced from Prof Otto Scharmer, MIT: The Theory of U

information that does not conform to our pre-existing opinions and ideas, and we can focus on and retain those ideas. We are even open-minded enough to be able to explain their rationality. However, we are in a defensive debate mode.

At this level of listening, we do not filter out "inconvenient truths", but our willingness to be swayed in our reasoning and conviction is minimal. We listen to and digest ideas, not to challenge our existing points of view, but to refute the arguments of the other more effectively. We are unwilling to listen with empathy and an "open heart" or bring our "established" truths into question. You might compare this to sitting down and engaging in a game of chess—with the intent to win rather than learn.

3. Empathetic—Open Heart
   Level 3 is the point at which we are willing to consider all available information with an "open heart"; ready to mingle our pre-existing ideas with opposing facts and opinions. We acknowledge there might be a bigger picture worth considering.

   At an OECD Integrity Forum in Paris (April 2017), Professor Le Menestrel of INSEAD was asked what he thought of President Trump. He responded, "You have to see the good in Trump before you judge him". Whereas many in the audience laughed at the counter-cultural suggestion by the professor at the time, the professor was evoking the level 3 listening rule. We might well have observed a similar reaction amongst a crowd of Trump supporters at a Make America Great Again rally if the object of the question had been Hilary Clinton. Until you can see the world from your counterparty's perception of reality and objectives, and perhaps acknowledge that some of their views may have some merit—or that their background orientates them to focus on matters differently—it is difficult to judge either their actions or their impact.

   Are the supporters of an accepted truth so determined that no matter what another suggests, that view will be denigrated as madness as a matter of principle—or are they ready to consider the merits and new perspectives the other brings to the table? Might they be willing to integrate these new realisations into their own revised views of the world? Scharmer likens this level to getting out of your chair and going to the window to have a good look at what is happening outside; a preparation, perhaps, before venturing out the door.

4. Generative—Open Will
   The final, ultimate and transformative level of listening is the one that changes your life, your business, your values. Impossible without mastering "Open Heart Listening", we can relate this to the individual's ability to see the writing on the wall, or as Scharmer puts it, the emerging future. From standing with an "open heart" at the window looking out, you are now stepping out into the reality that is not your own domain; one that is outside your comfort zone. In doing so, you start to look at your personal existence from the outside, re-evaluate your position and status, and gain a fresh understanding of what is happening around you. You understand your own context from a new perspective and are free to see and

explore the full potential of alternative future paths you can follow. You listen and reformulate the reality around you, discover the "emerging future", and transform your own—seeing the writing on the wall and taking heed of its portent.

12.3   Preparing Ourselves for Dialogue

We are, by and large, entrenched in our cultural roots and carry with us the legacy of unchallenged tradition, mythical stories that rationalise and justify our history. Stories of the "enemy without" threatening to destabilise our community is part of our narrative; those "others" we imagine will remove our privileges, be they plentiful or pitiful, established through the efforts of our forefathers. This is as true for a White dominant culture as it is for a Black minority deprived of privileges.

A conversation between the more and less privileged on equality, discrimination and mutual respect requires empathetic listening by both parties. It also requires a willingness to embrace and act on new-found realities. The power to instigate conversations of mutual respect in the search for equity and inclusion falls to the more powerful dominant grouping. In the age of #BLM, the dominant group concerned is predominantly White—and in the Western context, previous slave-owning and colonial societies. It will not always be an easy task. There are members of excluded communities who are so far entrenched in their distrust of White supremacist behaviours—past or present—that they cannot believe that acceptable change is achievable within their lifetime other than through confrontation and conflict. Fortunately, there are others who are willing to invest their goodwill in those they perceive to be allies to their interests. All parties have to adjust to an open mindset for constructive dialogue to take place.

At the start of any difficult conversation between two parties who may be perceived or suspected of having differing agendas, there will be an anticipation of conflict. If this is true of two individuals, it is equally correct of a group setting, a town hall meeting or a discussion forum. Hence, the calling of a meeting to start a living, learning and constructive dialogue cannot just be a mandatory invitation to join colleagues to sort out the question of racism in the organisation. People have to feel that their presence, even if "required" by their superiors, is unthreatening and that all participants are in a safe place.

The first point of order is to discuss how participation will make life better. Clarification needs to be provided as to why a D&I policy and programme is being introduced, along with the facts, figures and stories that evidence the need for it. Importantly, fears about the consequences of engaging in the conversation need to be addressed [4]. The onus must be on what we, the organisers and facilitators of the programme, can do for the participant, not what the participant employee can do for the organisation. The question, therefore, as to how to convince those who are amongst the dominant, more privileged grouping to ally themselves to the cause of promoting equality, diversity and inclusion, is only the second topic to be raised. Empathy then is a prerequisite for open minds and dialogue, humility another.

Humility at the Root of Empathy

Yet, surveying social media in the 2020s, you would be forgiven for believing that the arrogant have taken over the world. Humility is a "feeling or attitude that you have no special importance that makes you better than others" (Cambridge.org); it is a state whereby you acknowledge that you have no monopoly on truth and accept that others are just as deserving of attention and respect as you would hope to be. It is not rocket science to assert that a conversation between two humble people is likely to be more constructive than one between two arrogant individuals. If we are to succeed in our quest for a living dialogue leading to enlightenment and greater inclusion, we need to consider how best to engage with those who have been educated to believe that they are more special than others; to dissuade them from the notion that their perceived superiority is a consequence of destiny and ability rather than merely a social construct resulting from the vagaries of history.

Our worldview, including what is commendable or ethical, is determined by our narrative about that world. Our perspective is limited or expanded by the extent of our knowledge of that world. How can an individual question conventional wisdom if the only information available to them supports their existing worldview? Churchill once said that history is written by the victors with the implication that failures are temporary and glorious and victory a proof of justice; even atrocities will be rationalised as heroic. We all cultivate a legacy of which we can be proud. No wonder then that dominant groups are generally blind to discrimination happening around them; it is not part of their narrative.

Research has shown strong correlations between individual recognition of racism in the USA and their level of historical knowledge of Black history [5]. Raising consciousness of the history of racism will enable citizens to view the current distribution of wealth, opportunity, and social standing in a different context. The imagined "superiority" born of ignorance will be diminished. Naturally, an individual who feels that the respectability of their cultural identity is being eroded will tend to feel under attack, potentially even to the point of self-loathing or denial. A White American or Bristolian whose family wealth is shown to be born of the slave-trade will naturally seek to disassociate themselves from guilt. They point to the passage of time since the misdemeanours of their forefathers, interpreted as they are by modern-day standards. Frequently, their attitude will be defensive, and their strategy to ensure that the material and structural privilege they hold is not lost.

This loss aversion, the tendency to prefer the avoidance of losses rather than an accumulation of gains, was first identified by Professor Kahneman and has been written about extensively since [6]. Further research on self-affirmation or core self-evaluation, call it self-esteem, has shown that a counter to this loss aversion, or fear of threat to self-esteem, can be found in re-educating the subject on their self-perception; by accentuating other aspects of their self-worth [7].

Citizens of the Moment, Not the Past

It is helpful to consider White denial in light of perception and narrative rather than any negative personal characteristics. The challenge is to make those who fear the loss of esteem accumulated from a questionable and inherited common history and culture—about which they can do nothing—see their identity instead in terms of who they are in the present; to focus on their personality traits, their values and the importance of the impact they have today or can achieve in future.

This reorientation is cumbersome, complicated and involves the psychology of the individual. The creation of a merit and recognition framework within the organisation that highlights the personal qualities that promote corporate objectives, be they financial or non-financial, is critical in laying the structural foundations for individuals to see themselves as worthy on their own achievements rather than merit bestowed by the cloak of the social standing of one's parents, or the schools one has attended.

If we look at the reverse side of this particular psychological coin, the outsider minorities are also in need of self-affirmation. To be aware of how history and discrimination have hindered one's progress both socially and professionally when measuring up to meritocracy—as institutionalised by the dominating classes—is likely to express itself either in anger and resentment or shame and inferiority. None of these sentiments helps establish a constructive, living dialogue. All participants, be they of the more or less advantaged grouping, need to see the world in terms of the present, as far as possible unburdened by the past [5].

> Unless we bind up the wounds of the broken-hearted, we cannot hope to create a just and durable society where everyone has a place in the sun, ... [8]
> Father Michael Lapsley

The Power of Empathy

We cannot ignore the fact that there will be members of the hitherto more privileged ranks that will carry a heavy emotional attachment to their negative views of those asking for, even expecting, equality of treatment and opportunity. There will be those amongst the more disadvantaged communities who will find it very hard to engage with and trust people they see as having been, or who they suspect remain, oppressive and counter to their well-being. Phrases like "guilty of driving while Black" speak to the common distrust Black Americans have of their own police force. Stories of injustice and negligence, at the hands of UK and other European authorities, that disproportionality impact People of Colour abound, both from official investigations as well as in the shape of rumour and gossip on social media [9].

As with any fear induced by personal or reported experience, individuals suffering from anxiety at the prospect of having to find a middle ground of respect for their foe, may require help. From the perspective of inclusive leadership, the minimum objective is to ensure that people so influenced will not assert themselves as Blockers or Resisters to the cause of diversity and inclusiveness. For many, however, the threshold of minimum compliance may simply be to remain neutral in the face of greater diversity and inclusiveness in the organisation. The leadership objective is to ensure that those who stay in the organisation and who cannot "believe" in the mission of D&I do not become Blockers or Resisters, but instead become resilient enough to live with the change and to be accepting of, and compliant with, expected behaviours.

When Sheryl Sandberg of Meta[1] wrote her book "OptionB: Facing adversity, building resilience, and finding joy", her trauma was very different from those discussed in this book [10]. She experienced the very real loss of her husband and life partner, and the imagined loss of a future: A loss of hope. However, she emphasises two fundamental aspects of empathy as exercised towards those in distress, and its role in building resilience in those experiencing it. They provide some insight on how to try to place oneself in the shoes of others.

- To replace the adage "treat others as you would want to be treated" with "treat others as they would want to be treated". To follow what Ms. Sandberg calls the platinum rule requires a level of empathy that goes beyond relating the situation of others to our own experience. Instead, as with level three "open heart" listening (see Fig. 12.1), Sandberg suggests we seek to empathise with the background and experiences, or the worldview, of the one in need of comfort and security. Nobody likes to feel obliged to argue their corner ad infinitum. The Black worker should not have to put the case for change. Instead, this case should be championed by the White colleague, either informally as a curious co-worker who wants to play their part in creating an equitable and equal workplace, or formally as an ambassador or ally. This ingroup co-worker needs to ask the question as to how their Black colleague experiences bias before together exploring how to avoid prejudice in future. As Citigroup CEO Mike Corbat wrote to his employees, "While I can try to empathise with what it must be like to be a Black person in America, I haven't walked in those shoes" [11]. Yet, empathy is the starting block of dialogue and reconciliation—we have to try.
- To encourage those impacted by anxiety to respect their emotions. Those affected have to be persuaded that their fears are grounded in their personalised experience and observations of the world. If we actively suppress these feelings, then we cannot confront them and find constructive ways to deal with and dissipate their cause. Give your employees, on both sides of the exclusion divide, the safe space to be angry, afraid, disenchanted or passionate. Until we accept our vulnerability—our own and that of others—we shall not be able to construct a rebirth of confidence and self-esteem.

---

[1]Previously Facebook.

These aspects of the need to help members of the majority and minority community to live with, or overcome their concerns, provide an extreme example of what is required from not only the leader promoting inclusivity, but the whole community engaging in this living dialogue.

12.4   The Enduring Conversation

Keeping a conversation on-subject and supportive of defined visions and goals does not happen without curation [12]. This work only starts once the groundwork and preparation are done, and we have established a thorough understanding of the state of equality, diversity and inclusion within the organisation. Whereas there can be no single recipe for the successful facilitation of a living dialogue for all organisations, there remains a generalised series of steps and processes that will help engage those involved and keep it that way.

1. Conduct an assessment of the cultural orthodoxy of the dominant group and that of the minorities in the organisation. Conventions and conduct that need to be addressed and modified should be mapped. For example, one might examine the ways workplace culture creates pressures for minorities to code-switch their behaviours.
2. Locate the flashpoints of discrimination and prejudice that most concern those subjected to them, as well as those cases of injustice that the dominant class—were the situation reversed—can most engage with. We now have the topics of conversation that cause not only friction and obstacles along the path of inclusion, but also those that are most likely to generate a common pursuit of justice and fairness.
3. Create forums, channels and platforms upon which a facilitated discussion may develop. Whereas unchecked exchanges might fall back into a "them and us" debate about who is "most right", the rules of participation in the conversation must be unfalteringly based on mutual respect, and policed within the behavioural norms and expectations defined by the leadership. Help-lines and anonymous speak-up reporting tools must be put in place as advisory and safety-valve precautions. Before trust is fully established, those with disturbing experiences to relate, or concerns to raise, must be able to do so without fear of being labelled, ridiculed or targeted for retaliation. However, their stories provide valuable insight and material for identifying beliefs and behaviours that fuel exclusive practices and provide material for group and case study discussion in forums and working groups.
4. Accompany the conversation and discussion with constant reminders as to the purpose and objective of the living dialogue process. Participants need to be provided with success stories and witness inclusive behaviours being rewarded. The joint cause of equality, diversity and inclusion must be kept front and centre at all times. It is the leader's responsibility to set the pace and tone of this process,

preferably by sharing their own unique stories and even confessions of failure to meet the standards now being sought.

5. Do not allow the conversation to go stale. The subject matter must stay fresh and up-to-date with those cultural flashpoints that keep members of the organisation engaged. A perfect inclusion culture is a distant, if unrealistic, destination. The diversity debate has expanded from gender balance to LGBT+ to racial inclusion, and we are still grappling with gender pay gaps, distrust in women leaders, and social pressures for women to "raise the kids" [13]. Even should the day arrive when racial exclusion is considered a matter largely settled, the inclusion debate will need to move on to ageism, religion, or co-workers with visible or invisible disabilities or impairments. The desk of the Diversity and Inclusion Officer will surely never be cleared.

The Changing Conversation

Organising an effective dialogue that drives change is a governance issue. To persuade an audience to listen, understand and absorb new lessons is a human affair. Pat Wadors, Chief People Officer at Procore, outlines four principles to evoke when seeking to win others over to a new way of thinking [14]:

- Do not hesitate to hold the mirror up to those who need to understand how, in context, their behaviours or mindsets are destructive or ugly.
- Encourage a sense of self-awareness amongst the congregation, making them mindful of how workplace wellness impacts both personal enjoyment of being at work and business performance; how these cannot and should not be separated.
- Use the tools available to you to provide evidence of areas that need attention or proof of progress. For example, most companies have employee satisfaction surveys, and some use smaller scale and more frequent pulse surveys. These need to be opened up to allow consideration of the extent to which a culture of trust, diversity and inclusion, is present or not. What must not be forgotten is that minority views and concerns may be lost in the melee of consolidated feedback. Consequently, other hard or soft modalities of obtaining data on how minority workers experience the workplace, including specific social audits, will also need to be employed.
- Do not underestimate the power of storytelling. It is the number one communication method to engage with an audience and create empathy for the cause you are promoting.

Let not the epitaph of the D&I programme be "We've been here before"; rather, it should be "another day, another lesson learned, tomorrow will bring the same".

Setting the Agenda: Together

Thus far, we have advocated a bottom-up approach to identifying issues, concerns and complaints that need to be confronted with empathy to resolve misunderstandings, wrong-headed assumptions and even unethical conduct. A grassroots approach is an important aspect of empowering those impacted by exclusion and inclusion to express their emotions and engage in the process. Left to its own development, however, outbursts will be haphazard and incident driven.

The random nature of this hunter-gatherer approach to conducting a living dialogue risks some topics being over-emphasised and others being omitted. Some discussions will gain traction and draw much attention. In contrast, one that is less well understood or is inadvertently overlooked may be lost, even if its impact could be very significant. For this reason, there has to be a top-down governance process that makes use of experts, and a leadership determined to leave no stone unturned. We need to construct a methodical management process to monitor and analyse progress and discoveries. In fine, our human experiences must be surrounded by a governance framework that ensures transparency.

12.5   The Stakeholder Dialogue Process

If we are to be inclusive, the experiential impulses received from the social networks within the firm will provide optimal impact if accompanied by social audits that implicate all stakeholders. A systematic approach will allow us to identify the full scope of our D&I challenge, ensure that we forensically identify the stakeholders impacted by diversity and discrimination issues, both in and outside the organisation. The detail discovered in the pursuit of this two-pronged methodology will evidence, inform and fuel the living dialogue otherwise taking place and extend the project's scope to include individuals or communities not immediately included in an otherwise introspective conversation—the invisible stakeholders. Our objective must be to ensure that all known, and potentially unidentified, stakeholders to the organisation's D&I strategy are identified in order to assess the impact of the firm's actions on each of them. One such, generic, stakeholder map is depicted in Fig. 12.2.

The workforce Amongst the immediately identifiable stakeholders are those generally grouped under management and employees. These may be segmented into further clusters to include executive, senior and middle management as each will have different perspectives on the implementation of the D&I strategy. Employees might differ by location, include freelance and temporary project workers, or even divide into groups working at the office or from home, or between full-time and part-time workers. There should be room for consideration of how retired colleagues might benefit from a holistic D&I policy, or even assist in facilitating or adding to the living dialogue itself.

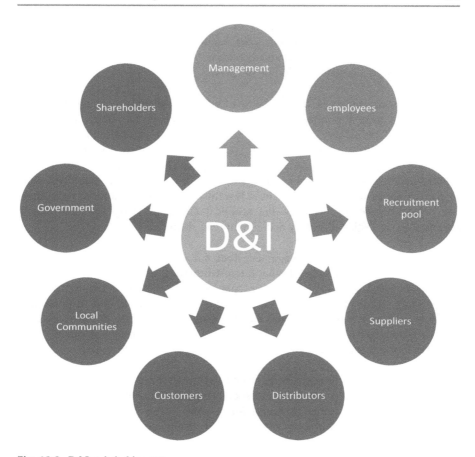

Fig. 12.2   D&I stakeholder map

Recruitment pools   One of the consistently popular reasons quoted for the absence of diversity is the scarcity of talent within the recruitment pools of the excluded minorities. Considering where recruitment is typically sourced, seeking out more diverse schools or regions where "scarce" talent may be more concentrated or easier to encounter. Even engaging with schools and universities to sponsor education for members of minority communities within the required fields could have unexpected results.

Customers   Consultation with existing and potential customer groups may provide intelligence on brand image and the effectiveness of marketing communications. For example, does the corporate message attract or alienate certain groups? Are your products accessible to minority communities, be they minority ethnic, disabled or others?

Contract partners Are your supplier or distributor networks skewed towards non-diverse networks? Diversifying your supply chain might offer competitive alternatives and even provide innovative ideas to make your product or service more attractive to a broader section of society.

Society Western society is in the process of political and ethical change. Over the past decades, under the influence of internet transparency, the public has become ever warier of politicians and big business. Confidence in institutions has been eroded and left citizens with a sense of social injustice, not least in the matter of inequality of opportunity and discrimination against Black, Minority and Ethnic populations. We observe that the new generations of the Millenials and GenZ who have or are about to enter adulthood have less trust in political institutions today than ever was the case for even for the sceptical GenX or Baby Boomer. Social expectations on justice, diversity and equality are shifting.

Shareholders Stakeholder management does not exclude shareholders; it merely places them alongside a range of other interested parties. Board directors have long since understood the importance of maintaining a close relationship with shareholders. Until recently, this has been presumed to be limited to providing investors with sufficient performance data to persuade them of the business model's durability and satisfy their desire for financial rewards through dividends and increases in the share price. However, life is no longer so simple.

In the guise of ESG (Environment, Social and Governance), investors are paying increasing attention to governance and social responsibility. In 2021, the financial news was replete with stories of shareholder revolts. A few years ago, shareholder activism was associated with corporate raiders, break-up merchants and demands for higher financial returns. Recent shareholder rejections of board proposals at AGMs have been on subjects related to CEO pay (Pearson, Glencore, BAE, Aston Martin, AT&T, GE and Informa, to mention a few) or sustainability:

- Exxon, Chevron and Royal Dutch Shell, for inadequate clean energy strategies
- Facebook, for disclosures on social issues like online child exploitation
- Amazon, on topics ranging from facial recognition to the use of plastics
- Goldman Sachs, on the disclosure of arbitration outcomes of harassment complaints

At Exxon, the shareholders voted for the replacement of directors; in the Netherlands, Royal Dutch Shell was denounced by the law courts for inadequate environmental action, harming its financial value and catching the attention of shareholders. Some of the most significant pension and sovereign wealth funds now track and vote at AGMs based on ESG performance. At Cop26, the Norwegian prime minister, Jonas Større, said the following regarding the current and future investment policy of "Oljefondet", the world's largest sovereign wealth fund: "Our goal is to make it the leading fund in responsible investment and the management of climate risk" [15]. The shareholder is always a significant stakeholder, but their interests and direction of influence are changing. Companies need to be ever more vigilant and attentive to investor relations.

The Generation Gap

Those who study demographics and the behaviours and mindsets of different generations come to relatively similar conclusions. The younger generations appear to understand that if they want a sustainable and socially just planet, they have to demand it and hold those who stand in their way accountable; they see the need to take proactive decisions to further their objectives. In marketing terms, this translates to judging companies on their impact on the environment and where they stand on social justice issues such as #BLM [16].

The company that narrows its focus only on its closest identifiable stakeholders has failed to account for the virulent impact of social media. Increasingly, the CEOs and board members of companies who fail to learn the lessons of ESG best practices are being held to account. Rio Tinto is an example of an organisation that made the mistake of disregarding (in this case) social minority rights when they destroyed an ancient aboriginal archaeological site in Australia to expand mining operations. This modern-day oversight led to a loss of reputation, share value, customer loyalty and court cases. The CEO, Jean-Sébastien Jacques, was made to pay the price and forced to resign. To the board of Rio Tinto, marginalised aboriginal society may have seemed a stakeholder some distance away from everyday concerns; no longer.

Stakeholder Management

If the enterprise can be positively or negatively, directly or indirectly, impacted by the good or bad will of partners or adversaries, then it would be wise to understand their concerns and ambition. It is better to engage with and educate them, manage expectations, and avoid or manage any conflict of interest that might arise before they occur rather than to leave their eventual reaction to chance.

Much as every stakeholder relationship will be unique to the balance of interest and influence of the parties involved, it may be helpful to position our identified stakeholders within a power matrix, such as is depicted in Fig. 12.3. The matrix plots the potential of a third party to be of strategic importance in meeting the firm's D&I (or any other policy) objectives, and the power and ability of that party to impose their demands on the organisation.

Regarding the four quadrants of the matrix, we have the following possible combinations:

- *The Strategic Partner* to the firm is a stakeholder who may be considered an important enabler of the company in meeting its goals and who can exercise a powerful influence on how the firm is to set about achieving its objectives.

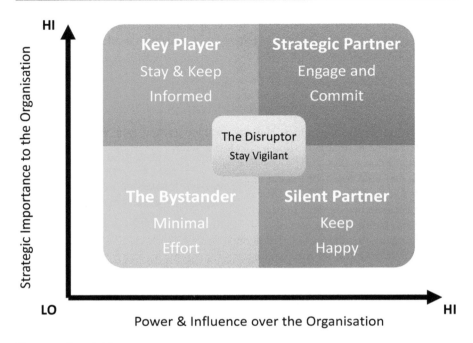

Fig. 12.3 Stakeholder management

Internally, we have highlighted the need for strong and inclusive leadership. The institutional power of this leadership, including the Chief Diversity and Inclusion Officer, is a function of their mandate, resources and access to the board. Without this power, the mandated executive will never be a Strategic Partner to the mission. They can only be a Key Player at best. Externally, joining with outside commercial interests who share the company's D&I aspirations may offer role model opportunities amongst your employees and within society itself. These stakeholders should be recognised for their strategic value and treated as valued partners and allies in the pursuit of a shared D&I objective. Not least, a vital stakeholder is the shareholder who, as Exxon discovered, can elect members to the board or dismiss those who ignore their priorities. Clarifying their expectations and gaining their long-term engagement in the project is essential.

- *The Key Player* is a stakeholder of significant value to the organisation, but whose opposition would not usually de-rail your efforts. Once one starts to populate this quadrant, it can become surprisingly large. Arguably, it is a list of opportunities, both existing and unexplored. The majority of the firm's existing employees may fall into this category as supporters of the D&I initiative. An unexplored opportunity may be those firms outside your traditional networks previously excluded due to prejudice. Too many Black-owned or managed contractors and suppliers are not considered for collaboration simply because our "dominant group" consciousness has been blinkered to them.

Externally, non-government organisations who act for greater social justice for excluded communities may fall into this category, providing help in educating staff and organising events where the firm may stand out as a sponsor of a movement for equality and justice. The Key Player employee requires the self-assurance to trust and rely on the organisation supporting and rewarding desired behaviours. If not, their willingness to actively support change may conflict with their pursuit of private interests, such as career and optimising family welfare. Within this category, we will also find the recruitment firms and education career officers who have access to minority group recruitment pools, not to speak of the potential minority recruits themselves. Staying informed about their priorities and keeping Key Players up to date with the organisation's strategic plans for D&I will help maintain their support or allyship.

- *The Silent Partner* is the sleeping bear you prefer not to awaken. Relationships are stable, but they usually have little interest in influencing your strategic direction—nor do you seek their attention or support. The Silent Partner is often of more significant concern as a potential threat than a contributor to your success. The Silent Partner may be an Ombudsman concerned with worker rights or a litigator representing factions of society opposed to more diversity and inclusion. It may be untrusting non-government organisations or a hostile media, whose attention you (1) prefer not to attract or (2) should it be unavoidable, wish to make sure that they give you advance warning or a right of reply before publishing a harmful report or headline. Ensuring that Silent Partner expectations are met (frequently a matter of reporting accuracy or transparency) is often the first step to keeping them happy and focused on problems other than yourself.
- *The Bystander* represents the final quadrant; actors who have little power to harm your achievement of organisational purpose and are of little strategic significance to help or hinder your success. The Bystander may include agnostic employees who see neither benefit nor threat resulting from the culture change, or the non-customer public. Even if your clients are overwhelmingly only interested in obtaining the lowest price or best quality of product possible, without concern about what social changes are occurring outside their community, they may still feature in this quadrant. The occupants of this quadrant have, however, been identified as a stakeholder, even if one of "low-value". They should not, therefore, be ignored. But relative to other stakeholders, the effort spent addressing their concerns may be minimal. But do keep an eye on where the bear is sleeping.
- *The Disruptor* is the stakeholder on the move. In their destruction of aboriginal cultural sites in the Australian outback in the development of new mines, Rio Tinto miscalculated the growing social influence of a Minority Ethnic interest and paid a heavy price. In the USA, we have witnessed the rising political power of Black, Asian and Latin-American voters driving social justice issues to the highest levels of the political agenda. However, this has been met by an equally passionate rise of overt White supremacism and charges of an "unamerican" tendency towards an overprotective and overly government-controlled welfare state. Changing values in society might have unexpected consequences in terms of customer or even non-customer ability to disrupt corporate strategy. This is an

important reason why the stakeholder risk map needs to be assessed, re-evaluated and considered by the board on a regular basis in line with the business strategy itself.

The Work Has Just Begun

In part A of this chapter, we have scanned the horizon and prepared our field of operations. We have identified the need for more profound listening skills within the community and researched the very human fears, hopes and emotions that need to be dealt with. We have analysed the landscape in terms of stakeholders and their respective roles in the change process, and we have determined what the target outcomes of that change should be. However, the project is only beginning. Just as the farmer who prepares the ground for a particular crop, a ready field is far distant from the harvest festival. The planting of ideas and care for their development are paramount if we are to keep weeds and random growth of wild plants at bay.

References

1. Sandel, M. (2020). *The Tyranny of merit.* Farrar, Strauss and Giroux.
2. McCluney, C. L., Robotham, K., Lee, S., Smith, R., & Durkee, M. (2019, November 15). The costs of code-switching. *Harvard Business Review.*
3. Scharmer, O., & Kaufer, K. (2013). *Leading from the emerging future.* Berrett-Koehler Publishers.
4. Solheim, D. (2020). *The leadership PIN code.* Lioncrest Publishing.
5. Henderson, F. A., & Kinias, Z. (2020, September 24). *Understanding the origins of white denial.* INSEAD Knowledge.
6. Kahneman, D. (2013). *Thinking, fast and slow.* Farrar, Straus & Giroux.
7. Kinias, Z. *Bolstering White American's ethnic identity resiliency.* INSEAD Working Paper Series 2016/56/OBH.
8. Father Lapsley, M., & Karakashian, S. (2012). *Redeeming the past: My journey from freedom fighter to healer.* Orbis Books.
9. Afzal, N. (2020, June 11). Black people dying in police custody should surprise no one. *The Guardian.*
10. Sandberg, S., & Grant, A. M. (2017). *Option B: Facing adversity, building resilience, and finding joy.* Alfred A. Knopf.
11. Roberts, L. M., & Washington, E. F. (2020, June). US businesses must take meaningful action against racism. *Harvard Business Review.*
12. Holt, D. (2016, March). Branding in the age of social media. *Harvard Business Review.*
13. Ro, C. (2021, January 19). Why do we still distrust women leaders. *BBC.* https://www.bbc.com/worklife/article/20210108-why-do-we-still-distrust-women-leaders
14. Wadors, P. (2021). *Diversity, inclusion and belonging.* LinkedIn Learning course.
15. *Statement at the UN climate change conference in Glasgow.* Accessed December 14, 2021, from www.regjeringen.no/en/aktuelt
16. de Chenecey, S. P. (2019). *The post-truth business.* Kogan Page Publishers.

#LivingDialogue2: The Imperative Condition of a Living Conversation—Cultivating the Ground

13.1 Organising for Dialogue

The list of preparations is extensive. So far, we will have elected inclusive leaders drawn from multivarious backgrounds, bolstered trust in the integrity and fairness of the corporation, primed our organisational community in the art of listening, engaged with legacies of the past and confronted the difficult questions they raise. We have established a shared vision of the future culture of diversity and inclusion amongst our stakeholders. What must the Chief Diversity and Inclusion Officer now do to create the platforms and meeting places necessary to provide the soil fertile enough for inclusive ideas to take root and rustle up the energy for culture change? In this chapter, we shall explore the roles of allyship, training, group meetings, including Employee and Business Resource Groups, online forums and other intranet social media tools.

Before we consider some of the various tactics available to us, we must offer a disclaimer and a reminder. This book aims to explain, elaborate on and exemplify the three imperative conditions for change leading to an inclusive culture: Inclusive leadership, a trust culture and a living dialogue. Each company will face challenges in achieving this trinity. The tools and paths to success are limited only by the imagination and experience of those mandated to drive and implement culture change. The examples of "tools" explained below only exemplify and demonstrate some of the types of measures that may effectively promote the inclusive mindsets we seek.

Combining Empathy and Collegiality

We have argued that one of the most effective tools of influence is social proof (aka "word of mouth"). In this case, the most significant messengers are to be found amongst ambassadors and allies. A close cousin of the D&I Ambassador, the diversity "Ally" is frequently found amongst ingroup people-managers within the

A. Smith-Meyer, *Unlocking the Potential of Diversity in Organisations*, Diversity and Inclusion Research, https://doi.org/10.1007/978-3-031-10402-2_13

organisation; a person in authority who stands up for others in the advancement of an inclusive workplace. Whereas the low-level majority member subordinate also has a role to play in confronting prejudice, micro-aggression and discrimination, they will only do so if they are secure in the knowledge that their superiors will support them and protect them from retaliation.

The D&I function will have its officers strategically embedded in the central operating units of the organisation. Their mission can be strengthened by identifying and empowering assigned ambassadors willing to broadcast the inclusion message to colleagues proactively. Supported by convincing and inclusive leadership, the function and its ambassadors will embolden staff to support D&I values and even champion them as an ally to their excluded colleagues. Educating employees on what inclusive values and behaviours consist of in addition to the basic principles of allyship will encourage the adoption of new behaviours and help regulate unjust behaviours as and when they occur. As understanding amongst sympathetic colleagues increases, so will the number who are willing to speak up civilly against discriminatory behaviours.

Dr Stephanie Creary of Wharton University has researched and developed a framework to improve the workplace experience of Black employees in corporate America. Her ideas are encompassed in the acronym LEAP. In her words, it is "based on the idea that relating to people who are different from us takes hard work and can be anxiety-provoking. Yet, doing the necessary work to notice, connect, value, and respond to others' needs results in more effective working relationships" [1]. LEAP highlights four behaviours required of those willing to become allies of Black or minority colleagues who dare to bring the full range of their talent and potential to the workplace:

L: Listen and learn from your Black colleague's experiences.
E: Engage with Black colleagues in racially diverse and casual settings.
A: Ask Black colleagues about their work and their goals.
P: Provide your Black colleagues with opportunities, suggestions, encouragement and general support.

Listening

Experience and research show that when a disadvantaged individual raises issues of equality or the lack of access to opportunity, they are often attacked as "moaners", "apologists for poor achievement", "having a chip on their shoulder" or viewed as a "trouble-maker", and treated accordingly. The fear of repercussions is the prime driver of the code-switching practices that Black and other minority individuals use as a defensive mechanism to avoid confrontation and survive in an environment dominated by a more privileged group. Consequently, we cannot easily expect or demand a member of a deprived minority to lead on the call for culture change. It is too easy to accuse them of self-promotion or trying to use guilt and conscience to gain an unfair advantage over those they claim are acting in a discriminatory way towards them. The ally has to take on the role of advocate or supporter for their cause and be the one who intervenes against micro-aggressive behaviours, discriminatory language, or faces up to the racial elephant in the room in a group meeting.

To be able to speak up on or against inappropriate behaviours at the right time, the ally must at least be able to recognise the discomfort experienced by the minority group employee. Ingroup employees need education on how to engage with their outgroup colleagues through being curious about their colleague's everyday work-place experiences, such as how they feel after reading about the latest #SayTheirName atrocity against their community, or the previous evening's White supremacist demonstration. We cannot teach emotional intelligence, but we can train people to listen as a path to learning.

Engagement

To engage with colleagues of colour on topics such as racial discrimination is to make a big ask on trust. The White ally may be authentic and sincere, but the discussion they solicit may still be difficult and frightening. Conversation in the office, even in the corridor, may seem unsafe and discouraged by concerns of who might be watching or listening. However, we can facilitate safe speaking opportunities in formal town-hall meetings, group discussion forums and other online platforms. Engaging with a disadvantaged group member will be more relaxed and natural when they are empowered by their superiors and in familiar surroundings, including being together with others within their community.

Ask about work

Ask a person who has experienced loss or disappointment "how are you?" and your attempt at constructive help may be misinterpreted as an offer of pity instead. Asking questions that provide your colleague with a sense of agency, or an offer of support, might be better received: "What did you understand by so-and-so's comment. How would you like to react to it?" A work colleague, but especially the manager of the minority worker, needs to convince the person concerned that what is on offer is not only sympathy but also tangible help and support. "Your idea didn't get enough airtime in that meeting. Can we go over it again with (insert decision-maker's name) tomorrow when they have more time?" Discussing the minority experience in the context of their work tasks reinforces the standing of the subordinate as a profes-sional and competent co-worker. "I like the ideas you put forward in the meeting. Is there anything I can do to support them?" The greater the self-esteem thus gained by the minority group subordinate, the more openly they will express their unique mix of experience and talent.

Recent surveys show that even though 87% of major companies have an employee sponsorship programme, only 23% of Black employees consider that they experience support in advancing their careers [2]. The manager, of whatever background, has a particular responsibility to take on the role of mentor or coach for talented employees who do not "look the part". When the minority group or female worker explains the barriers to opportunity or progress they encounter in the workplace, the sponsoring or mentoring ally can provide valuable advice on how to tackle dominant culture colleagues and superiors on difficult questions. These may include compensation, promotions or simply opportunities to grow. Diversity implies the interaction of different cultures; inconveniently, that includes diverse customs, assumptions and even communication methods. Sometimes, an interpreter or even a mediator is required.

Provide opportunity and support

The people-manager can be trained to be more aware of their unconscious bias regarding the abilities or mindset of their subordinates and how to mitigate the impact of biases that already exist in the system. Managers conducting performance appraisals with a deeper listening style might better understand the ambitions and frustrations of a minority subordinate. For a manager to explore how they can generate growth opportunities suited to an employee's unique ability and motivation is always wise. On the other hand, in the context of minority employees, such analysis is vital if the prejudice of stereotypes is to be overcome. To be an ally also requires active support; being there for marginalised group colleagues, and speaking up when injustice starts to appear on the horizon even if minority group colleagues are absent from this space. For the peer group colleague, this may be cutting off potentially prejudicial behaviours by dominant group colleagues before it fully manifests itself, like pointing out that an idea voiced in a meeting has already been made by a colleague working under the challenge of prejudice.

Sometimes, just being there is more powerful than trying to be the great avenger for someone who is hurting. After the death of her husband, Sheryl Sandberg said: "Don't ask me how I am. 'How are you?' feels really insensitive even though it's said with the best of intentions. My husband just died. How am I? Really? Instead, ask, 'how are you today?' How are you today is a shorthand way of saying I know you're suffering, I'm acknowledging your pain, but I want to know how you're getting through it today". It is not just about being an ally; it is about being a good friend and colleague [3].

To be an ally is not to carry a label; it is simply to be a good and caring colleague. If properly encouraged throughout the workforce, it may, one day, even render those afore-mentioned corridors and water coolers safe zones, even for controversial discussions.

Scenario Training

Many forms of training can be undertaken. Sessions that raise awareness of unconscious bias are commonplace and widespread, even in companies where the sentiment is less one of conviction and rather one where "we must be seen to be doing something". The participant may typically, but not always, come away from such training feeling much more aware of the workings of prejudice and even feel inspired to "do something" about their personal behaviours. However, once back behind their desk or with equipment in hand, they are at a loss as to how to go about implementing what they have learnt. Awareness of a situation does not necessarily prepare someone to know how to deal with it—change happens when employees understand not only that bias exists, but when they have access to techniques to mitigate the impact of that bias.

Awareness without knowledge of how to apply it is like an engine without fuel. The change management programme may have a framework to keep D&I concerns front-of-mind amongst decision-takers. Inclusive values and codes of conduct may provide a moral compass on how to avoid discriminatory behaviours and outline the outcomes to strive for. By establishing forums and mentoring programmes, we may even facilitate the living dialogue necessary to ensure that information exchange and feedback loops lead to continuous improvement of the trust and inclusion culture. But, these are governance arrangements; they provide a stage for protagonists to occupy—it does not make good actors of the protagonists.

In ethical training programmes, experience has taught us that practice makes perfect—or almost perfect. To properly understand the correct application and consequences of implementing ethical, or in this case expected diversity and inclusiveness behaviours, the employee—privileged or less so—needs to experiment and experience the impact of their interventions, protests, negotiations, expressions and offers of sympathy firsthand, in a safe environment and in the spirit of learning.

Traditional D&I programmes frequently start with unconscious bias training. Without all the other elements required for a culture change programme, this will tick a box, but prove ineffective. It may even be counter-productive as it can highlight stereotypes without adequately explaining the benefits of ending prejudice [4]. The serious D&I contender will, therefore, look for a more practical behavioural training education, including how to deal with contentious situations. Labelled Workplace Civility or Bystander Intervention Training, enabling participants to recognise prejudicial circumstances and providing guidance on how to safely de-fuse such situations, helps avoid conflict and harm to established relationships [5].

Those asked to confront their long-held attitudes and behaviours need to be given the opportunity to develop their minds and engage in critical thinking [6]. Experiencing the role-play of situations that require swift evaluations and determined, sometimes courageous, action, provides a discussion and learning opportunity. The employee versed in the potential consequences of their actions or inaction will be more confident in their response to conflict. We all know those pangs of guilt or feelings of inadequacy that follow when, 10 min after the time for reaction is passed, one thinks of what would have been the "smart thing to do"; or worse, realise that one has done more harm than good. Having the advice of outsiders who are experts in their field and listening to the experiences and lessons learnt by others will provide fertile ground for collaborative discussion between the diverse participants in the training session or forum. Learning principles by rote sitting behind a desk is no substitute for role-playing and workshop experimentation.

Promoting a diverse and inclusive society is an ethical choice; it will generate conflict touchpoints. The scenarios involved are predictable, however. An ethical training programme intended to explore and prepare for the many grey zones of moral choice may, therefore, be broken down into four primary conflict areas [7]:

1. Speaking the truth versus loyalty to a community or ideal
2. Individual and personal interest versus what is right for your community as a group
3. Short-term versus long-term priorities and outcomes
4. Uphold expectations of justice versus mercy to preserve human dignity and compassion

At times these conflicts may happily co-exist. For example, speaking up and telling a truth as an ally against a discriminatory act or comment may marry perfectly with the ideal advocated by your organisation; but what if, in so doing, you harm the promotion prospect of a friend? Your reputation as an ally may increase your esteem in the eyes of colleagues if you intervene in a situation, and at the same time serve the objectives of your community to become more inclusive; but what if, in doing so, you open the door of opportunity to a minority colleague, and it so happens that you yourself wanted to enter through that door? And so, we can go on.

13.2 The Meeting Place

Using a formal training programme, ambassadors and allyships, leading by example and producing corporate coffee mugs decorated with inclusive messages and symbols are part and parcel of the roll-out of the culture change programme. The outcome may well be a spontaneous and genuine communication process throughout the organisation. Without further direction, however, the energy of ambassadors may be depleted, the vigilance of allies diminish, and the novelty of gadgets such as mugs and mousepads fade. We can schedule regular reminders, typically to celebrate "International Days" against racism, for LGBT+ inclusion or gender equality. One firm installed "nail varnish stations" to greet workers arriving for work on a Gay Pride Day, inviting arrivals to varnish one fingernail purple in support of their LGBT + colleagues. A similar gesture involving black nail varnish or offering brightly coloured bracelets to symbolise diversity could be on offer to help mark the International Day for the Elimination of Racial Discrimination or the UN World Day for Cultural Diversity for Dialogue and Development. The only limitation to such opportunities and reminders is our imagination.

If the evolution of the corporate dialogue is to stay energised, active and properly aligned with organisational D&I objectives, the discussion needs to be curated and facilitated by a dedicated team for the organisation and management of D&I activity. One-off events featuring invited speakers, fundraisers or community engagement initiatives will cause a buzz and a spate of enthusiasm. However, to drive a continued curiosity and learning process, there need to be permanent platforms available for the dominant and disadvantaged groups to mix and exchange experiences. Individuals confronting their prejudice need to engage with those who feel the impact of daily discrimination and micro-aggression. In the absence of an opportunity for reconcili-ation, the effort to find joint solutions and acceptable behaviours that lead to greater inclusiveness or a sense of communal belonging will flounder. Crucially, these meeting places must be safe from fear of retaliation or anger; participants have to be able to find comfort as well as the confidence to speak freely.

Employee Resource Groups

Frequently referred to under the acronym ERG, an Employee Resource Group is a formal employee-led affinity group, often based on individual identity. The forum is an opportunity for people to exchange opinions and ideas on a particular issue. If we are to ensure that the third imperative of the Living Discussion is kept alive and thriving, the organisation needs to provide the time and space for employee participation. The ERG is integrated into the organisational structure and contributes to the better management of human resources and corporate culture. Whereas the ERG is already a step on the way to creating a safe environment for dialogue and reducing prejudice and stereotyping in the workplace, the so-called Business Resource Groups form part of the strategic business plan of the company. The BRG ensures that dialogue and understanding are leveraged to focus on how diversity can drive business as well as social objectives [8].

The forums or ERGs may be multiple; they may be large enough to encompass interested parties from across the organisation or limited to accommodate a team of co-workers. They may be formal with moderators and panels taking questions from the audience, or informal social gatherings featuring (culturally appropriate) snacks and refreshments. The larger the meeting, the greater the need for formal planning and leadership. But even in smaller get-togethers, it is helpful to follow certain routine governance steps to ensure that the primary purpose of the meeting does not deteriorate to a point where the original purpose is lost. For example, consider an equality forum where participants are consistently distracted by the release of monthly or weekly business-critical numbers. If the forum is always the first meeting point after publication, covering and commenting on the news might quickly become a habit ending with conversation no longer focusing on equality, but on business numbers instead. There are, of course, many ways to cook an egg, but one approach might involve the following steps:

1. Nominate a team to manage and organise the forums or events.
2. Define the desired, long-term outcomes of the forum, including identifying stakeholders and the rules of participation (e.g. showing respect to all speakers).
3. Consider the nature of the event (formal or informal; a lecture or for group discussions; or a hackathon event with mingling in mind?) and how this might impact preparations.
4. Generate publicity for the event in memos, on noticeboards and posters, via intranet media, etc.
5. Target ambassadors and people-managers, as well as those for whom the forum is specifically intended.

6. Plan an agenda to focus minds on the topic for discussion. Consider presenting a survey or other data to feed discussion around experiences and views. Make it a learning process with clear take-away observations or conclusions.
7. Conduct the forum with an identified moderator or coordinator. Plan tactics to overcome "first-mover paralysis" where no one wants to speak first.
8. Follow-up on the meeting conclusions immediately after the forum meeting. Find ways to preserve and use the energy and interest generated by the meeting.
9. Within the management team, reflect on the quality of dialogue generated and how to improve it. Define lessons learnt for communication back to the office of the Chief Diversity and Inclusion Officer.

Box Inc is an American internet company based in California. Its business is cloud content management and file-sharing services for businesses. Employee resource groups (ERGs) at Box are employee-led affinity groups based on a person's identity. Box ERGs included Box Women's Network, Women in Tech (specific to women in technical roles), Pride (an LGBT+Q group), Black Excellence Network, Latinx, Veterans at Box, and Families with Special Needs. "In the current climate, I think there's a desire to homogenise people or question the need for separate spaces. However, it's so important for people to have safe spaces. All of the groups are open to allies, but they will sometimes have closed meetings if necessary".
Megan Dalessio, D&I Lead at Box.

The Clorox Company is a California multi-brand manufacturer of health and household goods. Faced with increasing remote working, both by individuals and location, Clorox established Business Resource Groups to connect workers otherwise separated from one another. They developed a virtual forum network under the acronym ORBIT (originally Offices Remote But Integral Teammates). Its mission today is to "enable Clorox employees and teams to thrive wherever they live or work". In 2017, ORBIT was applied to the D&I programme to help generate awareness of how unconscious bias can influence decision-making. Since then, Clorox has established ERGs representing Asian, Black, Latino, multicultural, LGBT+, women's and veterans' interests. There is also a group representing Millennial workers.
Information sourced from company websites (2021)

13.3 Online Forums: Their Shapes and Sizes

Since the onset of the 2020 Coronavirus pandemic, "Working From Home" has become a concept with its own acronym, "WFH". Meetings, large or small, had to move online as lockdowns forced millions of office-based workers to clear their kitchen tables to make room for computers and monitors. As a result, what used to be considered the exception of remote working became mainstream.

Once outside the office, diversity is invisible and inaccessible, interaction difficult and forced rather than natural. The individual—be they of the dominant group at work or part of the minority—will revert to whatever represents the easy option. At the physical office, suggesting taking a coffee break to a familiar colleague is natural, yet, there is still the chance of encountering less familiar colleagues in the break room. Even if that favourite "coffee companion" is not available, then reaching out to "that person you have meant to talk to" but have not got round to doing so yet is a low threshold to cross. Video chat precludes chance encounters, and the likelihood is that efforts to contact others to brainstorm a question will be limited to those already on "speed-dial".

In a pandemic world, physical forums and group meetings may not be possible, but there has been a revolution in online meeting software in recent years that has accelerated in 2020. Baby Boomers and Generation X people may have a strong preference still for the physical get-together. In contrast, Millenials and GenZ workers have less aversion to technologies that enable virtual meetings conducted on their smartphones. In a workforce context, however, there will be some who are not interested in navigating the login and "allow access to microphone" buttons appearing on the computer screen. The pandemic has accelerated the use of virtual meetings, webinars and even conferences. The pendulum may swing back to crowded and noisy auditoriums, but the online forum will not disappear; the virtual event will become a complement to the physical event and is here to stay.

We can define two types of online forums:

- The synchronous virtual audio-visual event
- The asynchronous internet discussion forum using written or audio messaging

Live, public webinar or "Town Hall" style discussion groups moderated by the D&I function should allow questions and comments to be made without fear of retribution. As with auditoriums, where speakers are easily seen and identified, so it should be with online discussion. This live discussion forum should be open to all community participants. Still, the D&I function should carefully evaluate the need of the organisation they are monitoring to decide on the needs and access rights to a range of possible virtual communities. In the early stages of cultural change, if trust is not yet established, there may be a need for those who feel discriminated against to safely explore personal experiences and opinions with others in a similar situation. Those from a more structurally privileged position hesitating to ask "sensitive" questions should similarly be allowed to explore and learn. What is of the most significant importance is that these forums should be moderated by D&I professionals able to manage and inform the debate within them. The ultimate objective must be to work towards complete transparency, a prerequisite of a trust culture. However, to push along a strategy, it may be helpful to start small and appoint forum spokespeople to shield nervous contributors from being identified as an interim step.

Internal Communications

A word of warning. In non-media organisations, the hierarchical and reporting distance from the executive to the events organiser or facilitator can be significant. Even in organisations where communications are considered key, the priority is typically accorded external communications. The tradition is for internal communications to be organised by business lines, largely reflecting the lines of the organisation chart. The message prepared for group consumption leaves the office of the CEO to land on the desks of the other executive officers. They pass on the message (amended as they consider appropriate to their function or business line) to their direct reports. In this manner, the message cascades through the organisation. The larger the group, the greater the variation may be between its content and tone by the time it reaches employees in general—especially if these are spread between Asia, Europe, the Middle East and the USA, for example.

For a change in process-oriented matters such as procedures, protocol or general policy, messaging by diktat may be adequate. However, there is little or no allowance for feedback to be delivered back through the hierarchy. In matters involving culture change, value-led decision-taking and even such matters as remuneration and reward systems (often applied without consultation), this is an ivory tower, top-down approach that can be badly misinterpreted or misapplied. In the dynamic world that we have previously argued will leave the corporate tree at risk of being snapped by the gales of changing circumstances, this approach cannot meet the increasingly important function of feedback and dialogue with all parts of the organisation. Directors seated in the ivory tower cannot see beyond their horizons. There is too much happening beyond their view to believe that we can afford to allow early warnings available from the lower reaches of the organisation to go unheeded.

The argument, therefore, is that internal communications has become far more central and critical to organisational culture management than it has traditionally been credited with. In fashioning an infrastructure of supportive social networks such as ERGs and online forums, it would be the equivalent of playing with fire if left to inexperienced, if intelligent, subordinates as an "interesting experiment". The management of online forums, the creation of the safe environments necessary to ensure their success requires expertise, either acquired through specialist recruitment or contracted in for the purpose. To properly succeed, we need advanced analytics to assess the scale and source of the challenge. Employee polling, feedback interpretation, and even meeting facilitation are all critical factors that require either training or experts available to perform.

The synchronous virtual event needs to be organised similarly to the physical group gatherings described above. Differences relate to the restrictions imposed or fresh opportunities provided by the technology used. Adjusting to them requires members of the organising team trained in how to optimise the use of software solutions that best suit participant engagement, cyber-security and connectivity requirements. Factors beyond those of the physical event may include (but are not limited to) the following:

- Ensuring that access rights and privacy arrangements, including protection against hacking or illicit listening attempts, are appropriate for the host and the participants
- Choosing software that does not require the processing power of only the most up-to-date computers on the market
- Considering how participant behaviour differs from an event where physical presence precludes other distractions or where absence cannot be hidden by the mute button or switching out of video mode. The moderator might encourage participants to keep their web cameras on at all times.
- Activating participants to keep engagement high (such as real-time polling and the occasional use of breakout "rooms") and limiting time per session to align with the concentration span of someone in a WFH scenario
- Whereas a physical event will be timed to accommodate logistical realities, the online event can be timed based on participant convenience.
- In discussion groups, encourage and refer to participant questions forwarded by the Chat function. Ensure there is a Q&A manager to monitor and select the most relevant questions. Some software even allows participants to "like" questions posed by others, thereby helping to identify those questions seen as most pressing amongst participants.
- Consider what materials might be helpful to provide to participants in advance of the session, ensure the appropriate level of recording (it may not be at all appropriate) and make access to supporting materials easily accessible to participants after the session.

Well-designed entry portals, technology that works, dynamic content pages and attractive, user-friendly interfaces will encourage participation in virtual events and usage of online discussion forums. The employment of specialists in these functions may appear an expensive luxury to some, but in terms of effective communications, it is penny foolish not to do so.

Careful planning, testing and even rehearsals are indispensable for any event, particularly for online events, as the peer pressure of colleagues asking "will I see you there" is absent. The excuse of having to "take an important call" or even "dealing with the dog" appears far more prevalent and acceptable in the virtual world than in the real one.

The asynchronous internet discussion forum offers an interesting alternative to the conference call. It can be a dialogue that works in shorter bursts yet lasts longer than a coffee break at the office. As with the organisation of an event, the discussion forum should be managed by a specific team and feature moderators able to remove content and mail participants directly, if necessary. The rules of the forum should be clear, short and enforced. Once again, the recruitment and use of experienced and trained social media experts should be a prerequisite. In addition to increasing the chance of generating successful discussion, the social media officer will generally know how to use analytical tools and evaluate the data that such discussion groups can produce, including tracking trends amongst topics and identifying favourable or unfavourable mood swings.

Discipline in the enforcement of code of conduct rules on the forum and diligence in monitoring discussion is essential. For most purposes, there ought not to be any anonymity, but the organisers will need to decide if this is always the case.

Anonymity may be appropriate in some contexts, such as a helpline forum where people may be encouraged to ask questions they otherwise might fear asking. To avoid any aspect of "trolling" (the practice of intentionally upsetting or enraging others on social media through the use of deliberate misunderstanding and other forms of online harassment), the D&I Communications role may wish to curate submissions, subjecting them to review before publishing comments to the forum.

Intranet and Social Media

There are many benefits to developing an internal social media strategy:

- It can promote more openness and interest in exploring difficult subjects.
- It can connect communities that are remote from each other, especially in an environment of WFH.
- It can be tailored to the specific needs of certain sub-groups within the community and encourage complex topics and discussions to be brought to the surface.
- It can be used to feed information, knowledge, studies or statistics to various discussion forums, all to improve understanding and empathy.
- It can provide valuable information to the D&I function on hot topics or highlight business units experiencing particular challenges so that they may assist where needed.
- By moderating the discussion forum, the D&I function can educate, inform and offer to help individuals or specific groups dig deeper into a particular subject area to identify the possible source and solution to the concern raised.

More than all of these, a well-designed, fit-for-purpose, internal social media strategy will be a valuable tool to ensure that the living dialogue, the third imperative of culture change, is kept alive.

13.4 The Elephant in the Room: We Are Human After All

Part One: We Are Lazy

There are many ways to "lead a horse to water, but you cannot make it drink". There are ways to provide opportunities for discussion and exploration of the subject of diversity and inclusion, but we are, after all, dealing with human beings, not algorithms.

The role model effect of inclusive leadership, our first imperative of culture change, is the most powerful influence on employee behaviour. Leadership behaviours satisfy our inherent instinct to avoid danger and discover a safe passage to a brighter future. Hannah Arendt, in her book "The origins of totalitarianism", explains how the tyrant makes use of an "audience (that) was ready at all times to believe the worst, no matter how absurd". It is a human trait used for evil in the past, but it cannot be ignored. The leader who acts as a role model and solution provider to what may seem inextricable dilemmas can change mindsets for good, as well as bad. It is up to us to choose our leaders wisely.

Beyond good leadership, however, it is a fact of neuroscience that as much as humans may be emotional and unpredictable, our behaviours are indeed hard-wired to some fundamental cognitive biases. Our role model leaders must not only be wise and committed; it helps if they have a skilled communications manager who knows how to sell the message also. Some of the strongest influencers of behaviour are [9]:

1. The bias of social norms
2. The bias of relativity
3. The bias of anchoring, and
4. The bias of zero cost

The bias of social norms
Social proof has been discussed in various contexts throughout this book. It is the power of group ethics, namely, the expectations of behaviour placed by the group on the individual. The other three cognitive biases mentioned contain hints as to how to present one's argument to have the best chance of persuading your metaphorical horse to drink the water in the trough.

The bias of relativity
Neuroscientific research explains that our primal brain is programmed to make quick decisions—a decision to fight or flight in the face of a dangerous enemy is both stark and crucial to the decision-maker. We also know that when faced with two options that do not offer a clear choice based on personal advantage—i.e. choices that are difficult to differentiate between—it can lead to procrastination or indecision. Consequently, when promoting D&I, the alternative visions of the future must be obviously, even radically, distinct. A case made with whole-hearted conviction and passion is more likely to engage the audience than any monotone argument for gradual change. It is the unwavering show of determination of the leader that D&I is not only desirable, but that it is the only vision that is worth considering that will engage employees or community members.

The bias of anchoring
Neuroscience often exposes human weakness. The human instinct is to prefer the easy option rather than a more challenging one. The decision to fight or flight in an emergency may indeed produce a leader who takes on a challenge. Still, the motivation to change is more likely to respond to the bias of relativity explained above than a permanent desire to be exceptional. Anchoring bias is at the heart of habit, repeating a successful action recurrently—thereby avoiding any need to rethink our options. Hence, the first decisions we ask our audience to take are crucial

to shaping group ethics and establishing behaviours we wish to be norms; in our case, to be welcoming and open-minded to diversity and be inclusive in our working relationships with people of different cultures than our own. This is why the objective of D&I cannot be left to well-intentioned randomness, but instead must be governed by a carefully planned campaign. We know the phrase "first impressions matter"; it is as true for an ideal as it is for an individual.

The bias of zero-cost

Neuromarketing of this bias is visibly on display whenever we visit the supermarket, the bookstore or the online shop. It is the "buy two and get one for free" offer, or a promise of free delivery. This is closely related to the loss-avoidance bias that makes us keener to take advantage of what we have rather than working towards a more distant, more considerable gain. To the change manager, it teaches us that to "ask" employees to take risks, to act on courage rather than instinct, or to carry additional burdens is less likely to engage them than promises of praise and recognition for merely participating in an ongoing parade. Morin and Renvoise express this as "we always prefer free options over fee options". We should not ask our employees to lead the charge and take the risk of change. It should not be our Black, minority or ethnic colleagues who are asked to challenge and confront discriminatory practices in the firm. Taking risks is a leadership responsibility; followers should be allowed to do no more than follow, if that is their wish.

Part Two: We Are Emotional

People who write books generally like to do research, and people who have done research most frequently want to share their knowledge. In 2016, shortly before the UK referendum on Brexit, this author (a non-British convinced European with a fair understanding of trade finance and the Institutions and procedures of the EU) discussed the merits of Britain leaving the European Union with an English friend of long-standing. He was voting to leave the EU, and I wanted to understand why. I was determined not to counter-argue his viewpoint. Instead, I was attempting to complete his less detailed understanding of the workings of the EU. After a long conversation where he stated his arguments, and I calmly explained how almost all the complaints he held against the EU were either inaccurate or exaggerated, he replied with a phrase that told me we could never agree on the subject: "Anthony, you clearly know a lot more about these matters than I do, but all we want is to get our independence back".

My chat with my close friend had gone well enough that we had avoided an argument—in fact, he admitted that many of his reasons for wanting to leave the EU were not grounded in rationality or facts. At the core of his argumentation was the attempt to rationalise an emotional desire for a simpler world where there need be no more talk of the EU or globalisation. Institutional procedures and political influence in a world dominated by the USA and China did not appear to matter to him. My discussion with him helped me to understand that in the face of faith or emotion, "facts and figures" have only a limited influence in actually changing minds. What I also realised was that, although our discussion had been calm and a two-way conversation, I had played the role of the "expert" versus the "recipient"—a role sometimes referred to as the "logic bully". What I had encountered was what psychologists already knew, that providing knowledge alone to change minds is of trivial importance in the face of deeply held worldviews [10]. Indeed, what does not sway people may simply strengthen their previously held beliefs.

Professional mediators and negotiators seek to guide or persuade their clients or partners of a course of action that is to the mutual advantage of all parties. They know not to allow a discussion to become emotional or agree to debate deeply held beliefs, such as religious faith. In recent years, many of us have discovered the dangers of confronting opponents to what we consider apparent truths. In the USA, the advent of Trumpism split the country into two political halves. In the UK, the debate surrounding the meaning, let alone the impact or cause, of Brexit divided the country. Also, as the Coronavirus pandemic encircled the world, some religiously followed government advice on masking, social distancing and self-isolation; others stubbornly disputed the existence of any serious threat. Trying to "speak sense" or discuss with a person persuaded to an incompatible viewpoint often ends in frustration and anger, even in the ending of previously good relationships. We come back to our earlier assertions about the art of communication—if we cannot listen with empathy, we cannot understand the reality as perceived by our discussion partner; if we cannot let go of our convictions to explore other views of the world, we cannot understand, let alone successfully argue for our own.

During the writing of this book, the Palestine-Israeli conflict once again manifested itself in a rain of rockets in the region. In his Hidden Brain podcast, Shankar Vedantam referenced the work of Professor Lee Ross of Stanford University on attitude formation and social cognition. In it, he shows the inability of those on each side of suffering to allow empathy for the other to co-exist with the sympathy they demand for themselves. "When Arabs and Israelis think about their conflict, each group desperately want their observers to know they have been wronged. To acknowledge the pain on the other side is to limit this claim somehow. That's why two groups can look at the same reality and see completely different things" [11]. It is a tragedy that our minds are so structured to protect our narratives, our hurt and our trauma. Yet, this is the challenge that we must overcome if we are ever to reconcile our experiences of pain—to find it in our hearts to be vulnerable to new realities and have the courage to forgive.

Motivating a Change of Mind

How, then, should we proceed in our forums or one-to-ones? Our conversation partner (such as a long-standing victim of prejudice) may be either emotionally fragile and on guard against signs of micro-aggressions or less than fully trusting of our intentions? Alternatively, and frequently, the colleague of the dominant social grouping might find it hard to accept that experiences of discrimination, prejudice, dismissive behaviours and even gaslighting[1] are being enacted by peers they hold in high regard [12]. Psychologists find that when we listen carefully and allow our conversation partners to explore the complexities of their own argumentation, they become less extreme and more open in their views. To ask how their ideas might work in practice, rather than asking why they favour those opinions, is more effective in opening their minds to the complexity of the problem and gaining acknowledgement that their knowledge is only partial [13]. The recommendation is that rather than trying to convince people to change by confrontation, it is more effective to help them find their own intrinsic motivation to change through a process known as motivational interviewing. Professor Grant of Wharton University explains how motivational interviewing is used to change the mind of the intransi-gent, "by interviewing them—asking open-ended questions and listening care-fully—and holding up a mirror so they can see their own thoughts more clearly. If they express a desire to change, you guide them toward a plan". He warns that it is not a matter of attempting to manipulate the subject. "It requires a genuine desire to understand people's motivations and help them reach their goals".

In certain political quarters, this process is described as "giving grace"—taking the time to listen to a political opponent's concern in search of a shared interest [14]. It is a process where, by sharing personal experiences, we make it easier to reflect on the discrimination or marginalisation of others; for example, a gay man and a White woman sharing their respective experiences of prejudices encountered, before together exploring the impact of racism. Persuasion happens in that by talking about themselves, individuals generally realise that a more tolerant attitude is consistent with their self-image. The science does not guarantee a result, but within the worlds of anti-vaxxers and politics, research evidences that methods such as motivational interviewing achieve material results. Leadership consultants will recognise this as the power of a coaching style of leadership.

On the subject of race discrimination, Anré Williams, a Black executive at American Express, said: "It's not a topic that you look forward to discussing at work at all, because it gets you into a conversation with a lot of people who may not be well-informed, who may ask a lot of questions which are full of bias. It takes your energy away from the positivity you're trying to keep to excel in your business career" [15].

Starting a conversation on a subject with someone reluctant to explore a topic or with people who "won't understand" (i.e. do not have the range of experiences that will allow genuine empathy) is difficult. The challenge for the instigator who wishes to improve understanding and find ways to make life better for those on the receiving end of discrimination is to generate trust. The sensitivity of the discourse means that the six building blocks of trust previously referred to in Fig. 10.1 (Respect, Fairness,

---

[1] Gaslighting is the "psychological manipulation of a person usually over an extended period of time that causes the victim to question the validity of their own thoughts, perception of reality, or memories and typically leads to confusion, loss of confidence and self-esteem, uncertainty of one's emotional or mental stability, and a dependency on the perpetrator". Definition as provided by Merriam-Webster.com (16 December, 2021).

Predictability, Competence, Communications and Support) need to be integrated into your communication style. What you say and how you say it will either remove barriers to vulnerability or lock the door on them firmly shut.

Words Matter … Along with the Rest

Neuroscience explains mirroring or code-switching as behaving similarly to others to remove barriers that might arise from perceived cultural differences or values. In everyday situations where values are not as much different as merely expressed differently, we can gainfully mirror the behaviour of another to form trust relationships. When we act like our conversation partner, it helps us live an experience from the standpoint of the other party. By activating and relating to memories of our own experiences, we can connect emotionally with what our partner is experiencing; we trigger what might be called genuine empathy [16]. It is only through connecting emotionally on the same plane that we can show that we do understand; that we care about the emotions being experienced by our opposite number; that we really want to help and educate, not dominate and convince without merit. But if the person we are mirroring holds significantly different values and worldviews, the trust created is insincere and false.

We know from Professor Mehrabian's research that there are three elements of communication that have to be congruent if they are not to lead to scepticism and distrust. These are the words spoken, the tone of voice used, and body language—most frequently in the form of facial expressions. We are all familiar and, perhaps, agree with the phrase "words matter". And they do, but it is clear from studies that the weakest form of communication is, in fact, the choice of words. The phrasing may be clumsy or imperfect, but if the tone and body language are sympathetic and unthreatening, Mehrabian's research indicates that words only import 7% of the combined words/tone/body language package. Further studies even suggest that in telephone conversations, when body language is unseen, tone impacts 86% of the listener's interpretation of the intended message compared to only 14% of the words spoken [17]. It is clear from the research that the worst form of communication is the written word, unsupported as it is of either tone or positive body language. Combined with our primal predisposition to look out for signs of threat, the phrase "words matter" takes on enormous importance when writing messages by letters or email, on chat, on internet forums, etc. When breaching a sensitive subject, about which your interlocutor is already defensive, it should always be done when the tone of voice and friendly gestures are readily observable.

13.5 Authenticity Matters

Public speaking coaches instruct politicians amongst others on how to sound convincing, trustworthy and credible—however, the most crucial requirement is to be authentic. Faking a smile will be noted, unconsciously, if not consciously.

Although psychologists will tell stories of how sociopaths can convincingly fake sincerity, this is not an option for most of us. Consequently, the best practice is to only engage with the person opposite if your desire to have the conversation comes from a place of genuine concern for your conversation partner. Sometimes, we are not convinced of the benefit or need to engage. In that case, it is probably best to discuss only the peripheral aspects of the question, making efforts to understand without judgement. When encountering a group who are uncertain of what is expected of them, they rarely say anything meaningful until after the senior person in the room has spoken, effectively pre-judging the outcome. This so-called Sunflower Bias is often compounded by the fact that the same leader, frustrated by the lack of diversity in the ensuing conversation, continues to seek fresh input on how to deal with the issue at hand using closed questions. Suppose the topic is tricky for some to open up on. In that case, the approach must be open-ended, and any input acknowledged and encouraged without any hint of surprise, judgement or exaggerated sympathy. A respectful pause, clarifying questions and gratitude for the sharing of information combined with follow-up feedback shortly after is more trust-inducing than any show of outrage or promises for action that are not reflected by subsequent actions. To return to the words of Professor Grant quoted above: "I no longer believe it's my place to change anyone's mind. All I can do is try to understand their thinking and ask if they're open to some rethinking. The rest is up to them".

What language should we use when trying to motivate someone to question if their worldview is one-sided and based on myths and stories with no or little substance? At their extremes, the deeply traumatised individual and the convinced conspiracy theory advocate are beyond the ability of most of us to either win their trust or alter their mindset. But the vast majority of those the organisation has actively recruited to join our community will have a desire to be in harmony with the majority of their new colleagues. They will want to please both their peers and superiors and will react positively to the incentives and rewards offered to those who support the culture promoted by the leadership. The underlying assumption is that (1) we are attracted to organisations and processes that advocate values we already share, and (2) we all want to be liked and accepted by the social grouping of which we are a part. All that is needed is a language and a communication process that invites the fragile to take the first steps to share their fears and for the sceptics to examine their assumptions. Words matter, but the authenticity of their meaning matters more.

The Full Package

We have to accept that the flow of information through the organisation cannot be placed in the straitjacket of a pre-defined governance framework. A chain of command is designed specifically for delegation and the delivery of instructions; it does not generate a conversation. Only by focusing on the ecosystem of dialogue can we produce a productive and beneficial exchange of information. In nature, there is a concept of the trophic cascade, that by influencing one element of the ecosystem, it alters its entire functioning. For example, in 1995/1996, wolves were re-introduced into Yellowstone National Park to dramatic effect. The wolves changed the behaviour of deer as they sought refuge from the threat the wolves represented. As a result, the flora changed as previously grazed areas saw bushes and trees reappear, in turn attracting a greater variety of birds and smaller animals. The growth of trees reinforced the banks of rivers, and even the rivers started to flow differently [18]. Culture and the behaviours we experience within them are like trophic cascades. As leaders, we can create platforms for productive exchanges of information and knowledge. We can promote, reward and demonstrate values and qualities that engender trust within the organisation. We can even orchestrate the agenda and establish common goals for the community to pursue together. However, there comes the point where we have to stand back and let the dialogue take place. We have to remain vigilant, ensure that the conversation remains civil and that, at the end of the cascade, the outcomes align with our expectations and aspirations. We cannot control mindset; we can only hope to create the right conditions for the values we hold dear to take hold.

References

1. Creary, S. (2020, July 8). How to be a better Ally to your Black colleagues. *Harvard Business Review*.
2. Hancock, B., Manyika, J., Williams, B. R., & Yee, L. M. (2021, April 15). The Black experience at work in charts. *McKinsey Quarterly*.
3. Sandberg, S., & Grant, A. (2018, March). *Option B: Building resilience*. Linkedin course.
4. Atewologun, D., Cornish, T., & Tresh, F. (2018, March). *Unconscious bias training: An assessment of the evidence for effectiveness*. Equality and Human Rights Commission.
5. Langer, Harward, & Taylor. (2021, May 11). *Speak-up and call-out culture*. Ethical Systems.
6. Hodges, C., & Steinholz, R. (2017). *Ethical business practice and regulation*. Hart Publishing.
7. Kidder, R. (2003). *How good people make tough choices*. HarperCollins.
8. *What's the trend with ERGs and BRGs*. Interview with Leah Kyaio in the Affinity Inc. Magazine on December 20, 2017.
9. Morin, C., & Renvoise, P. (2018). *The persuasion code*. Wiley.
10. Hornsey, M. J., Harris, E. A., & Fielding, K. S. (2018, April). The psychological roots of anti-vaccination attitudes. *Health Psychology*.
11. Vedantam, S. (2021, May 21). *Tribes and traitors*. Hidden Brain podcast.
12. Mallick, M. (2021, September 16). How to intervene when a manager is gaslighting their employees. *Harvard Business Review*.
13. Grant, A. (2021, January 31). The science of reasoning with unreasonable people. *New York Times*.
14. Resnick, B. (2020, January 29). How to talk someone out of bigotry. *Vox.com of Vox Media*.

15. Abelson, M., Basak, S., Butler, K., Leising, M., Surane, J., & Tan (2020, August 3). The only one in the room. *Bloomberg*.
16. Preston, S. D., Standfield, R. B., Damasio, H., & Mehta, S. (2007, September). The neural substrates of cognitive empathy. *Social Neuroscience*.
17. Betts, K. (2009). Lost in translation: Importance of effective communication in online education. *Online Journal of Distance Learning Administration, Summer*.
18. *How wolves change rivers*. Video by Sustainable Human viewable on YouTube. Posted February 13, 2014.

Part IV

The Governance of D&I: Best Practice Standards

It is no accident that the third part of this book is the most substantial. Drawing on the discoveries of Parts I and II, we have sought to illustrate how leadership, dialogue and trust might make the challenge of transformation and culture change a manageable proposition. Yet, the organisation cannot sustain all of these imperative drivers of change without help. In the absence of continuous encouragement, we grow satiated with dynamic dialogue and are tempted by the comfort provided by new presumptions and conventions. Eventually, trust will be taken for granted, and new "accepted behaviours" be confronted by new, emerging conflicts. Leadership roles will change, key opinion-leaders will depart, and fresh influences arrive as the CEO baton gets passed on to the next successor.

Much as people may protest against systemic bias and injustice, the sustainably inclusive organisation will need to institutionalise constant dialogue, learning and leadership principles. Governance is often presented as bureaucracy in the pursuit of predictability. However, in a world that is ever less predictable, the role of governance is changing to accentuate the creation of a resilient organisation capable of discovering, absorbing and adapting to change. Inclusive governance is no longer about the cold numbers of risk and profit calculations; it is about the monitoring and management of lived experiences and sentiment. In this part IV, we look at what this means for the governance framework, the organisation, and its members.

#InclusiveGovernance: Making It Happen 14

14.1 The Governance of Culture Change: Positioning the D&I Function

For many, the question is a glaring one. Why does society, and more specifically, company boards and executives, find it so challenging to drive cultural change on a subject that, in and of itself, is so obviously in need of correction? It is a topic that goes to the heart of the challenge of modern governance. If boards are incapable of instilling cultural change in their organisations, then how on earth can they expect to enjoy any success in addressing the "Social" of ESG demands. If their actions fail to do more than merely try to erase the worst of social policy mishaps, how can we hope to access the power of purpose, culture and values? [1]. Token gestures might quiet the waters in any given press conference, but they will not subdue the risk of scandals and mishaps. To address the "S" in ESG, there has to be cultural change; a change in organisational behaviour and mindset.

Too often, the burden of organisational leadership is placed on a single individual: most frequently, the CEO. This image of leadership, reinforced through a thousand years of portraits depicting conquering heroes on horseback with a sword in hand, is (perhaps disappointingly) misleading. Where is the general without their sovereign and their army? Where is Napoleon without his allies, lieutenants and administrators? One person can inspire a crowd, but implementing intent requires organisation and resources as well as hearts and minds. The CEO might appear as the figurehead for change and provide meaningful leadership qualities that encourage followers and supporters. Still, without the unequivocal support and empowerment from the board or the firm's owners, such leadership will likely flounder and result in only superficial change. There is an adage that says, "the fish rots from the head". It implies that the observed and evidenced mindset and behaviour of the leadership reflects itself in the main body of the organisation. Unless the organisational direction is convinced of the need for change, promotes and internalises that change, then change will not happen. This leadership for change, in this case, inclusive

© The Author(s), under exclusive license to Springer Nature Switzerland AG 2022
A. Smith-Meyer, *Unlocking the Potential of Diversity in Organisations*, Diversity and Inclusion Research, https://doi.org/10.1007/978-3-031-10402-2_14

leadership, starts at the level of the owner-entrepreneur or the board of directors. Therefore, the role of the board and its members warrants a closer look.

The Central Role of Boardroom Leadership

The board of directors has a responsibility to shareholders, but they also have their own identity as "the company". Just as a paymaster may instruct a subordinate to perform a particular act, it does not excuse the outranked agent from responsibility or accountability for the consequences of such an act. There is, therefore, a conflict of interest already established at the point where shareholders entrust their capital to the care of the board of directors. The director is not just an agent without an independent duty to reflect on his or her actions. They have an obligation to exercise independence of mind that ensures personal awareness of the impact of, and personal responsibility for, their decisions [2]. Once an organisation is committed to a vision and ambition for D&I, the director should embed that objective in all aspects of its decision-making, policy formulation, and design of governance and control frameworks. The entirety of the corporation must be able to match the words and actions of the board with the pursuit of its stated objectives.

Article 88 of the EU Capital Adequacy IV Directive addresses the governance arrangements it requires amongst regulated financial service companies [3]. The directives' instruction and recommendations are, however, just as applicable outside the financial sphere as it is within it. It highlights several issues of particular relevance to our focus. Firstly, it confirms the principal responsibility of the board:

> Overall responsibility for the institution; approve and oversee the implementation of strategic objectives; risk strategy and internal governance . . .

The board has "overall responsibility for the institution" and, consequently, also stands accountable for all actions undertaken by the company on its behalf. It is primarily expected to "oversee" the implementation of strategy by the executive or third-party agents, and its duty is to ensure that the intended outcome is achieved. To do this, the board must establish an appropriate internal governance framework.

In the execution of its duty, it falls to the board to appoint, evaluate and reward or dismiss management in an independent manner. This expectation is repeated by the OECD [4] and most corporate governance codes issued by various authorities worldwide, including the UK's Financial Reporting Council [5].

Board Delegation of Authority

The relationship between the board and the executive is that the executive officer (s) acts under the delegated authority of the board. The executive is accountable to the board, which is responsible to shareholders and other stakeholders. This hierarchy explains all aspects of the CEO-Board relationship. The executive is not the originator of diversity and inclusiveness initiatives within the organisation. Instead, he or she is an individual who has been chosen as the best person to spearhead and implement the strategy and policies of the board. It may happen that the CEO will try to educate a board on the necessity and benefits of D&I. But in the absence of a convinced Chairperson and board members who believe in its strategic value, the CEO will have to fight the good battle on two fronts; seeking the continuous approval of mandate by the board, and the hearts and minds of employees.

The Chief Executive Officer

The CEO will often be an executive board member, but principally is the main interlocutor between the company's daily management and the board. In addition, the CEO will chair the management committee composed of the other chief officer executives such as those responsible for finance, operational risk, human resources, IT and other strategic functions considered key to success.

Executive Duties

Whereas the CEO carries the primary responsibility for fulfilling daily management duties delegated by the board, each executive officer has the same obligations within their specific field. Although in this section, we address the responsibilities of the CEO, these apply equally to the other executive officers responsible for their expert area of activity—including risk, compliance, audit, finance, etc.—eventually also a Chief Diversity and Inclusion Officer.

Various laws on limited companies expand on the duties of the CEO [6]. Many of these relate to operational, controlling and financial reporting tasks, but they also instruct them to:

- Manage and execute the company's business in accordance with the policies and instructions provided by the board.
- Prepare reports as required by the board and proposals for deliberation on subjects reserved for the board.
- Abstain from any activity or action that may have a material impact on the condition or strategic direction of the company without explicit board approval.

It should be clear that the power relationship between the board and the executive is driven by, and under the full responsibility of, the board.

Board Delegation of Mandate

Hence, every power possessed by the executive has been delegated by the board, which remains accountable for the outcome. Usually, this power is extensive so long

Strategic Matters	Operating Matters
Ambiguous, non-routine	Routinised
Organisation-wide impact	Operation-specific
Transactions bringing significant change	Small-scale change
Environment- or Social-driven change	Resource-driven

Fig. 14.1 Defining matters reserved for the board

as it is applied within the firm's board-approved strategy, conforms to the policy framework created by the board, and is used following the organisation's governance processes. These deliberations and decisions include the definition of organisational purpose, vision, mission; and the values and behaviours that serve such purpose and vision.

The CEO represents the whole executive team, individually and collectively, and is responsible for their performance. This mandate is too large for the board to control beyond strategy formulation and the policy framework. The board cannot micro-manage the activities of the CEO and the executive team. Instead, it has to determine which objectives may be pursued by the executive with significant tactical freedom to act as they choose, and which matters should be reserved for the board; in other words, those matters where the power of decision is withheld from the executive as exemplified in Fig. 14.1.

The board has to decide how far powers delegated to the executive should go, i.e. defining "matters reserved for the board". At a superficial level, one can merely make the distinction between strategic and operating matters [7].

It follows that non-routine decisions, such as the acquisition or disposal of significant assets or activities, cannot be described as "daily management". In like manner, the design and governance framework of culture change is hardly a routine matter. Arguably, once the cultural change is fully embedded, it may be viewed as "routinised" as "the way we do business around here". That, however, would be to ignore the fact that culture is constantly subject to changing impulses and influences. Suppose we accept the idea that culture is a strategic matter and a critical success factor for the business over time. In that case, the reins of power can never be entirely entrusted to the executive—the responsibility of the board to maintain constant oversight of developments and supervision of executive performance in this regard is never diminished.

Field Marshall Grav Helmuth von Moltke [8] (1848–1916) defined strategy as "the evolution of a central idea according to continually changing circumstances". Hence, when internal factors such as staff changes or resource restrictions impact the implementation of a strategy, the CEO and the executive team might be expected to make any necessary adjustments to maintain a realistic pursuit of the "central idea", such as D&I. The executive's obligation would be only to report such changes to the board after-the-fact, albeit in a timely fashion. On the other hand, a strategic adjustment may be imposed by influences beyond the control of the executive, such as a significant change in competitive circumstances, new or arising environmental or social expectations, or other concerns regarding the impact on stakeholders, etc. In this case, the CEO would be expected to prepare a file and proposal to the board regarding the appropriate response—leaving it for the board to make their evaluation and conclusion. If circumstances require a change in strategic direction, then the onus falls on the board to determine the new course to be set.

14.2   Diversity and Inclusion as a Control Function

In a previous chapter, we discussed the profile required for the nomination of the Chief Diversity and Inclusion Officer. The candidate should be someone the board and the executive are confident can competently manage the governance and managerial task of running a culture change programme. The CDIO position requires solid persuasion and team management skills. Hence, charisma, insight, empathy and an ability to bring the collective best out of a team of managers is essential. Together with their team, the CDIO will have to meet the expectations of the excluded groups within the organisation while being visibly influential amongst the leadership itself. In like manner with the CEO, we also specified that this person could only be as influential and effective as is permitted by their delegated mandate, empowerment and resources. In this regard, the perceived authority of the CDIO to exercise independent judgement and actions is a matter of "seeing is believing". This observable impact is not possible without the actual and practical power of an independent-minded function.

Within any organisation, there will be a natural tension between those chasing business targets set by the executive or even the board, and those who are the gatekeepers of prudence, governance or social equality. The temptation to see them as in a state of competition is strong. To counter this, the board and the executive have a responsibility to maintain a sense of shared purpose, as well as a culture of transparency, mutual trust and a willingness to speak up and challenge.

A culture that allows for the ready exchange of ideas and information, and the experimentation and failures that accompany success, can only exist if there is a high degree of trust between colleagues, employer and employee, manager and subordinate. Staff must be convinced that the sharing and voicing of ideas and opinions, at times challenging the existing order of things, will not be abused or retaliated against. Trust, guided by a common understanding of purpose and objective, is the essential ingredient of a culture that fosters innovation and progression.

In the ideal world, rules and regulations would be redundant. But the human mind is quick to rationalise non-conformist behaviour to justify the accommodation of conflicting interests, performance pressures or even personal convictions that deviate from that outlined by the firm. Based on long experience of financial scandal and abuse, regulatory institutions have been created, common accounting standards established, laws and regulations introduced. In business, there is no room for naïve trust. Organisations need to apply a "trust but verify" policy so that individuals know their actions are monitored and that miscreants will be held to account, irrespective of who they are. This is why internal control functions exist and are a natural part of the business. Regrettably, this applies also to the fight against prejudice and discrimination. For this reason, the role and function of the CDIO must be viewed as having not only an "evangelical" purpose, but one of monitoring and control also.

This chapter seeks to establish an orderly definition and understanding of the responsibility and expectations placed on the D&I function. However, the full scope of any function assigned to supervise organisational behaviour and culture is never complete.

> Succession planning, attracting and retaining diverse talent, mentoring, where we go to recruit people. All of that are things I play a role in.
> Desiree Ralls-Morrison,
> General Counsel at Boston Scientific
> (encompassing the D&I function)

The "Three Lines of Defence"

Since business owners started recruiting employees to further their business capacity, there have been controls placed on them to verify that tasks are completed as intended. In the modern era of limited companies, whereby ownership is separated from daily management and directors are charged with the fiduciary duty to oversee the use of the corporate funds, the concept of governance has evolved. For most of the twentieth century, businesses operated with the idea of Internal Control, a set of checks and balances entrusted to senior management and an internal audit function to guarantee four principal outcomes:

- Safeguarding the assets of the enterprise from fraud, abuse or theft
- Ensuring that financial statements are accurate, consistent and trustworthy
- Improving the efficiency of operating performance through the generation of management information
- Compliance with management objectives (policies), laws and regulations

The CDIO mandate is to ensure the proper implementation of policy directives relating to D&I. It is a mandate that covers educating staff, advising on the implementation of policy, monitoring policy outcomes and reporting on trends and developments, including investigating and handling any cases of misconduct. The extent and length of the ISO international standard on diversity and inclusion (ISO 30415) demonstrates the time and resources needed to execute this responsibility [9].

Some disagree with this scope and argue that D&I policy can be adequately monitored and policed by general management. Until the end of the 1990s, it was, indeed, commonplace for the oversight and control of the activity and behaviour of subordinates to be left to business management. The only independent check would be performed through the annual visit by Internal Audit. In some quarters, this approach has become known as the "Maginot Line of Defence Method". The

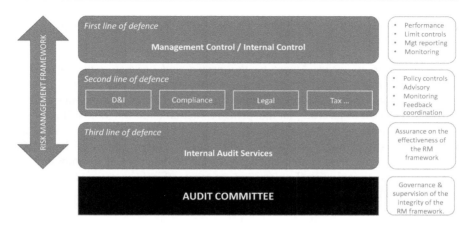

Fig. 14.2 The three lines of defence risk management framework

concern with this approach was that if that line were successfully bypassed or breached, then misconduct would have a good chance of remaining undetected, at least until it was too late to rectify. It was only in 2003 that the UK Financial Services Authority first mentioned the "Three Lines of Defence" method and brought the concept into mainstream banking risk management, since replicated in most complex or regulated sectors [10].

The basic presumption behind the Three Lines of Defence ("3LoD") approach is that where any one line of control may have gaps through which misconduct or errors might pass unnoticed, it is unlikely that three lines, one controlling the completeness and efficacy of the other, will have the same gaps. Hence, any mishap escaping the first, or even the second line of controls, would be unlikely to escape the attention of the third (see Fig. 14.2).

The Chartered Institute of Internal Auditors offers an explanation of the 3LoD. We might apply this to D&I implementation in the following manner [11]:

1. *The first line of defence—functions that own and manage risk*
   Under the first line of defence, operational management has ownership, responsibility and accountability for directly assessing, controlling and mitigating risks. The manager has a primary responsibility for being aware of organisational policy and expectations concerning D&I and will be accountable for the inclusive conduct of subordinates and share responsibility for the equitable behaviour of peers.

2. *The second line of defence—functions that oversee or specialise in risk management and compliance*
   The second line of defence consists of various internal functions such as ethics and compliance, risk management and other control departments. D&I within this line of defence would monitor and facilitate the effective implementation of functional inclusiveness practices by operational management and assist the

executive and board by reporting appropriate diversity-related information up and down the organisation.

3. *The third line of defence—functions that provide independent assurance, above all internal audit.*
   Internal Audit forms the organisation's third line of defence. Applying a risk-based approach to its work, an independent internal audit function will provide assurance to the organisation's board of directors and senior management as to the efficient implementation of D&I policy and the effectiveness of the CDIO function in facilitating, monitoring and reporting on outcomes. It encompasses all categories of organisational objectives: strategic, ethical, operational, reporting and compliance.

The application of the 3LoD approach to D&I in a bank trading room may be experienced as follows:

Traders generally operate in a demanding environment that is frequently stressful and often boisterous. Tempers may flare, but the toleration of conflict needs to be high and mitigated by a "band of brothers/sisters" sense of loyalty and understanding. It is an environment where politically incorrect, even hurtful things may be said amongst colleagues, irrespective of race, gender, colour or creed. All behaviour will be subject to the first line of defence supervision by the Chief Trader, who maintains close relationships with their subordinates and is sensitive to frictions or other relationship matters between them. The Chief Trader would have to be aware of D&I policies, sensitive to the impact of words and the expression of prejudice, and quick to intervene with immediate admonishment or coaching regarding what constitutes appropriate behaviour and response to provocation. Part of the Chief Trader's required profile and performance objectives are the tasks of role model, mediator and referee.

Still within the first line of defence, the Head of the Dealing Room and the Chief Traders may be supported by trading room D&I ambassadors who can act as a safety valve for any instances where the Chief Trader's efforts prove insufficient. The ambassador will maintain a general awareness of D&I objectives and behavioural expectations. By raising the need for "clearing the air", the ambassador might also ensure that hot spots or concerning developments are not kept hidden from view.

The second line of defence of a D&I function will verify that those first-line efforts comply with policy objectives and are adequate in the face of the constantly changing language and understanding of what constitutes inappropriate racial or other discriminatory behaviours. In addition, they act to protect the organisation from serious misconduct by specifically monitoring for signs of inequity, favouritism and discrimination. The Legal department performs second-line supervision of the correct application of equal opportunities laws and regulations, while human resources would be a natural partner to the D&I function in handling employee complaints of bullying or other forms of discrimination.

As indicated in Fig. 14.2, Internal Audit is the third line of defence tasked with evaluating the effectiveness of the D&I role in the second line of defence. The mission is to ensure that they and other second-line contributors are adequately resourced and capable of performing their mandate. In the 3LoD system, Internal Audit is furthest from the business activity, and therefore the most independent of the internal control functions. In many organisations, the Internal Auditor will report to the Chair of the Audit Committee, a sub-committee of the Board of Directors.

Reporting Lines: First Line of Defence

The first line of defence reports to the head of the business activity. Suppose the business operates a system of appointed ambassadors who can liaise between the D&I function and department employees. In that case, they can be trained and equipped to perform a valuable role as facilitators of forums, inclusion discussions, and provide advice on tackling "difficult" conversations or situations. Such ambassadors should be closely aligned and in regular contact with the Diversity and Inclusion Officer appointed to oversee their business area. Their activity serves the head of that business who needs to ensure that the ambassadorial role is recognised by all and is empowered to enquire and advise on minor situations before they are allowed to fester and undermine the culture of trust. Equally, however, the ambassador must also understand that any situation that cannot be resolved by a quiet word or expression of support should be reported to both the responsible business hierarchy and the D&I function. The ambassador should not be required to do the firefighting on their own and should not be deemed accountable for any mishaps incurred by collegial misconduct. At most, they are there to act as firewatchers and potentially as guides. Responsibility for exclusive or discriminatory behaviour within a department remains firmly with the head of the business unit concerned. It would be naïve to believe that the head of any business is not facing a perpetual conflict of interest between precisely measured business generation and profitability indicators and the less measurable behavioural objectives established for them by their superiors. Unless monitored by a second line of defence that is independent of business management in a way that the first line is not, it is all too easy for priorities to be tempted away from long-term cultural stability to satisfy short-term profit, convenience or laziness when dealing with subordinate relationships.

Reporting Lines: The Second Line of Defence

Many sources describe the second-line function, including the ISO 30415 discussed in Chap. 17. Arguably, due to the strategic and systemic importance of the banking sector to the global economy, one of the most evolved descriptions of the second line of defence is to be found in financial sector regulations. Consequently, we shall refer to the guidance provided by the European Securities and Markets Authority (ESMA) [12].

ESMA specifies five specific roles that compliance functions in the second line of defence are expected to perform and which can be translated to the Diversity function:

- Identifying how and where exclusive, prejudiced and discriminatory behaviours and decision-taking may be experienced and observed.
- Assessing the extent to which these risks are likely to occur and the level of attentiveness, monitoring and control required by location or activity.
- Advising the board, but more urgently, the business unit heads on how to best discharge their duties under D&I policy and in the context of the nature and urgency of the risks identified.
- Monitoring of actual employee behaviour and the general ambience and indicators of the degree of trust and fairness experienced by departmental employees.
- Reporting its findings to front-line business managers and the board in a systematic, regular, consistent and timely manner.

This description of the second line of defence's responsibilities is not exclusive to financial institutions. It is inspired by and developed in line with standard risk management best practices. Therefore, it can easily be applied to ethical and conduct risk, of which non-inclusive behaviours are one.

The European Banking Authority ("EBA") outlines its expectation of outcomes from the organisation of compliance as a second line of defence, here again, adapted to the D&I function [13].

- The establishment of a permanent, effective and global D&I function to safeguard a consistent benchmark of acceptable practices and behaviours, uniformity in awareness and training approach, and consistency in performance recognition and disciplinary decisions.
- Regular and effective assessment of how a business activity may negatively impact compliance with diversity policy objectives and the provision of advice on the implementation of inclusive initiatives and control procedures.
- Continuous ability to "verify" that the initiation of new roles and activities are mindful of D&I objectives and compliant with D&I policy.
- Continuous "verification" that any new or amended procedures, including impactful policies such as remuneration, remain compliant with D&I policy.
- Ensure D&I policy as established by the board and the executive is implemented and observed.
- Provide regular reports to the executive and the board on the evolution and trends of the cultural environment, specific non-compliant behaviours and any indicators of success or failure related to goal setting.
- That the D&I function findings will be "taken into account" by management.

The extent of supervision and interaction implied by the above list of expected outcomes is impressive. Still, comparable lists may be found in ISO standard descriptions of operational risk management, IT security and HR. For the D&I function to perform its duties and render the best possible service to the business and the board of directors, resources allocated to the function must be significant and adequate, and independence of business influence guaranteed.

ESMA specifically addresses the issue of adequacy of resources by specifying that:

- The compliance function should be allocated a budget consistent with the level of compliance risk (in this case, the risk of non-inclusive behaviours) the firm is exposed to.
- The D&I Officer should be consulted before the budget is determined.
- All decisions for significant cuts in the budget should be documented in writing and contain detailed explanations.

Even the EBA acknowledges that economic reality may moderate the extent to which a business can maintain an independent compliance function. Hence, they apply the principle of proportionality: that the compliance duties may be combined with other risk or support functions if necessary; for D&I, most naturally with an ethics or HR function.

There are occasions, especially in US-inspired organisations, where functions such as ethics and compliance, even D&I, are entrusted to the Legal department. Supporters of this combination will reference the influence and standing of in-house counsel and the legal profession as the gatekeeper of justice and ethics. From a governance perspective, however, the legal function has a first duty to protect the organisation from legal liability. Yet, this duty can easily be at odds with the fair and socially responsible treatment of an aggrieved employee. It is, therefore, highly recommended to maintain a professional distance between the D&I function and the Legal department.

Reporting Lines: The Third Line of Defence

The third line of defence is the internal audit function. Those of us with grey hair may recall the auditor as someone who came to inspect the books and make detailed reviews of files to check for clues of poor quality, negligence or even fraud in the business line. In the three-lines-of-defence model, modern practice has evolved. Now, internal audit is more concerned with the effectiveness of the second line of defence functions in terms of outcome relative to their objective. They may also perform roles such as investigations where foul play may be suspected and where the second line of defence's independence may be compromised due to their closer relationships with the business.

Best practice and regulators in financial and other business areas like pharmaceuticals require that the third line of defence be entirely independent; the head of internal audit should report directly to the board or the chair of the audit committee. Even so, there is no guarantee that even the internal audit function cannot be pressured to express their concerns with "greater sensitivity" to political dynamics and business "realities". This is where Internal Audit's relationship to the external auditor provides an additional check and challenge to the quality of independent findings and recommendations of Internal Audit.

14.3   Ensuring the Independence of Internal Control Functions

Independence allows the Ethics or Diversity and Inclusion Officer to view the assigned field of activity with greater objectivity and fewer conflicts of interest. Without a clear reporting line into an independent divisional or group function, a local D&I officer reporting sanctionable conduct to the head of the business unit they supervise will live in fear of retaliation in terms of compensation and promotion at best, and dismissal and exclusion at worst. Even so, an officer of the second line may still gain an undeserved reputation as "inflexible" or "difficult" if they are seen as too distant to the business they supervise; the "them" to the "us". Unless the business manager accepts D&I as part of business strategy and success, and the D&I officer as a trusted advisor and partner, any pressure from superiors demanding greater profits or business growth can quickly place a spanner in the works of collaboration between the first and second lines of control.

The risk of internal control functions being pressured to put the corporate "best foot" forward in their reporting and conclusions will always be present. Even the external auditor may fear the loss of a significant contract when dealing with a major company. Therefore, the best guarantor of integrity and independence-mindedness within an organisation is where organisational culture already is one of transparency, challenge, values, trust and integrity. It is the role of the external auditor and eventual regulators to act as the final "backstop" to ensure that functions such as internal audit and compliance are free to perform their duties independently.

Suppose the board is determined to promote a culture of integrity that supports ethics and inclusiveness. In that case, it will reflect this objective in their appointment of executives, the formulation of remuneration policies and the governance of decision-making. Any attempt to curtail independent oversight and reporting will be very difficult. Once, when discussing changes in the culture of integrity within a firm before and after being acquired by a larger company with a strong hierarchical lean, the CEO explained: "Before the acquisition, it was impossible to hide anything—everyone considered quality and integrity their business and felt free to challenge their peers and superiors if something looked wrong. Now, staff do not dare say anything; they only look at the files on their particular desk. If I wanted to, I could hide almost anything I want". If we want to empower certain functions to help maintain integrity in the firm, we have to create the right conditions for them to operate in.

The Reality of the Remote Diversity and Inclusion Officer

We have previously considered hierarchy and reporting lines. A manager who evaluates a subordinate's performance has the power to decide on pay increases, bonuses, promotions and the work ambience and pressure on a daily basis. There is no doubt that the subordinate will heed the cues provided by that manager as to what denotes on-the-job "success" or not.

It is a particularity of the second-line defence functions that its staff needs to be close to the business units they monitor and report on, both geographically and in knowledge. Whereas the Internal Audit function conducts sporadic visits to a given office, potentially resulting in audit reports critical of local management to their Head Office manager, the second line of defence has a far more exposed relationship with local colleagues and superiors. A D&I officer is expected to ensure daily supervision of the business and have a duty to intervene in the event of a potential breach of regulation or corporate policy. Whereas exceptions to the best practice of ensuring control functions have reporting lines separate from the business they are linked with, there are many instances where this is still not the case.

A challenge to this hierarchically aligned reporting is the distance between manager and subordinate, which is not uncommon in global organisations. For example, when the manager is located at Head Office in Paris, and the subordinate D&I officer is situated in Sydney, Australia, communication technology, time zone differences and remoteness all conspire to weaken the hierarchical link. There is a greater risk that local colleagues and non-hierarchical superiors will exercise a more significant influence over the remote officer's actions and behaviour than the Head Office manager. A Group Compliance Officer colleague of mine went to great lengths to emphasise the lines of reporting, duty and reward power he held over his distant reports; literally. At the time of bonus allocations, he would travel the world to all of his remote direct reports to personally hand them their bonus cheques. This symbolic gesture never went unnoticed.

It is in the nature of all internal control officers, including the Diversity and Inclusion Officer, that they have to be willing and able to "speak truth to power". Their ability to do so relies on their belief that the "power" in question will not be able to retaliate against them. They must believe that the manager to whom they report will not only support them as they fulfil their duty, but also reward them for doing so. This is the threat facing the first line of defence ambassadors, which must absolve them from direct responsibility. But it is a threat that must be avoided at all costs by the second and third levels of defence. It is therefore essential that the remote manager of a local D&I function is (1) in regular communication with the distant subordinate, (2) has a public profile within the organisation as a person of influence at the highest levels of the firm, and (3) that they will not hesitate to intervene at the slightest sign of their direct report being placed under pressure by local management or colleagues for performing their role. At the first hint of fear or concern on the part of a subordinate that they are threatened or actually being retaliated against, it is critical that there is an immediate response on the part of the superior—even to the extent of making an unscheduled visit to the office concerned to both comfort and embolden the remote subordinate, but also to apply pressure and, if necessary, "read the riot act" to local management. There are times and situations where an apparent disproportionate response is needed to ensure that not only the independence of one officer is assured, but that by extension, example and reputation, the independence of other officers reporting remotely to a particular function is enhanced.

Reporting Lines of the Diversity and Inclusion Function

The strength of the independence of the D&I role is a function of:

- The degree to which the officer's straight reporting line leads to the highest levels of the group function
- The quality and frequency of communication between the officer in the field and the remote supervising manager
- The degree to which the performance evaluation of the remote officer is conducted and rewarded by their non-business line superior (and is free of undue influence from local management)
- The degree to which the remote officer believes that their superior can protect them in the face of local pressure and threats of retaliation

The final bullet emphasises the credibility of the remote superior officer or group function in terms of power, competency and willingness to protect and intervene on behalf of the subordinate. In an organisation where (say) the Group or Chief Diversity and Inclusion Officer is not considered able to influence executive management or to have a voice at the board of directors, such perception of power is significantly reduced. For example, a CDIO who reports to a Chief Risk Officer or Head of Human Resources who does not have any notable reputation in diversity or organisational behaviour matters will immediately lose influence within business units when compared to the CDIO who reports to the CEO and has a direct line of communication with the Chair of the Audit Committee.

Furthermore, it requires that the profile of an influential and confidence-inducing head of an internal control function must have the personality and leadership instinct for sound judgement and relationship building, and possess the courage required to be visible and, indeed, "speak truth to power".

Of Sticks and Carrots

To readers used to the machinations of risk management, the policy and implementation duties of the diversity and inclusion function fall naturally to a second line of control function. However, to readers more familiar with culture management, this labelling might appear restrictive, focusing more on preventing misconduct than on the propagation of ethical behaviour. In response to this apparent dichotomy, two aspects of the 3LoD model need explaining.

Firstly, the 3LoD model has evolved out of the internal control and internal audit tradition—inarguably, both of the risk management tradition. Indeed, traditional governance is centred on the task of ensuring that accidents, mistakes and misconduct do not happen.

Secondly, the diversity and inclusion function's duties as a second line of defence is only part of their story. The US tradition of compliance has evolved from legal compliance aimed at adherence to prescriptive rules and regulations. In contrast, the European view of twenty-first-century compliance has a greater focus on conduct: Adherence to principles-led behaviours as exhibited by the organisation's members. This comparative difference is part of the reason that the concept of the Ethics Officer first took hold in US governance circles and has since found its way into global business language. This author's standpoint is that a compliance function cannot be effective unless supported by a strong ethical culture—it is perfectly feasible, and even desirable, to have compliance control and ethics management activities managed together, as two sides of the same coin. The goal of any regulation is effective behavioural influence [14]. In the words of the Dutch central bank, when explaining part of their regulatory approach, "..., we investigate group dynamics, behaviour patterns and mindset. Group dynamics looks at how people interact in a group setting .... Can everyone make themselves heard? And does everyone realise how their own behaviour can affect the functioning of the group as a whole?" [15].

References

1. Smith-Meyer, A. (2018). *Surviving organisational behaviour.* Kindle Publications.
2. (2017, September 26). Final Report – Joint ESMA and EBA Guidelines on the assessment of the suitability of members of the management body and key function holders under directive 2013/36/EU and directive 2014/65/EU. eba.europa.eu
3. Directive 2013/36/EU of the European Parliament and of the Council of 26 June 2013. *Official Journal of the European Union.* eur-lex.europa.eu
4. OECD. (2015). *G20/OECD Principles of Corporate Governance.* OECD Publishing, Paris. https://doi.org/10.1787/9789264236882-en
5. *The UK Corporate Governance Code 2018.* https://www.frc.org.uk/directors/corporate-governance-and-stewardship/uk-corporate-governance-code
6. The Companies Act, Norway. *Lov om aksjeselskaper.* https://lovdata.no/dokument/NL/lov/1997-06-13-44/KAPITTEL_6
7. Strategic Business Direction, Director and Board Development Programme, Institute of Directors, London. (2009).
8. https://en.wikipedia.org/wiki/Helmuth_von_Moltke_the_Elder
9. International Organisation for Standardization. (2021, May). *ISO 30415 – Human resource management – Diversity and inclusion.*
10. UK Financial Services Authority. (2003). *Building a framework for operational risk management.*
11. Governance of Risk, The Chartered Institute of Internal Auditors. https://www.iia.org.uk/resources/audit-committees/governance-of-risk-three-lines-of-defence

12. ESMA – Guidelines on certain aspects of the MiFID compliance function requirements (Ref: ESMA/2012/388 Sept 2012). esma.europa.eu
13. EBA guidelines on Internal Governance (ref: GL44 September 2011). eba.europa.eu
14. Khan, A. (2021, December 28). *A behavioural approach to financial supervision, regulation, and central banking.* An IMF Working Paper (WP/18/178). www.imf.org
15. *Supervision of governance, behaviour and culture.* As quoted on the DnB website, December 28, 2021. https://www.dnb.nl/en/reliable-financial-sector/supervision-of-financial-institutions/supervision-of-governance-behaviour-and-culture/#idqhno9bkjj

#InclusionMetrics: Defining Success of Diversity and Inclusion

15

15.1 Getting Past Blinkered Vision: Or Blinded by Numbers?

The saying goes, "a decision is only as good as the information that goes into it". The inference is that without information, no sensible decisions are possible. Peter Drucker is the management guru who coined the phrase "what gets measured, gets managed". By extension, we can infer that what gets reported influences behaviours. Ambiguously, what we measure is subjective, what we manage is elective, and what we act on depends on our willingness to be held accountable. If we want to measure culture and behaviours, we are surely capable of observing them; if we prefer not to change the status quo and remain within a comfort zone, we will choose not to see or listen to the evidence before our eyes. If it is a change in D&I outcomes that is the objective, we need to focus more on real-world consequences and less on cold numbers.

Humans have the power of observing and evaluating behaviours and the impact they have on others. We measure these against our values and can determine if acts conform to the ethical standards implied by the values we hold. In governance terms, however, if we are to hold an employee or actor accountable for their actions, we require evidence. If we want justice to prevail, we must have a fair process; we must have scales that weigh the good against the bad. We quickly conclude that we need good information to make a good decision. The challenge is that whereas diversity is relatively easy to measure, inclusiveness is not. Vernā Myers, VP of D&I at Netflix, said, "Diversity is being invited to the party. Inclusion is being asked to dance". It is easy to register diversity at the check-in to the party, but far harder to measure the quality of social interaction once the music starts.

Suppose we believe in the maxim that we tend to see what we want or expect to see (aka confirmation bias). In that case, the person who experiences belonging will be largely oblivious to the exclusion that is going on around them. For example, the White person who prefers to imagine that there is no "inclusion problem" will note the number of Black and other minority individuals present at the party and will particularly notice one or two mixed couples on the dance floor. However, they will

A. Smith-Meyer, *Unlocking the Potential of Diversity in Organisations*, Diversity and Inclusion Research, https://doi.org/10.1007/978-3-031-10402-2_15

not see that most couples dancing are not mixed. The art of measuring inclusion is not to seek positive confirmation of the absence of exclusion, but to actively monitor for incidents of exclusion [1].

Creating a Social Accounting Database

Like financial accounting, social accounting seeks to record and verify the impact of the company's activities. Over the past century, the introduction of financial accounting standards made it possible to reliably see variations in performance from one reporting period to the next or to compare one company's profitability with another. However, the criteria for social accounting are not yet universal, although the EU Non-Financial Reporting Directive and the Corporate Sustainability Reporting Directive [2] are heading in this direction.

Some do not see the value of tracking and tracing performance on environmental, social and other corporate responsibility matters. For them, the absence of a universal standard opens the possibility of engaging in window-dressing, issuing sustainability or similar reports that are vague or do not allow for easy comparison with other actors. This, however, is to miss an opportunity to nurture a meaningful culture that engages with employees, clients and other stakeholder contacts and which can enhance financial performance over time.

The European Directive on Non-Financial Reporting [3] recognises the pitfalls of companies focussing on financial reporting only: It encourages short-term rather than long-term decision-making, and it understates the importance of investment and the cultural drivers of innovation, such as trust, integrity and predictability. The importance of the Directive is in its ambition to raise the level of transparency of social and environmental impact of undertakings across the EU, and eventually to set the pace for the world. Regarding diversity, its focus is described as "diversity issues, such as gender diversity and equal treatment in employment and occupation (including age, gender, sexual orientation, religion, disability, ethnic origin and other relevant aspects)". Reporting on the more cultural and behavioural aspects of inclusion is not mentioned. However, importantly, the text also points out that transparency and the provision of non-financial information is "a continuous endeavour".

This omission of inclusion in the context of regulatory enforced non-financial reporting is understandable. Much of the reportable data on social issues, in particular, is hard to measure, and we are still trying to find reliable indicators. On the other hand, diversity numbers at various levels of the hierarchy can be detailed, but they say next to nothing about how a minority employee feels embraced by the organisation. There is nothing to indicate the extent to which they are free to express themselves and bring their uniqueness to the table, how much they trust their White managers, or if they feel empowered or fully recognised for their ability. The challenge is reflected in the guidelines issued by the official world of regulators. Of the 74 D&I measures suggested by the ISO 30415, all of 47% focus on listening and evaluating praise or complaint feedback received from employees, external stakeholders or from social listening, while 20% involve "evaluating" the effectiveness of measures intended to help implement D&I policy in the organisation [4]. There are several suggestions, such as monitoring demographic pay gaps, promotion and career development activity, and the presence of minority actors in the procurement chain—but practical measures of this type are relatively rare.

Hence, much of the social accounting of equality, diversity, and inclusion will be qualitative in nature or rely on proxy indicators that require interpretation. One path to establishing a data set upon which to review and evaluate performance on D&I topics is a social account of the stakeholder dialogue. In the context of the EU's CSRD, the European Financial Reporting Advisory Group (efrag.org) is further developing guidelines and taxonomies for ESG reporting.

15.2 Basic Diversity and Inclusion Reporting

By the logic of our progression through this book, we allow ourselves to presume a leadership in place that believes in the cause of greater equity, diversity and inclusion. We have outlined the necessary conditions of a trust culture that favours the sharing of experiences and transparency, and the creation of communication arenas and platforms that allow for the efficient exchange of information on the topic.

These are necessary pre-requisites for the establishment of meaningful monitoring and reporting processes. It is not conjecture to ascertain that 40% of S&P companies discussed D&I in their Q2 2020 earnings calls versus 4% in the same quarter of 2019 [5]. Executives and board directors have discovered that they require regular and reliable, objective indicators of the outcomes of D&I measures. In consequence, companies will likely engage in more extensive scope employment satisfaction surveys, which will provide valuable information of high quality. However, these are often conducted sporadically—and if regularly, not more than once a year in normal circumstances. The challenge is to identify key D&I performance indicators that can be included in monthly or bi-monthly management information reports. Unmonitored, trust conditions can be soured by a few incidents that go unpunished; communications can turn ugly at the intervention of just a tiny minority of miscreants.

To measure diversity is more evident than inclusion, but even so, this challenge cannot be underestimated. For example, the tracking of diversity in a multi-national company faces complex questions about what diversity means in its various locations, let alone how to produce comparable data; many jurisdictions forbid the mandatory compilation of demographic data such as race or religion. Nevertheless, statistics on staff diversity at their multiple levels of hierarchy should be compiled, monitored and policy targets pursued if fundamental change is to be achieved rather than merely be perceived.

At board level, the use of quotas to include more women has been much disputed and discussed. Still, supporters of enforced recruitment of minorities would argue that if we do not set the right example at the top, we will not promote the role models required to open opportunities for minorities in senior and middle management. The pressure to develop minority representatives as potential successors will be a natural consequence of increased demand at the top of the organisation. Indeed, a company with diversity on their board are twice as likely to set diversity targets within the leadership team. And it is not only in terms of representative numbers, but there is also a growing awareness that recruitment profiles should be more than skin-deep; there needs to be a broadening of background requirements and qualifications [6].

Measuring diversity amongst employees can be supplemented by more information on what is happening at the level of the selection of candidates for recruitment. For example, what is the variety of recruitment agencies and the communities they represent? Which demographics, cities, universities or communities are under-represented amongst applications? Does the company present itself as an attractive employer of diverse talent? The same questions can be asked of suppliers, contractors, distributors and even customers, the answers analysed, and policy objectives and strategies established. In the words of INSEAD Professor Henning Piezunka: "Spend less time being a good picker, and more time on being a good pick".

Inclusion is, as mentioned, harder to measure, but not impossible. Research and advisory institutions are busy developing proxy indicators based on behavioural sciences (discussed in a later section). As inclusion is a "feeling", and feelings are subjective and variable, measurement must be continuous, and findings acted on immediately. We cannot merely rely on slowly accumulated indirect indicators such as retention rates, promotion and attrition among the various demographics used to track diversity. Performing a company-wide employee satisfaction survey is an investment that requires very significant resources and, if carried out too often, leads to polling fatigue amongst respondents. It usually takes months of analysis and discussion before findings are published. Instead, the D&I function needs the feedback of more frequent, sporadic and informative pulse surveys that ask selected groups of employees to share their perceptions of the work environment, levels of engagement and overall employee experience [7]. Pulse surveys aimed at the historically disadvantaged working population might include questions on how pressured they feel to adjust their behaviours, code-switch or alter their language if they are to be accepted by their more dominant group colleagues.

Social auditing is growing in sophistication, but D&I functions responsible for regions, business divisions or units are already investigating reports received over the "Speak-Up" hotlines. Already, they should be collaborating closely with HR on reported bullying or harassment cases. Customer complaints registers and comments posted on external social media or employer assessment websites like Glassdoor provide valuable exclusion indicators. Even within traditional risk management monitoring and control processes, there is information to be mined.

In 2007, at a private forum, a global aviation company explained the range of sources they then used to gather intelligence on the ethical condition of the firm. The sources they described easily lend themselves to the creation of D&I data points.

- Investigative cases: Behavioural abuse takes many forms across an organisation. Both a high proclivity or absence of reported harassment, discrimination or intimidation are indicators of the presence of non-inclusive behaviours, can be closely tracked, and learnings extracted.

- Audit findings: An internal audit is present in most organisations. The function can be instructed to include D&I performance as a focal point. Still, even in the absence of any deep-dive inspection, a close reading of audit conclusions provides many clues as to the type of tensions that may exist within a culture, as well as the level of employee engagement present in the units concerned.
- Employee Opinion Surveys: The airline conducted these twice a year with a particular focus on the fear of retaliation, management reaction to reported misconduct and the promotion of diverse opinions.
- 360° Evaluations: Leadership evaluation of managers included collecting feedback on collaborative and inclusive behaviours from their subordinates, peers, superiors and customers. This feedback helped focus the mind of leaders on behavioural objectives, corporate values and how their role model behaviour impacts others.
- Performance Reviews: The inclusion of targeted behavioural traits in the annual performance review helped concentrate employees' minds on corporate values and provided feedback on employee behaviours and the general culture to the executive.
- Exit Interviews: Systematic collection of feedback from departing employees with consistent questionnaires highlighting areas of concern, such as D&I.

The Exit Interview Unmined

Generally speaking, the final litmus test mentioned by the airline—the exit interview—goes unused in many organisations. When a colleague decides to leave the company, we may be sad to lose a valuable team member or be relieved to have one less problem employee to manage. In the case of the former, we will have informal chats to inquire about the reasons for leaving, but all too easily be persuaded that "the other offer" represented an opportunity too good to miss. We prefer to believe that when we lose a talented subordinate, it is an institutional problem beyond our control. When we "lose a problem", we may still have a chat, but often we are not deep-listening to why they decide to leave, let alone investigate why the employee was such a problem in the first place. This inefficiency is not linked exclusively to D&I. Exit interviews ("EI") have always been available to HR, ethics and operational risk management officers. In some companies, EIs have been carried out diligently. However, the act of conducting an exit interview is without value if no importance is attached to the outcome of those conversations.

By convention, exit interviews are conducted by the HR department. Unfortunately, the information gathered often ends up being archived through no fault of HR other than the lack of interest shown by the stakeholders in the reports. In all the seven financial institutions I worked in during my banking career, I was never asked to participate in a formal EI. More importantly, as a manager, I was never offered any standardised EI procedure for my departing staff, nor offered any information if one took place. Like most managers, I had to conduct my interviews without the benefit of any training in the technique. Consequently, the interviewee was fully exposed to the discomfort of explaining what it is to be "badly managed" to their boss.

Surveys show that mine is not an unusual experience; most companies ignore the strategic value of exit interviews [8]. Research shows two principal reasons why EI procedures fail.

- The first is data quality—departing interviewees generally do not wish to burn bridges when leaving and will often not share their issues with the company or its management.
- The second is a lack of consensus on best practices. Most exit interviews do not follow a systematic questionnaire (4.4% of companies use questionnaires) and consequently do not objectively explore sensitive issues such as experiences of discrimination, harassment or integrity failures.

As commented by Spain and Groysberg, the exit interview is mainly regarded as "an operational duty rather than a strategic opportunity".

There are several best practice guidelines for conducting effective EIs. Following a prescribed range of topics; having the interview conducted by management levels once or twice removed from the interviewee's supervisor; timing the interview between the immediate emotion of resignation and before the moment of disengagement close to the time of leaving; training the interviewers and systematically reviewing and acting on interview output, are some. HR may have dedicated experts in interviewing techniques, but the responsibility for collecting and actioning the intelligence received should neither be hoarded by HR nor remain unexplored by other functions such as the business itself and D&I.

Raiding the Risk Management Archives

Anyone who has worked in risk management will be aware of the legacy of years of monitoring requests. New requests are frequently accepted and provided, but historical information generated that is no longer viewed is rarely discontinued. In pre-digital days it would manifest itself in boxes filled with computer printouts every day, much of which had to be archived for 5 years or more. In today's digital world of big data, there are arguably even greater seams of unmined, but relevant information available—some of which is utilised, but most of which is not.

There is no lack of data and indicators of all manner of risks. With some imagination and the recruitment of a data mining specialist, it is possible to discover gems of indicators directly or indirectly related to an absence of integrity, discipline, team spirit or a sense of joint responsibility. There is no reason not to believe that the same opportunities exist for D&I monitoring and reporting also.

The fact of the matter is that we have over 40 years of social science data documenting discrimination in society and the workplace. Using these same sources, it is possible to use the same indicators to help pinpoint where bias plays out in the workplace and target biased behaviours identified using new, inclusive processes [9]. In words written in a well-known book: seek, and you shall find.

15.3 Cultural Diagnostic Tools

The social sciences have developed an array of ways to analyse and evaluate cultural aspects of the organisation. Ordinarily, based on employee surveys and over time, we can create a picture of cultural maturity in terms of our objectives and trace improvements or deteriorations to highlight successful practices or identify areas that need remedial attention.

Culture diagnostic tools are generally designed to measure relatively universal dimensions of organisational culture, such as employee engagement. This may be adequate, but in a culture change context, it will not be exact enough. The culture survey may be quantitative (online questionnaire) or qualitative (interview-based). However, both will need to be tailored to account for the environment where the participants are located or the social context in which they find themselves. Aspects such as geographic, political, socio-cultural, industrial or even functional (e.g. women in engineering) [10] need to be incorporated into the tool's design. It is more than likely that in a niche aspect of culture assessments, such as inclusion, exploratory and qualitative initiatives like interviews, focus groups, meme and network analysis are needed to complement the quantitative assessment approach [11].

All the major consultancy firms offer cultural diagnostic services. Most of these use some information technology tools, but a significant part of their work involves organising online employee surveys and conducting extensive interviews throughout the organisation. Several alternative service providers advocate and use copyrighted survey tools based upon various psychometric and organisational behaviour methods. To explain these, a few respected diagnostic approaches are mentioned and cited below (but for lack of personal experience, they are not specifically endorsed by the author). Beyond the Employee Engagement Survey, some cultural measurement tools have become established methodologies taken up by major companies.

Barrett's Cultural Transformation Tools uses a Cultural Values Assessment and promises to provide a clear picture of what employees genuinely care about. It aims to flag gaps between current and optimal culture within a firm by highlighting any dysfunction in the organisation. They advise on a roadmap using measurable goals to achieve the organisation's culture objective [12].

MoralDNA draws its conclusions around three sets of ethical values, namely: (1) reason or logic, (2) care, love and empathy, and (3) obedience and compliance with the law. Combining a survey with interview activity, MoralDNA identifies sector or group level differences within the organisation, such as the state of ethics at executive, middle management and employee levels for comparison—valuable when evaluating the degree of trust culture within the firm [13].

The Inclusion Culture Niche?

New advisory institutions working on the cusp of academic research and business practices are busy developing proxy indicators based on behavioural sciences. The Gartner Inclusion Index seeks to build a benchmark for measuring D&I progress based on seven statements for "more or less" agreement by survey respondents [5]:

1. Fair treatment: Employees at my organisation who help achieve its strategic objectives are rewarded and recognised fairly.
2. Integrating differences: Employees at my organisation respect and value each other's opinions.
3. Decision-making: My colleagues fairly consider ideas and suggestions offered by other team members.
4. Psychological safety: I feel welcome to express my true feelings at work.
5. Trust: The communication we receive from the organisation is honest and open.
6. Belonging: People in my organisation care about me.
7. Diversity: Managers at my organisation are as diverse as the broader workforce (in society).

Through a series of pulse surveys, the organisation will create a baseline of employee perceptions with which to measure the evolution of "feelings" about inclusion throughout the firm. Potentially of greater practical importance, a sense of a baseline will enable management to identify outliers to the average—providing an opportunity to learn best practices from high-scoring business units and intervene where there appears to be a relative problem with the D&I implementation.

At Emtrain, they start from the premise that inclusion is a competence built on experience combined with personality traits such as openness and empathy. They, too, create a benchmark against which leaders can receive and evaluate D&I evolution in the company.

Emtrain adopts an approach that separates what behavioural economists refer to as social and human capital. Social capital builds on the organisational governance frameworks established by the firm to facilitate and encourage interaction between its personnel. Human capital evaluates and seeks out the skills and traits of those employees to help them realise their true potential within the firm. Consequently, they seek to measure key drivers of inclusion and equity at the level of the organisation, and of the individual [14]:

Organisational

- Fairness, consistency and the mitigation of bias in decision-making processes. Particularly around recruitment, career advancement and promotion, but also the daily operational management of meetings, task allocations and communications.
- Organisational awareness, acknowledgement and the valuing of differences in its workforce. Employees should experience that organisational frameworks create the space for diversity to be seen and flourish.

- Allyship role-model behaviours that create social equity, access and opportunity for those who would not otherwise have it. Allyship involves colleagues using their privilege to make a difference for those who do not have the same opportunities.

Individual

- The personal experience of colleagues gained through interaction with people from different races, gender, age, class and more. The more individuals live and socialise in diverse networks, private or professional, the less they rely on negative stereotypes and the more willing they are to create new relationships.
- Curiosity and empathy as expressed in the capacity to listen and learn about others without negative judgement. Curiosity reflects the ability to stop making assumptions in favour of discovery, while empathy is the ability to understand another person's point of view. Both are required to enable a growth mindset within the workforce.
- Social well-being is felt by the individual derived from the ability to express oneself authentically and their sense of acceptance and belonging. The higher this measurement, the less minorities will feel pressured to code-switch in order to gain acceptance within the firm.

These are but a sample of various methodologies applied to measuring culture, sentiment and specifically inclusion within organisations. Or as Janine Yancey, the CEO and founder of Emtrain, likes to say, "Helping to make the invisible visible so leaders can identify, measure, and track behaviour change to increase inclusion, diminish risk and increase organisational value."

15.4 Social Listening: Opportunity or Threat?

As part of the imperative for generating a #LivingDialogue, we have advocated establishing virtual employee resource groups or forums where those impacted by our shift towards greater diversity and inclusiveness can exchange experiences and information in a safe environment. We have also recommended that forums be either curated, moderated or monitored to ensure discussions stay on topic and any tension might be identified and eased. The D&I officer in the room hosting a physical forum discussion will sense the mood; interpret the language—both spoken and expressed through the body—to discern the direction of travel of sentiment. Is the conversation constructive and optimistic, or is it fearful, angry and pessimistic? Social listening serves the same function within the virtual forum by identifying keywords in combination with the emotional markers in the words associated with them. Brand managers are well acquainted with social listening as they track customer and social sentiment associated with their company.

Social listening is a relatively new science in the branding and marketing world. Still, there is no reason why the study of exchanges on intranet chats and forums cannot be subject to the same analysis practised by companies on Facebook, Twitter and Instagram. Current research ventures into topic modelling (searching for common themes), sentiment analysis (identifying positive or negative trends in communication style and language), and traditional keyword methods that track the usage of words known to have cultural connotations [15]. One surprising example is the research conducted on the relationship between code-switching and the use of language words and patterns. For example, we can measure inclusion by analysing the use of pronouns like "I" and "we" in our office communications. Studies show that language can reveal when individuals engage in internalised, empathetic code-switching, which helps us integrate by identifying with the dominant culture (e.g. the natural use of office jargon). This distinguishes itself from self-regulated code-switching, which is a more conscious alteration of expression deliberately adopted to gain credibility or acceptance within a group one does not feel a part of. In other words, our choice of words can reveal the degree to which employees feel included or excluded in the workplace [16].

There is a pitfall with social listening that must be heeded on scientific, ethical and even legal grounds. A review of internal emails for their terminology, sentiment and employee interactions is, one way or another, a form of invasion of privacy— even if anonymised. Such monitoring could provide valuable evidence of corporate health, but can be gathered with or without employees being aware that their digital work is being scanned. Furthermore, awareness by the staff of behind-the-screen electronic supervision can impact their use of language and phrases used, a.o., undermining the authenticity of survey conclusions [11]. Studies have sought to prove that the Hawthorne Effect (that behaviours under supervision may alter in the short-term, but revert to the previous norm with time) will always mean that humans gradually tire of artificial correctness if there are no consequences. The main takeaway is that when dealing with humans, we must remain vigilant of our moral obligations and that there is no absolute certainty with collected data.

There are legal issues of privacy to be considered, certainly, but in the larger context of the culture change mission, we have already identified that a culture of trust is imperative. Hence, the use of such surveillance must be considered in light of the level of trust in leadership and organisational justice. It would be counterproductive if participants are not made aware that their chatter is monitored, and ideally, it should be a subject discussed in the ERGs and forums to inform on their use and purpose. In any event, there should be guarantees of anonymity—such as engaging an independent provider to provide the social listening service. Depending on national cultures and other demographics, it may be that this avenue is closed due to the fears of retaliation it may invoke. However, if the culture of trust we have invested in is present and correct, then appropriate arrangements might be possible.

Privacy measures that might be considered include:

- Storing raw data on secure and dedicated servers behind the company's firewall
- Eliminating messages involving individuals outside the firm
- Removing identifying information such as email addresses

- Transforming raw message data collected by business line or division into cross-departmental or linguistic categories so that personnel identities cannot be deduced from message content
- Using external service providers committed to safeguarding the anonymity of staff

The Follow-Up

As we know, having the right tools does not guarantee a good outcome. Furthermore, in the words of President Ronald Reagan when debating the nuclear arms limitation negotiations with Soviet Russia, "Trust but Verify" puts meaning into not accepting initial findings at face value. Instead, diving deeper into the data provided and investigating potential red flags are essential if we want to ensure the proper outcomes. Culture surveys and social audits that seem too good to be believed, and those that appear untypically poor, should always be studied diligently to reveal hidden gems of learning.

- Do quantitative results match with expectations or qualitative information, or seem too exemplary?
- Do current outcomes align with trends indicated in previous reviews? Do other sources such as audit and risk management show similar findings?
- Reviewing outcomes with local D&I officers and conducting "Deep Dive" on-the-spot social audits as a sporadic reality check can be revealing, especially in remote locations.
- Remediation plans developed for local or regional business units run by local management and D&I functions should include regular progress reporting for committee review.

15.5   Monitoring Working-from-Home and Remote Locations

Organisations who rely on office workers have, to a large degree, been surprised with the success of the Covid-19 driven experiment in Working From Home (aka WFH). This has been particularly true concerning task execution and completion. However, what has been observed is that being away from colleagues at the office results in a decline of innovation, and distance from your superiors results in lower chances of promotion when compared with colleagues at the office [17]. It is intuitive to understand that remote workers can feel disconnected and eventually disengaged. Consider working with less than ideal internet broadband from the kitchen table, potentially living with the stress of feeling isolated or being surrounded by family, pets and children, causing distractions.

On the other hand, there are also reports from some minority employees that working via internet video conferencing has a liberating effect as we are inadvertently invited into people's homes, and formalities regarding dress codes and office language become more relaxed. Post-pandemic, there will be a return to the office for many. However, hybrid and permanent WFH solutions will be adopted in all sectors and cultures to one degree or another. The challenge of managing this new paradigm will not disappear. Managers in all manner of organisations are aware of these developments, and there is an abundance of advice on how to "check in" with subordinates regularly. For many, this may be sufficient, especially where the culture is already one of trust and inclusiveness. However, the reality for some will be very different.

The social commentator, Danielle Cadet, herself Black, states it thus: "Your Black colleagues may look like they're okay—chances are they're not". A social media message that went viral during the #BLM protests is striking: "There are Black men and women in Zoom meetings maintaining 'professionalism,' biting their tongues, holding back tears and swallowing rage, while we endure attacks from a pandemic and police. Understand and be mindful" [18]. Consider the risk to WFH workers, distant and isolated from the working environment, struggling with poor broadband and everyday office issues. Without the possibility of a safety-valve chat by the coffee machine or easy access to superiors and colleagues, they might quickly lose positivity and perspective. Some may even revert to less inclusive mindsets as the corporate working environment loses influence and communication style and behaviours become more selective and narrower.

McKinsey promotes what they call the "Influence Model" approach to monitor and manage colleagues across a virtual network. They maintain that this strategy is almost four times more successful in delivering results than those who do not proactively adopt an approach for managing culture in the current environment [19]. The Influence Model envisages an interplay between four drivers:

- *Understanding and conviction:* In demanding circumstances, people like to feel valuable and meaningful. Framing the current "sacrifice" in the context of the impact the organisation has on others benefitting from our services generates a sense of purpose, which will reinforce resilience. The product may be directly relevant to helping the crisis; the services provided may demand more creativity to aid customers through a tough time; it may even be that extra effort is helping to safeguard the lives and jobs of colleagues.
- *Reinforcement mechanisms*: Regular and supportive networking opportunities through employee resource group meetings, providing short updates on solutions and new practices being adopted through the organisation, and virtual coffee mornings will reduce the sense of isolation. For the lone worker or student, whose working days appear to blend into one another, having a disciplined routine to adhere to and shape their week around will increase the sense of teamwork and collaboration.
- *Confidence and skill-building*: Providing employees with opportunities to engage in re-skilling and other training programmes that help staff transfer from physical to virtual working will ease any sense of helplessness. Focussing on employee personal development and growth objectives by providing online training can

retain experienced staff and improve motivation as workers gain a sense of achievement and autonomy.

- *Role modelling*: The leadership must be visible to workers. Ideally, the executive and directors will endeavour to show that they too are making change efforts to help navigate the company through the crisis—one might see them declining or deferring part of their compensation until the situation is stable enough to promise job security. Leaders might host weekly virtual "town hall" meetings to answer employee questions or drop in on ERG or departmental meetings. Employees are expected to "follow" the lead of their superiors—but to do so, leaders must be visible.

Reinforcing Virtual Inclusion

Despite the growing availability of virtual office networking software [20], the pandemic has forced managers to become more structured regarding their connectivity with their teams. The remote manager is not merely a delegator of tasks, but also has to maintain a distant supervision of its execution and the quality of results. Estimating any feelings of inclusion or exclusion of a remote subordinate (for the sake of argument, called "Nico") is difficult. No longer can the manager rely on casual observations of Nico's stress levels; there are no collegial warnings or offers of support readily available. The isolated remote worker will typically hide their anxiety or sense of weakness and manage their communications on video links or telephone accordingly. When interacting with Nico, the manager has to rely on their listening skills and observe facial language as well as tone. Conversation must not be limited to task and results only, but include human, empathetic contact that is open and invites Nico to share how they feel in the moment—not how they know they are expected to be. For a small number of workers, such interaction skills may come naturally, but the greater majority need training in positive psychology management. This is true even at the office, especially when contact is minimal and distant. An incomplete list of remote management techniques might read [21]:

- Ensure Nico is at ease with their level of responsibility in these new circumstances. Tailor your contact style to suit Nico's preferred style. For example, in a situation where everyday contact is conducted through periodic, scheduled video meetings, the use of hierarchical power will need to be lessened, but only to the extent that the remote worker is not left with a responsibility they are not used to [22].
- Are you leaving room for Nico's voice to be heard? Some meetings will be one-to-one when the conversation can be a blend of checking on personal well-being and progress on tasks underway. Other meetings will be with several colleagues participating where everyone must be made to feel included and relevant. The manager must avoid starting a session by inadvertently declaring their expected outcome. Instead, they need to adopt an enquiring and learning stance and be

ready to calm domineering participants to make room for less known, polite or timid colleagues, like Nico, to express themselves.

- Adopt a coaching management style to help guide Nico. Nico used to experience a lot of on-the-job training by default as supervisors, and more experienced colleagues offered informal advice and help. The manager will need to create room or platforms for Nico to approach superiors or peers for help and advice without feeling inadequate for asking.
- Reflect Nico's feelings on their inclusion or exclusion relative to the team in group discussions. Encourage his team members to set individual inclusion commitments. Remote working poses a threat to a D&I culture irrespective of cultural mix and should not be ignored. The manager needs to raise the topic and highlight the benefit to the organisation and its mission from ensuring that everyone feels included, starting with the higher importance of collegiality in remote working conditions. Rewarding members for showing patience, curiosity, offering support and encouragement for others is critical.
- Ask Nico for advice on how to become a more inclusive manager. Managers must discipline themselves to exemplify the behaviour they want all their team members to exhibit. The manager might consider declaring what inclusive behaviour they are trying to master and role model "this" week or month and encourage team members to hold them accountable, rewarding them when they do.

Finally, take notes and find time to pause in the moment and reflect on your observations and discuss these with superiors and peers. Expressions of concern are meaningless if not acted on.

15.6 Putting the Horse Before the Cart: The Role of Reporting Formats

As we have seen, there are many ways to determine the status of, monitor, manage and report on D&I within an organisation. The temptation is to look for "quick wins" to demonstrate encouraging progress. There is a singular danger with this approach, however. We have to avoid the lure of defining our outcome objectives in terms of what we find easiest to measure. Instead, it is crucial to ensure the horse is placed firmly ahead of the cart. In other words, ensure that the end objective of behaviours and culture are well defined before considering any diagnostic help proposals. We cannot allow our tools to compromise our ambition for the sake of persuasive models that appear either more complete than necessary or too narrow in their application.

These aims and objectives will form part of the strategic discussion on "how" to achieve the "what" of the D&I vision. One tool that can be applied to this exercise would be formulating a balanced scorecard approach to address the D&I agenda specifically. The economists Kaplan and Norton published an article introducing an early form of social audit in 1992: the Balanced Scorecard—itself a refinement of ideas that emerged in the 1980s [23]. It is a model designed to enable managers to

Investment Value	
GOALS	MEASURES
Availability of D&I support	Shareholder engagement
Investor Attraction	ESG Reporting quality & innovation KPIs
L/T Financial Performance	D&I inclusion led financial KPIs

Value Creation	
GOALS	MEASURES
Employee diversity	Recruitment & pipeline trends
Market diversity	BAME market development
Supplier diversity	Procurement policy & BAME supplier KPIs
Reputation	Social Media KPIs

Core Competence	
GOALS	MEASURES
Inclusive Leadership	C-suite & board profiles
Leadership Communication	Clear policy objectives
#LivingDialogue	ERGs; events & forums
D&I Management	Monitoring, training & resources

Cultural Values	
GOALS	MEASURES
Employee Engagement	Culture diagnostics
Employee trust	HR complaints
Innovation	Ideas tracking
Inclusiveness	ERG, events & forum outcomes

Fig. 15.1 The balanced scorecard

define and set goals that are expressed more broadly than financial terms. It seeks to integrate financial, operational, client and investment performance into one multi-faceted scorecard where the chief value-creating measures stand alongside one another, avoiding the domination of one only (generally profitability).

The original questions asked by the Balanced Scorecard are:

- How do customers see us?
- What must we excel at?
- Can we continue to improve and create value?
- How do we look to shareholders?

The methodology provides an expedient framework to ensure that long-term success factors are always kept in the limelight.

A revised schedule of questions for the purpose of diversity and inclusion might be:

- How do our employees evaluate the inclusiveness of our organisation?
- What are the core competencies that enable us to promote diversity of talent?
- What behaviours and values within our firm enable us to share, learn and innovate?
- How can we secure the commitment of shareholders to grow through diversity?

The basic premise of the balanced scorecard, such as that depicted in Fig. 15.1, is that it tries to define success as multi-dimensional. To focus on success in one or two dimensions only is to neglect vital success drivers in other parts of the business or within the D&I objective. To achieve long-term success, the company direction and executive must take a "balanced" view of company performance.

Each of the four success criteria described in Fig. 15.1 supports each other. Value creation cannot be optimised without a culture of engagement and innovation, which in turn requires a focus of effort on core competencies and a convinced investor community willing to support new ESG projects. Core competencies cannot be maintained unless attuned to the various forms of value creation. Confidence amongst employees in organisational justice and a sharing, learning and innovative culture will further financial performance and increase conviction within the investor community. A culture of excellence and innovation that springs from a workforce more interested in corporate achievements than personal advancement will create value. We could continue.

The goals and measures provided in Fig. 15.1 are merely random examples. For example, the perception of value creation may be linked to evidence of the company's social responsibility, such as environmental and social actions that improve reputation and customer loyalty. Measures that showcase governance are a high priority in the company, aiming to increase investor confidence and willingness to provide additional capital. Employee training might increase core competencies or loyalty to the organisation. A focus on sustainability may be a core competence essential to ensure new products are future-safe.

The fundamental consideration in the balanced scorecard is to ask the right questions. What are our goals? Why do we want investors to support us (hint: it is not to maximise the value of CEO bonus share options)? What makes our customers willing to spend money on our product or service? What makes us a unique proposition? What do we do better than our competitors? What types of behaviour do we want to encourage in our workforce that protects and improves our overall performance?

The answers to these questions will tell us what our key success factors are. Only then can we consider how to track performance and progress in all aspects of the business and create the relevant key performance indicators.

15.7   Success: You Know It When You See It

Significant studies and reports have been produced annually since the 1990s evidencing the long-term financial benefits of greater diversity—initially in terms of gender diversity, but later concerning LGBT+ and ethnic minority communities; several of them are cited in this book. Such gains are comparative and show superior growth, profitability and solidity amongst upper quartile inclusive companies compared to lower quartile non-diversified companies. Qualitatively, we can sense the positivity and "hear" the hum of sharing and innovation in the office where relations between diverse colleagues is one of smiles, openness and collegiality. On the other hand, we can also "hear a pin drop" in an office culture where fear and loathing dominate the atmosphere. Diversity and inclusion are part of the employee engagement equation. It feeds team spirit within the organisation and its good reputation as a "best places to work" employer.

A social audit will essentially capture this positivity in terms of environment and performance, retention and recruitment of talent and the vibrancy of communication across the firm. There is one last process that is ever-present in any organisation and in evidence every day. We can help evaluate the presence of the inclusivity ethic in the organisation by observing the decision-making process introduced in Chap. 5. We recall the five stages of rational decision-making as follows:

1. Identification of the challenge, problem or opportunity
2. Generation of options and choices to deal with or solve the question
3. Evaluation of the multiple alternative solutions available and selecting one, based on purpose and desired impact and outcome
4. Acting upon the decision and implementing the solution chosen
5. Monitoring and obtaining feedback on the implementation of the decision in terms of achieving expected goals while making any adjustments necessary to ensure an optimal outcome

This model lends itself easily to the description of the ethical decision-making model by insisting that at each stage of the decision process, the decision-makers are taking due account of the purpose of the organisation and the moral values that support its strategy in achieving its ambition [12]. As inclusivity is the outcome of a culture built on the ethical values that underpin openness, curiosity, learning, trust, fairness and respect amongst others, then the definition of an inclusive decision-making process is only a matter of emphasis. The desired outcome is the same—decisions that abide with the group ethics established by the community it serves. Hence, we can consider our academic, rational decision-making model and compare it with what we see in the meeting rooms, offices and on the shop floor within the firm.

- Stage One
  Ensure you understand the nature of the problem, including ethical and inclusivity concerns. The way you frame the question at hand defines how the question is interpreted. Do you consider the identification of the problem to have taken full account of any ethical or inclusivity behaviour that may be hiding behind the apparent cause of the issue?

- Stage Two
  Generate two or more alternative solutions to choose from. A problem has presented itself. It may include ethical or D&I concerns that need addressing. However, even if not, there is every reason to consider how the decision might not also serve a moral or inclusive objective—or at least ensure that the decision does not go counter to ethical standards and values being nurtured in the organisation.

- Stage Three
Having generated alternative solutions to our problem, now is the time to evaluate them and set them in order of priority. Financial performance expectations will surely feature, including the acceptability of rates of return, some profit now or more gain in 5 years, or how much operational risk to take. However, a constant, unwavering factor in determining the best choice of the options available should be the questions: Is it ethical? Is it fair? Does it sustain enduring values of diversity and inclusiveness?

- Stage Four
This is the point where we are looking for someone to accept accountability for the execution of the decision. Assigning responsibility to an individual and holding them accountable for an impossible task is, in itself, unethical. Along with a delegation of responsibility, it is necessary to check and verify that the basic resources exist for the person to succeed.

- Stage Five
Check if your decision is performing as expected, both operationally and concerning its impact on stakeholders, including the minority groups you seek to treat inclusively. If this is not the case, the causes need to be identified, and decisions made for new actions if adjustments need to be made.

All processes can be improved or made more effective. If we are to ensure that our ethical stance and our D&I policies translate into competitive advantages for the firm, our governance framework should ensure that feedback on implementation and outcomes (e.g. by using social accounting techniques) are transparent, disciplined and made available for review.

References

1. Gaudiano, P. (2019, April 23). Inclusion is invisible. *Forbes*.
2. EU Commission. *Proposal for a Corporate Sustainability Reporting Directive*. Accessed July 14, 2021, from eur-lex.europa.eu with further information available at ec.eurpoa.eu
3. European Parliament, & the EU Council. (2014, October 22). *Directive 2014/95/EU as regards disclosure of non-financial and diversity* information.
4. International Organisation for Standardization. (2021, May). *ISO 30415 – Human resource management – Diversity and inclusion*.
5. Romansky, L., Garriod, M., Brown, K., & Deo, K. (2021, May 27). *How to measure inclusion in the workplace*. HBR.
6. BoardEx, & Odgers Berndtson. *UK Leadership Diversity Report 2021*.
7. Kaji, Khan and Devan. (2019). *The inclusion imperative for boards*. Deloitte Insights.
8. Spain, E., & Groysberg, B. (2016, April). Making exit interviews count. *Harvard Business Review*.

9. Williams, J. (2020, June 12). Companies have the tools to fight racism. Will they use them? *Bloomberg*.
10. Smyth, J. (2021, July 13). BHP rape cases shine spotlight on Australian mining culture. *Financial Times*.
11. Ethical Systems. (2021, January 27). *Corporate culture assessment*.
12. Hodges, C., & Steinholz, R. (2017). *Ethical business practice and regulation*. Hart Publishing.
13. Steare, R. (2006). *Ethicability*. CLE Print.
14. McKinnon, L., Sorensen, Pereira, L., & Todd, R. (2021, May). *Workplace culture Report – Inclusion 2021*. Emtrain.
15. Kessler, B. (2018, December 12). Algorithms to decode an organisation's culture. *INSEAD Knowledge*.
16. Doyle, G., Srivastava, S., Goldberg, A., & Frank, M. (2017, July). *Alignment at work: Using language to distinguish the internalization and self-regulation components of cultural fit in organisations*. Stanford University.
17. Hidden Brain podcast, NPR. (2020, November 16). *When you start to miss Tony from accounting*. Interview with Nicholas Bloom.
18. Roberts, L. M., & Washington, E. F. (2020, June). US businesses must take meaningful action against racism. *Harvard Business Review*.
19. Dagan, N., Baz-Sanchez, L., & Weddle, B. (2020, August 9). *Driving organizational and behavior changes during a pandemic*. McKinsey.
20. Seal, R. (2021, May 8). Can virtual meeting spaces save us all from Zoom fatigue? *The Guardian*.
21. Ellsworth, D., Imose, R., Madner, S., & van den Broek, R. (2020, July 22). *Sustaining and strengthening inclusion in our new remote environment*. McKinsey & Company Insights.
22. Hofstede, G. *The 6-D model of national culture*. www.geerthofstede.com
23. Kaplan, R. S., & Norton, D. P. (1992, January). The balanced scorecard – Measures that drive performance. *Harvard Business Review*.

#BeTheChange: Corporate Responsibility and Impact Beyond the Firm 16

16.1 Leadership in a Leaderless World

If there is one thing that the twenty-first century and the impact of social media have taught us, it is how it can shape popular opinion. Algorithms, originally intended to do no more than increase advertising revenues at Facebook and other similar platforms feedIng news and information to its users, have resulted in users being fed curated information based on their "likes" and click activity. Given our propensity for confirmation bias, we enjoy reading about stories and "facts" that reinforce our existing beliefs or prejudices. As a result, many of us are now on the receiving end of one-sided views of the world. Consequently, societies are facing relentless pressures to divide rather than to gather. Special interests thrive on the now separate, exclusive news feeds being delivered to the smartphones of different groups in society. Certain politicians, whose main objective is the accumulation of power and privilege, have ridden on the waves of information turmoil to their advantage; others who have ambitions to shape the world into their own vision of a better, more complex world are left, like King Canute, trying to master those same waves. It is an unequal fight.

The world still suffers from the aftermath of the financial crisis of 2008/2009, with no fresh political leadership appearing to offer meaningful hope of new promise for the future. The subsequent vacuum of leadership has led people, consumers and other stakeholders to turn their attention to the behaviour of the "other half" of society; or rather the other 1%. Resentful eyes turn towards the holders of disproportionate wealth, to the owners of capital, and to the executives perceived to be earning multiples in their hundreds more than their workers. Out of this malaise, 2019 saw "Environment, Social, Governance" gaining currency. Ideas of stakeholder capitalism—capitalism with a social and environmental conscience—executed in an air of transparency and accountability is slowly overtaking the shareholder capitalism of the 1970s. The mood and the demography of the people, the consumer, have shifted. To ensure long-term survival and success, companies can no longer stand as a casual bystander to social chaos, political failure and

A. Smith-Meyer, *Unlocking the Potential of Diversity in Organisations*, Diversity and Inclusion Research, https://doi.org/10.1007/978-3-031-10402-2_16

injustice. Company boards and executives have to engage with a broader society of citizens, consumers and employees, or else they will turn their back on them. Companies no longer have the option to disregard the political and social sentiment of the crowd—they have to be seen to engage and to prove that they are sincere in doing so. The old option of maintaining a low profile and remaining silent is no longer possible [1].

Beyond the Firm

We have mentioned before that an organisation cannot truly convince others of its sincerity or authenticity unless it is seen to be consistent in its behaviour and true to its values. Hence, the company that has successfully engineered a culture change within the firm cannot rest on its laurels without simultaneously embedding the same principles in its business with third parties and in their interaction with society also [2].

The inclusiveness process requires the organisation to demonstrate to its members that the leadership is serious about promoting its principles and values beyond its walls. A company should know their business partners and customers. Verifying the true identity and trustworthiness of suppliers and business partners is part of robust governance, due diligence and compliance procedures. Increasingly, firms are required to check that supply chains do not involve the use of slave labour, conflict minerals or any involvement with UN-sanctioned countries, etc. Equally, firms that are serious about being authentically true to their inclusion culture should audit and determine the diversity and attitudes of suppliers and distributors.

The "S" of ESG stands for social impact. To be credible in the eyes of all the players on the stage upon which the organisation acts, it must also evaluate the social impact it has on issues it pretends to care about:

- Are the products and services of the firm properly available to, and appropriate for, minority groups on a non-discriminatory basis?
- Is inclusiveness a subject that is a challenge for the communities it serves or benefits from?
- If there is a lack of qualified candidates from minority groups to recruit from, can the firm help find or develop the pipeline?
- If schooling and education is an issue, what can the company do to support talent development in underprivileged schools?
- Can the firm make available scholarships and paid work experience opportunities to students who would otherwise be unable to fund their studies or obtain internships?
- Can the company act as an employer role model for under-represented communities to inspire ambition and a belief that there can be progress and achievement for them also?

It is easier to ask questions than to determine any quick answers, but solutions are best found on the ground, on the shop floor. Fine speeches and colourful, annual sustainability reports filled with diversity statistics will not produce answers.

It is said that imagination knows no bounds, yet we tend to live our lives in a habitual routine based on unquestioned convention. Suppose we can discipline ourselves to listen, empathise and learn. In that case, we can discover a plethora of possible initiatives and actions that can create a path to a diverse and inclusive culture within our organisations and even in our society. Below, we shall look at the actions taken by Microsoft and Ernst & Young in the USA as they seek to embark on a path of change and inclusion inside and outside the firm.

16.2   The Case Studies

Many firms are doing good work currently to improve their inclusion cultures, and each story is both individual and no doubt experiencing progress and setbacks simultaneously. We are going to look at two companies from the outside, based on their public response to the #BLM protests in June 2020. Our purpose is not to evaluate the success or otherwise of their actions, but to use them as examples for debate and inspiration.

Case Study One: Microsoft

As of June 2021, Microsoft ranked 183rd on MITSloan/Glassdoor's D&I listing of 577 companies. In the category Tech Giants, they ranked 6th behind companies such as Facebook and Apple, themselves occupying the 108th and 117th slots, respectively. On 5 June 2020, the CEO, Satya Nadella, emailed all staff. It starts: "Seeing injustice in the world calls us all to take action, as individuals and as a company. Sometimes this action is personal—what do I do to change? Sometimes it is organisational—what changes do I need to make around me? And sometimes it is reflected into the world—what can we do as a company to accelerate the change we desire?"

On the official Microsoft Blog, on 23 June 2020, Satya announced what he called "three multi-year, sustained efforts" dedicated to:

* Increasing the culture of inclusion within the firm
* Engaging the ecosystem; impacting business relations
* Strengthening Communities by supporting Black and African American citizens in the communities in which they live

We shall look at the measures that Microsoft advertised that they will take within each of these focus areas.

Microsoft Culture

Microsoft intends to improve what it believes is already, at least partially, an inclusive-oriented culture. The intention is to deepen the company-wide understanding of what it means to be a minority, provide additional assistance for Black Americans to enjoy successful careers within the firm, and raise the profile and importance of achieving diversification targets at various levels within the organisation.

On Culture Change

Megan Carter is a Corporate and Executive Communications Officer at Microsoft, specialised in D&I. She expresses what appears to be a typical response from communities under attack from discrimination: "We are tired. I am tired. I am tired of the fear. I am tired of the hate. I am tired of feeling helpless. I am tired of worrying about the physical safety and freedom of the Black people in my life, every single day. But I am also tired of people who say they don't get it, that they don't know why we are making such a big deal out of this race thing, that they thought this was all in the past" [3]. These are sentiments that lead to workers disengaging with their employers, lead to talented individuals adopting low profiles, losing self-confidence and the will to grow. In her article, Megan highlights the importance of what Microsoft calls "Allyship".

Lindsay-Rae McIntyre is the (White) Chief Diversity Officer at Microsoft. She reminds us that "the brain processes exclusion the same way as physical pain." She goes on, "The reality is that when it seems like people don't understand or relate to what individual communities are facing—that in and of itself can be experienced as exclusion" [4]. Together these two Microsoft bloggers explain that "exhausted" minorities need the active support of "allies" within the more privileged communities to reverse the direction of exclusion. Through the "relentless" empathy of White allies, they help share the burden and bring the two communities together. In the promotion of Allyship, Microsoft has adopted our "Imperative #3", a policy of continuous living dialogue: encouraging the more privileged within the company to view their actions and circumstances as part of one work community, not separate from the problems facing minority groups.

Microsoft plans to accelerate its cultural transformation by encouraging its employees to act as supportive allies to those struggling for recognition of their competence or status by adopting three specific behaviours:

(a) *Engage with empathy and care*, so as to be more aware of what motivates us in a given situation, but also what is motivating the other, enabling us to work towards solutions and outcomes that integrate as much of both as possible.
(b) *Ask, don't assume.* We have already highlighted the impact of micro-aggression and prejudiced opinions on what motivates, or is expected by, those in a different social situation than those enjoying greater privilege. We project our generalised view of what the disadvantaged community is feeling or in need of, and fail to recognise that each individual is unique, with different feelings,

reactions and needs depending on the situation. If we are not careful, empathy can turn to pity and support to a negation of agency for the marginalised colleague. The discipline to overcome this bias of approach is a large part of what Microsoft appears to be aiming for when they speak of "Allyship".

(c) *Take accountability for our own learning.* "Accountability" is a call for employees to take responsibility for becoming more aware of the issues and challenges involved in dealing with prejudice and its outcomes. It is not for those in privilege to burden minorities with the task to educate them—the privileged can do this themselves, and it will lead to a better, more informed living dialogue with disadvantaged colleagues, the result of which will be more "Allyship".

This Allyship initiative, or continuous living dialogue, will only succeed in the presence of inclusive leadership from the top and an otherwise trust culture within the firm. It is perhaps comforting that the CEO announced that as of 2021, classroom training on Allyship and privilege in the workplace is to be mandatory for senior and executive management of the firm. On the other hand, the implication that executives usually consider themselves exempt from staff training requirements might indicate that the existing leadership style is less inclusive than one might hope. As mentioned before, if the leadership only walks the talk of inclusion, and fails to talk inclusion while they walk, then no programme will achieve the culture change we all desire.

Minority Representation in the Workforce

Microsoft intends to strengthen its career planning and talent development efforts throughout the workforce, but will pay particular attention to Black employees.

Microsoft is amongst a tiny minority of Fortune 500 companies that dare publish its complete workforce demographic data [5]. Against the backdrop that approximately 13% of the US population is made up of Black communities, and even allowing for the fact that these communities are disadvantaged in terms of education and self-development opportunities, the 4.4% African American representation at Microsoft (up from 3.8% in 2017) still leaves room for improvement. Black representation is highest in retail roles where it has been relatively stable at 18/19%, but the number falls dramatically in technical and management positions. At the company's managerial, director and executive levels, the representation is consistently around 2.6%, having risen only very slowly from 2.1% in 2016. Microsoft has a challenge on their hands.

To succeed, Microsoft will need to apply meaningful diversity targets in terms of representation, promotion and hires. A recruitment drive of this nature needs to avoid raising the hackles of those who will claim that "preferential treatment" of minorities is "unfair". It is hard for many people to accept that the introduction of quota-like targets is an attempt to level a currently uneven playing field for the careers of minorities struggling under prejudice. More often, those in a position of relative privilege will perceive such initiatives as an attack on the "acquired rights" of the self-perceived "elite". Such career development plans need to be explained and understood as being for the greater good of company performance, and greater diversity as an enrichment for all employees. The problem needs fixing, but the price must not be perceived by the dominant majority as too severe; otherwise, social cohesion and organisational trust may be lost. As with all procedural change, a programme to increase minority representation in the firm's senior ranks needs to be applied with careful attention to organisational justice—transparency in objectives and methods needs to be a priority.

The Microsoft Ecosystem

The company recognises that prejudice within the firm will decrease if business and society in general also understand the need for change. As a major global company, Microsoft recognises its potential as a driver of such change. Consequently, it is looking towards its business stakeholder groups and partners amongst suppliers, bankers, distributors and more to join Microsoft in this crusade for change. In this endeavour, Microsoft has declared its intent to:

1. Double the number of Black-owned approved suppliers over the next 3 years and increase scrutiny of supplier demographics to favour companies with greater Black representation in the supplier evaluation and selection process.
2. Grow Microsoft's portfolio investment activity with Black and African American-owned financial institutions, doubling the (unspecified) existing relationship business volume channelled through Black-owned institutions to help develop their market presence.
3. Invest $50 million in Black-owned businesses to increase the number of Black-owned partners in Microsoft's US partner community by 20% in the next 3 years.

A global firm like Microsoft has the financial power to influence the behaviours and choices made by its business partners. It cannot ordain change, but it can communicate its intention to integrate D&I policy objectives into the business relations evaluation and selection process. How far this will affect business relationships will depend on the balance of power between the firm and its business partner—who needs who most. However, making clear that such objectives exist and promoting them in Microsoft's "ecosystem" can only help increase awareness and reactivity amongst business partners. Furthermore, "walking the talk, and talking while walking" will help convince employees that their employer is sincere and authentic in its desire to right past wrongs and strengthen the firm's integrity in the pursuit of its stated mission.

Strengthening Communities

Microsoft recognises that it cannot change society, but it is a stakeholder and can influence certain parts of it. A large part of the discrimination against Black minorities, in particular, is the unavailability of clear education and work opportunities that enable Black citizens to climb the social ladder. Indeed, even within Minority Ethnic, religious, or other excluded communities, breaking ranks with the mainstream destiny of its members may meet with objections. Addressing this issue, therefore, requires efforts to increase access to opportunities for the entire community.

Education

Leaning strongly into their industrial expertise, Microsoft is committing to broadening its work to help Black students develop the skills needed to succeed in the digital economy. Over 5 years, Microsoft is to expand its industry volunteer programmes to bring computer science education to an additional 620 high schools (from around 900 presently), primarily serving Black communities in 14 States. They also promise to do more to help retrain Black adults for the digital industry and provide cash grants to community-based nonprofit organisations.

It makes sense for companies facing a recruitment bottleneck to make specific efforts to help schools produce the right kind of skills in the communities they wish to hire from. It seems clear that Microsoft's approach to its community outreach programme is reflective of its business and data-centric orientation. Other possibilities might include targeting:

- Traditional Black majority universities for graduate hires and
- Minority groups for paid internship opportunities and
- Scholarships to enable talented students to more easily emerge from their social restraints

Initiatives like these are long-term investments that would increase the corporate brand profile as an ally against prejudice and discrimination amongst the general public, including one's clients.

Social Justice

Microsoft, amongst others, already works to diminish systemic problems within the US social justice system in its treatment of Black minorities. Microsoft has been working on this topic since 2017 and is increasing its funding budget by $50 million over 5 years. Using their technology and expertise, Microsoft will focus on the use of data and digital technology to improve transparency and accountability in the US justice system.

Likewise, Microsoft is committing to help expand the availability of quality broadband services in regions and cities where communities are poorly served and provide technical support for nonprofits that support, and are led by, People of Colour.

Charity Begins at Home

Microsoft's actions appear to reflect a stakeholder-led approach, aligning much of their social engagement initiatives with their immediate business needs and skills. Other companies might choose to broaden their efforts to help their minority community stakeholder groups across a broader spectrum; related to their businesses both directly—like Microsoft—and indirectly.

Case Study Two: EY USA

EY enjoy the top slot amongst management consultancies in the previously mentioned ranking of companies considered by employees to be supportive of D&I. Overall, they are an impressive 13th in the listing. As a result, its actions and recommended practices are all the more interesting to take a closer look at. On 11 June 2020, a few days after Satya Nadella's email at Microsoft, EY USA released a short video outlining the anti-racist actions they were committing to, more about which later [6].

EY has a valuable place in the public debate surrounding integrity and ethics in the workplace. They sponsor conferences, advise on compliance topics, and conduct workplace reviews on corporate culture. Before looking at how EY (USA) approach D&I within their own walls, we will look at the general recommendations they provide clients on their website. To do so, we shall reference their work on LGBT+ inclusion as a proxy for the seemingly absent equivalent on racial inclusion [7].

Their basic premise is that "diversity paired with inclusion drives business success and better outcomes". EY also identifies some of the key obstacles to the effective implementation of D&I policies in an international organisation. Their concern is that a global presence not only increases diversity amongst the workforce but introduces fresh diversity challenges as well. Social, legal and company culture are layered on top of personal beliefs, opinions and fears, creating a hotbed for conflict [8]. In a global consultancy group where members are independent country-based partnerships, the autonomy this implies is even more of a cultural challenge than a multinational conglomerate of subsidiary and sister companies might experience.

Do as I Say ...
The EY approach differs from the three-pronged Microsoft approach of "Culture, Ecosystem, Society" by applying a somewhat comparable, but more prudent step-by-step method of "When-in-Rome; Embassy; Advocate". EY makes the point that this is a progressive model that requires getting your house in order first, before moving through Embassy and Advocate Cycles.

- When-in-Rome considers how to drive D&I improvements within the four walls of the company modified by local laws and norms influencing citizens and employees.
- Embassy considers the impact and risks of engaging with entities and stakeholders outside the firm.
- Advocate is targeting social, even legislative change in the host country.

Nine Inclusive Steps
In 2019, EY published a comprehensive report on LGBT+ D&I strategies entitled "Making it real—globally". The recommendations relate only to LGBT+; the words "Black" or "race/racial" do not receive mention in the text. Although the challenge of racial inclusion adds an additional layer of complexity to the task, the D&I objective

is the one and the same and, hence, worthy of study. The report proposes nine ways to advance LGBT+ policy to practice within the firm or international group:

1. *Conduct an opportunity and risk assessment and identify priorities for action.* EY differs from several other sources by emphasising risk analysis that includes consideration of the general legal and social environment in which the company finds itself. Is the legal setting supportive of minority rights as in Scandinavia and the EU, or restrictive as in Russia and parts of the Middle East? [9].
2. *Set policy globally, calibrate implementation locally.* Whereas EY's When-in-Rome approach promotes discussion and raises awareness levels within the firm of the impact on colleagues living under the shadow of taboos and prejudices of society, they advise a softly-softly approach to avoid the awakening of potentially damaging cultural rifts within the firm itself.
3. *Keep making the business case for diversity, promoting 360 education and storytelling.* Many activists within ethics and civil rights movements dislike issues they consider to be moral imperatives being discussed solely in terms of improved business outcomes. However, the evidence is there, and for certain individuals whose background is firmly rooted in prejudice and stereotype, it may be the only way to start a conversation. The danger is that a focus on the business case might lead the firm to pursue behaviours that the leadership does not subscribe to. Permissiveness should not be confused with inclusiveness in terms of the establishment of trust cultures. Tolerance is no substitute for empathy if the objective is to promote the authentic confidence-building leadership required for real culture change.
4. *Engage LGBT+ advocates and allies at all levels of the organisation.* EY underline the need for a real commitment of the firm's leadership to inclusion, identified as "Imperative #1". The transmission of that leadership energy to empower role models, sponsors and ambassadors of the D&I cause throughout the organisation is essential if altered mindsets and behaviours are to happen.
5. *Build out strategies supporting successful career growth.* This statement entails a recognition that individual career development opportunities may prove a challenge for under-represented or suppressed minorities. This EY report does not address career planning for specific individuals working within a single business unit. Instead, EY addresses the problem of employee mobility, such as women or homosexuals moving to Saudi Arabia; a critical concern for multinational firms.
6. *Create opportunities for reverse mentoring and education of management.* This recommendation recognises that many executives and managers who have already achieved success in less tolerant times would benefit from personalised training and awareness sessions on new practices and behavioural expectations.
7. *Utilise social media and other technology, locally and globally.* In a world of dispersed business units and the COVID-19 practice of remote working, EY suggests conveying the inclusion message and an invitation to engage via social media networks that may, or may not, include external stakeholders like suppliers, distributors and clients.

8. *Develop LGBT+ networks and unify globally.* In line with our contention that no inclusion can properly evolve without a continuous, living dialogue within the firm—or across the global group—EY stresses the need to direct this discourse, online or otherwise, in a manner that promotes solidarity, strength and cohesiveness.

9. *Measure, solicit input and celebrate success.* On the argument that "what gets measured, gets done and what counts, gets counted", EY recommends the establishment of two or three goals to "measure and celebrate". Cultural change of mindset is the cornerstone of inclusiveness—and this is difficult to measure with any precision. As noted earlier, reviewing the outcomes of initiatives and evidencing success in advancing culture change is essential. To ensure awareness is increasing and micro-aggressions, a.o., are diminishing, there has to be transparency and data confirming that D&I strategy is making a difference. Culture change, as we have discussed in earlier chapters, involves behaviours that are complex to measure but can be easily observed. This effort to alter mindset must not risk being diverted by any obsession with what works to suit monthly or quarterly risk management styles of reporting.

EY's nine recommendations are well worthy of study and consideration. Still, as their discussion of the need to tailor D&I strategy to each localised business unit implies, there is no single recipe of success. How then has EY applied their advice to their US operations?

EY in the Real World of #BLM

As mentioned, EY in the USA published a document in 2020 entitled "EY's commitment to anti-racism in the US" [6]. Their declared objective is to eradicate racism and discrimination against the Black community within EY by introducing strategic change with the firm and influencing those communities where they are active. Likewise, they intend to act to influence public policy. In line with Microsoft, they distinguish between their own culture, their "ecosystem", and broader society in general.

Their list of intended actions includes the following (slightly shortened wording):

- Evaluating internal talent and business processes to further advance equity across race
- Investing $3 million in organisations committed to fighting social injustices in law, health and economic inequality in the Black community
- Contributing $4 million to four historically Black colleges and universities
- Funding an initiative to bridge the distance learning gap for underserved students
- Expanding the EY Entrepreneurs Access Network focused on Black and Latinx entrepreneurs to help connect them to peers, sponsors, capital and customers
- To drive policy change and lead actions for change in its communities with vendors and others they do business with
- Investing in EY-related communities through employee volunteer programmes

- Allowing EY staff to participate in the demonstration march in Washington, DC on 28 August 2020, commemorating the 57th anniversary of the historic civil rights march. Employees may also observe Martin Luther King, Jr. Day on 18 January 2021, "a Day of Service for our US professionals to participate in EY sponsored activities"

16.3 Case Study Conclusions and Comparison

In writing this commentary on Microsoft and EY USA, we have only considered the information readily available on the Microsoft and EY websites in 2020. It is therefore not possible to conclude on neither the extent of the commitment promised by the two companies nor their success. Both have emphasised the importance of establishing clear and measurable milestones. There is the evident danger that an organisation can talk a good game, yet do little in fact to enact change, or that a firm is quietly understated while earnestly implementing meaningful measures motivating culture change beyond the prying eyes of onlookers and commentators.

At the start of the chapter, we referred to the respective rankings of Microsoft and EY in the MITSloan/Glassdoor listings. In them, employees have provided their perception of inclusion and diversity within the walls of the firm they work for. As we have seen, publicly, EY discusses diversity primarily in terms of gender and sexual preferences. Their reaction to the #BLM furore in 2020 was markedly less emphatic and confident than Microsoft's, yet in the overall D&I rankings, EY comes 13th while Microsoft is 183rd. Without prejudice to these two firms, inclusion and exclusion are subjective feelings where one group (such as women), already included in the mainstream dominant population may enthusiastically subscribe to the inclusion practices of their employer, while the dissenting voice of another smaller and excluded group may not be heard.

In the case of EY and Microsoft, it is difficult to make any qualitative comparison. EY does not publish gender or minority representation which Microsoft does. On the face of their public actions, it may appear that Microsoft is more active in terms of the inclusion of minorities. Yet, in the Fortune 2019 listing of the 100 best workplaces for diversity, EY is ranked 17th while Microsoft does not make the list—in fact, no big tech company does. Then, in the spring of 2021, EY's ranking falls to 41st (with no publication of gender or minority representation), Microsoft again not making the list. It all demonstrates the care that we must adopt when evaluating numbers and comparative statistics [10]. As the saying goes, actions speak louder than words—or numbers. We are not our own best judge of character or fairness—for that, we are all too human.

Do as I Do ...
There is a difference between perception and prejudice, although one might influence the other. Just as prejudice must be challenged, so it also needs to be clarified. Perception is an opinion based on what we observe rather than what we have been taught, albeit through the lens of expectations. If we do not pay attention to it, it can

result in lasting "first impressions" that eventually evolve into prejudice. How others perceive your actions, as we have discussed, is an essential element in the communication of sincerity, commitment and authenticity. In this respect, Microsoft and EY differ significantly.

Satya Nadella, as CEO of Microsoft, took a personalised interest in the firm's reaction to #BLM. By communicating a very personal commitment to improving D&I at Microsoft and being transparent on his lengthy internal communications, he exhibited both leadership commitment and activated a broader discussion within the firm. In comparison, the short statement of Carmine di Sibio, EY Global Chairman and CEO, is far more reserved and limited to eight sentences, including one in acknowledgement that "words alone are not enough" [11].

Of Head and Heart

Both companies provide suggestions and comments that are well worth the consideration of others. Their approaches reflect their overriding business purposes. Microsoft pledges to bring their digital competencies and capabilities to bear on the internal and external focal points they identify. At the same time, EY promotes a very risk-based approach to their D&I strategy development recommendations, as befits one of the big four consultancy firms. Neither bow to the theologian's purist ethics and inclusiveness preference for the arguments of moral imperative. Consequently, they may be running the risk of trying to instil cultural change through the head and not the heart when both are required.

Through their public reporting, Microsoft has revealed that it is measuring and working on the critical inclusiveness indicators recommended by EY; and that they still have some way to go. However, EY has not made such information easily accessible on their US website, and when addressing inclusiveness, this is mainly focused on LGBT+ and gender diversity issues. The two companies have done their talking, but what counts remains what they say while walking the talk.

16.4   Be the Change: Ask Not of Others What to Do

A change management process is neither simple nor separate from the routine business of the firm. As with ethics, the strategy for ensuring non-discriminatory conduct cannot exist alongside a business strategy; it must be embedded within it, be part of its DNA and enacted in its "lifestyle". The vision and the values we prescribe in our quest to achieve diversity and inclusion have to be an integral part of the way we interact, take decisions and measure our success. Why then not stand tall outside of the firm in our dealings with our external stakeholders such as customers, suppliers, distributors and government?

A single organisation pursuing authentic equity, diversity and inclusiveness objectives in coming years will do so in relative isolation to the world around it. It can define its own ethics, it can pre-select the employees more likely to embrace diversity, and continuously educate, honour and reward the behaviours that support it. Our influence and control is high and depends only on the leadership walking the talk, and talking while walking. An organisation cannot exercise anywhere near as much influence in broader society, but it can choose its partners and create a shared story with its customers. We should never forget that knowledge never discovers itself—without Einstein, the Law of Relativity would only be a mathematical formula. The human element in decision-making is what makes the difference. In the words of Harvard economist Peter Drucker:

> Whenever you see a successful business, someone once made a courageous decision.

Beyond Performance Indicators

Mr. Nadella of Microsoft is undoubtedly aware that setting KPI objectives and throwing money at a cultural issue is no longer tenable. We know from painful experience that, just as we cannot have an ethics and compliance strategy separate from business strategies, we cannot divorce culture change initiatives from the conduct of business either. We know that if there is a conflict of strategies, where one is rewarded by business KPIs and the other is not, then it is the business targets that prevail—even if in breach of advertised ethical rules. The twenty-first-century corporate has to focus on three levels of inclusion if they are to be compelling and convincing:

- The culture and behavioural norms on show within the company itself
- The example the company plays as a business leader within its stakeholder grouping
- The company as a sincere and authentic voice for change in broader society

References

1. de Chenecey, S. P. (2019). *The post-truth business*. Kogan Page Publishers.
2. Hunt, V., Prince, S., Dixon-Fyle, S., & Dolan, K. (2020, May). *Diversity wins*. Mckinsey.
3. Carter, M. (2020, May 28). *Get it wrong for me: What I need from allies*. LinkedIn Pulse.
4. McIntyre, L.-R. (2020, May 28). *Relentless empathy: When hate demands critical leadership*. LinkedIn Pulse.
5. Microsoft. (2019, November). *Diversity and inclusion report*.
6. The video (Accessed July 2020) has since been taken down. Accessed June 2021. Refer to https://www.ey.com/en_us/purpose/ey-commitment-to-anti-racism for other information.
7. Kida, H., & Twaronite, K. *LGBT+ inclusion: Can you apply a globally consistent policy across an inconsistent world?* ey.com

8. Smith-Meyer, A. (2018). *Surviving organisational behaviour.* Kindle Publications.
9. Kurtanidze, E. (2021, April 30). *Dismantling LGBT+ rights as a means of control in Russia.* Freedom House Perspectives.
10. Egbuna, T. (2019, April 15). *The problem with company diversity rankings.* Chezie.
11. Di Sabio, C. (2020, June 23). *Our commitment to address racial discrimination.* ey.com

#BestPracticeStandards: From Compliance to Culture

17

17.1 The Role of Business Standards

Academic theory attempts to explain how the world functions—it cannot dictate how we should manage the real world. Academia provides us with concepts and theories that help us to understand the dynamic changes occurring around us. It helps us to ask the right questions and points at potential answers. It does not give us practical advice on what specific measures and actions to take.

The business world equivalent is the development (by committee) of common standards of best practice with the objective of improving corporate performance. Born of the need to establish common technical standards on matters such as equipment and machinery and food safety across industries and markets, collaborative organisations develop common standards at the levels of business sector, country, region or international. Over time, the globalisation of our economies created a need for standard definitions of best practice concerning issues like health and safety, human rights, IT and the fight against organised crime. Management, governance and risk management practices have been added to the brief to ensure a clearer understanding of terms such as bribery, human trafficking, hygiene and more. Recently, racial diversity and inclusion have been included in this brief. Encouraging the use of common standards is the equivalent of establishing a common language. Differences may still appear, but overall, the chances of understanding one another improve and negotiating contracts using a common standard of quality opens opportunities for trade and growth. The flagship organisation for such standards is the International Organisation for Standardisation, based in Geneva, Switzerland. Its membership is composed of over 165 national standards organisations, and its ISO standards[1] are much quoted and referenced all over the world. Its principal purpose is

---

[1] Somewhat confusingly, the International Organisation for Standardisation (also known by its French name of Organisation International de Normalization) has adopted the standard acronym, ISO as a descriptive across all languages.

© The Author(s), under exclusive license to Springer Nature Switzerland AG 2022
A. Smith-Meyer, *Unlocking the Potential of Diversity in Organisations*, Diversity and Inclusion Research, https://doi.org/10.1007/978-3-031-10402-2_17

to answer the question: "What's the best way of doing this?" [1]. In May 2021, they published the ISO standard 30415 on "Human Resource Management—Diversity and Inclusion".

NB. Certification Is Not the Answer

A board of directors has a primary responsibility to pursue the long-term success of the company including identifying and mitigating the main strategic and operational risk facing the company.

It is only too typical that when an organisation becomes subject to new regulatory or social expectations, the leadership immediately seek assurances of compliance regarding the expectations placed upon them. It is a risk aversion mindset that often takes precedence before any strategic evaluation. In a company where the "why" of diversity and inclusion is not placed ahead of the "how", a standards-based D&I programme may, in effect, encourage companies to do no more than the minimum necessary to tick all of the boxes required to pass an audit or achieve a certification—particularly if certification is thought to immunise against any liability for failures. During a panel discussion on ISO compliance standards in 2015, Alexandra Almy, then a certification manager at ETHIC Intelligence, said, "Standards are meant to help companies effectively mitigate the risk . . . in their business, not to provide them with a way of 'buying their way out of jail'" [2].

Alexandra went on to say that while compliance with best-practice standards "might show the existence of a program within any given company, they do not necessarily evidence a program's effectiveness in mitigating that company's specific risks". At the same event, Scott Killingsworth, law and ethics partner at Bryan Cave LLP, explained, "Any standard that tries to cover a very broad range of situations cannot be very specific or directive, or it will be a bad fit for many of those situations. But if a standard is general enough to cover all of those situations without controversy, it risks being redundant or insipid".

Compliance with a schedule of requirements, even if "certified" by an outside consultant, will not produce any lasting change in culture or mindset. Instead, the organisation that wishes to introduce change will have to do so through commitment, resources and continuous effort. At our panel discussion, Klaus Moosmeyer, currently the Chief Ethics, Risk and Compliance Officer at Novartis, concluded, "Based on the risk assessment, you have to carefully integrate these elements into the relevant businesses. For this job, you need skilled professionals who know their company and the business environment—and of course a clear commitment by the top management".

As a final word on the limitations of the usefulness of national or international standards on D&I, I would draw your attention to what is likely the most important recommendation of all—that of committing to continuous improvement, always.

17.2   ISO Standard 30415: Human Resource Management— Diversity and Inclusion

ISO standards are the result of diversity in action. The standards are debated in committees made up of national experts drawn from its 165 members. The final product is the result of the best minds from multiple cultures around the globe, but is beset by the conflict of emphasis that members bring with them from their national standards boards. We have previously stated that a common objective, vision and mission is necessary to focus diverse minds on a common objective. Equally, a diversity of interest can influence the definition of that common objective, rendering it, as commented above, "redundant or insipid". In the case of the ISO, it is not strange if that objective is to find a common standard that is sufficiently high level to incorporate the more specific interests of each of the national states that are to ratify it. Diversity applied to a blank page may well lead to a fresh and innovative solution to a given question. On the other hand, if the task is to find a common framework in which to fit diverse objectives, it becomes a negotiation.

ISO 30415 is the product of a committee negotiation. Its conclusions and standards revolve around six operational parameters, of which the human resource management life cycle is the most extensive.

ISO 30415:2021 Operational Contents
- Accountabilities and responsibilities
- D&I framework
- Inclusive culture
- Human resource management life cycle
- Products and services—design, development and delivery
- Procurement and supply chain relationships
- External stakeholder relationships.

Within Section 8 of the Standard, "Human resource management life cycle", there are many recommendations that represent HR best practice, irrespective of any D&I objectives:

1. Workforce planning—Identifying and ensuring adequate and appropriate HR resources to complete the set mission both for the immediate and the future.
2. Remuneration—Remuneration policy should include measures to ensure processes and procedures are fair, equitable and transparent.
3. Recruitment—The evaluation and sourcing of candidates should be organised to attract and employ the best minds and talents to fit the workforce planning requirements.
4. Onboarding—Recruits should be made to feel welcome and valued. Onboarding should create the conditions needed to assimilate and succeed in the organisation.

5. Learning and development—If human capital is genuinely considered the most important asset of the firm, it needs to be systematically nurtured and developed.
6. Performance management—The individual performance and behavioural expectations placed on employees should be clear and result in fair and constructive feedback.
7. Succession planning—The positioning of successors to important positions within the firm should be based on required skills and talents and without prejudice.
8. Workforce mobility—Mobility of workers between functions and locations can add value to the organisation. This should be managed with care and respect for those concerned.
9. Cessation of employment—There comes a time when employment is terminated, due to retirement, changing business realities or choice. Procedures should ensure that the individuals concerned are treated with care and respect during what is often a traumatic time.

To Tick or Not to Tick the Box: This Is the Question

In Annexe "A" of the Standard, there are a total of 177 boxes for organisations that wish to comply with ISO 30415 to "tick". Herein lies the continuing debate surrounding the split between compliance and ethics. Proponents of the ethics function often describe compliance as having a mission to ensure that rules and regulations can be certified as having been complied with—irrespective of outcomes—ethics, they argue, concerns itself with conduct and the all-important impact of those behaviours.

"Where there is a standard, a certification consultant is waiting in the wings". D&I is a complex matter, and we have discovered how our human mind prefers to simplify and find easy-to-execute solutions. As with other standards issued in the past, the temptation will be to adopt a sleep-walker approach to D&I implementation and merely demand confirmation that the actions required under the "gold standard" of the ISO are met. However, this alignment of procedures and policies ignores the challenge of actual culture and mindset change. In one simple sentence, the self-assessment boxes provided in Annexe "A" should only be applied in a continuous look-back exercise and not considered a one-off to-do list.

In section four of the ISO 30415 ("Fundamental D&I requisites"), there is a list of conditions that must pre-exist any implementation of the ISO guidance. The conditions necessary to evidence a commitment to D&I and the development of an inclusive organisation are:

- Recognising diversity by valuing all people equally
- Governing effectively through inclusive systems, policies, processes, practices and operations
- Acting accountably in the promotion of an ethical and socially responsible workplace

- Working inclusively by fostering an accessible and respectful workplace
- Communicating inclusively by recognising and responding to the needs of the recipient
- Advocating and championing D&I by influencing organisational practices and stakeholder relationships

Naturally, the espoused conditions of valuing employees, being consistent, promoting accountability, respect, communicating with empathy and engaging with stakeholders, all speak to fair process and organisational justice; values that every corporation should aspire to irrespective of any focus on D&I.

The D&I Function

In Section 5.4 of the guideline, ISO outline 15 responsibilities that should be delegated explicitly to the D&I function in their promotion of an inclusive organisational culture. These align with the general duties of a second Line of Defense control function described in Chap. 14 and include:[2]

- Assure that D&I principles adopted by the board are embedded in the policy and procedures structure of the organisation
- Promote, advise and educate on D&I knowledge, skills and expertise in the formulation of corporate policy, processes and practices
- Manage the resources allocated to the promotion of D&I principles
- To increase participation of minority groups by enabling access and ensuring necessary adjustments to the workplace
- Introduce evidence-based monitoring, checks and balances to mitigate the effects of bias in policies, processes and practices
- Create a safe environment enabling communication and the expression of diverse opinions without fear of retaliation—institutional or otherwise—including for whistle-blowers
- Ensure that stakeholder feedback received is properly taken into account and acted on
- Promote the organisation's D&I principles in its conduct of business with external stakeholders.
- Establish monitoring, information gathering and analysis of diversity data to review and report on the impact and effectiveness of measures implemented in support of D&I principles.

---

[2]The wording of these responsibilities are those of the author as inspired by that of the lengthier ISO 30415 guidelines and not an accurate reproduction thereof.

"A Good Compromise Is One Where Everybody Makes a Contribution"—Angela Merkel

In a 52-page document, the ISO highlight the many actions, measures and outcomes involved in meeting the challenge of D&I. Section 7 of the guidelines defines inclusive culture as one that enables fair and equitable access to opportunities and fosters a sense of connectedness and mutual respect. Much of ISO 30415 will be inspired by already existing ISO standards such as ISO 30405/30406/30408/30409/30410/30411 and 30414. These all deal with best practice on human resource management to optimise performance and social responsibility towards internal stakeholders. Throughout ISO 30415, the emphasis is to adjust and align best practice with the particular social responsibility to fairness and the absence of discrimination. In the search for a universal standard that applies to an emotive and subjective topic as the inclusiveness of cultural differences that appear foreign to the dominant majority, one might forgive some superficial guidance in cases where broad-based agreement between divergent interest groups is the goal.

Of the 177 action steps recommended by the standard, there are 3 dominant themes once the leadership has determined a D&I policy for implementation:

- Review and update the existing policy and governance frameworks to align, embed and ensure compatibility with D&I objectives.
- Determine an appropriate monitoring framework that includes collecting demographic data and ensuring its regular review and evaluation to confirm D&I objectives are being achieved.
- Educate, train and communicate the purpose and desirability of D&I objectives and expectations regarding collegial and business conduct behaviours.

Most recommendations primarily address the principles of supporting impartiality and fairness. In addition, we find the need to make sure of an adequate allocation of resources, leadership role-modelling of D&I behaviours, enforcement of behavioural expectations, and engagement with all stakeholders—internal and external.

At its time of publication in May 2021, ISO 30415 was greeted with much anticipation. It followed the prior publications of various countries such as the UK and Norway, but due to its global reach carries more influence. National standards were developed for local industries. Consequently, they are marginally less general on how the guidelines are to be interpreted and applied.

17.3   The NS 11201:2018—Diversity Management Systems Requirements

The British published their standard in 2017 (BS76005), and the Norwegians their NS11201:2018 in July 2018. We have chosen to review this recent Norwegian standard to illustrate what is considered the best D&I practice in a country deemed by many to be more egalitarian than most.

The Norwegian standard was published on 1 July 2018, following the work of a committee composed of representatives from business, government, trade unions, research institutions and non-governmental organisations. The report is available in Norwegian and English from the website of Standard Norge (www.standard.no). The standards were developed to:

– Allow for the further development of potential that comes from diversity
– Advance business sustainability, innovation and value creation
– Promote the organisation as an attractive employer to facilitate the recruitment of talent and competence

The Norwegian Standard for Diversity and Inclusion comprises seven parts which are summarised and considered below. The presentation is indicative only of the nature of the recommendations made within the standard. It is not intended to provide an accurate or complete rendition of the Standard published by Standard Norge.

NS11201:2018 Explanation of Topic & Document Reference
Context of the Organisation: Section 4
• Formulate a vision and specify the objectives of greater D&I.
• Formulation and promotion of the use of inclusive corporate language & communication.
• Integration of D&I objectives within strategic business goals.
• Evaluation of organisational maturity in terms of D&I objectives.
• Alignment of recruitment profiling and training objectives to promote greater inclusive traits.
• Conduct an operational risk evaluation on the impact of greater diversity on health & safety.
• Ensure all D&I information collected and stored in support of the programme conform to GDPR.
• Conduct a social audit of D&I amongst the external stakeholders of the organisation.
• Understand laws and regulations regarding D&I in your markets and guard against procedural discrimination.
• Conduct a complete stakeholder analysis for the firm and map their D&I needs and expectations.
• Establish a governance framework for D&I, clearly establishing the application and limits of policy that aligns with stakeholder interests and capacity.
• Establish monitoring and review of D&I policy execution in the spirit of continuous improvement.
Leadership: Section 5
• Establish terms of reference and leadership skills required to manage inclusiveness, including an open mind, emotional and cultural intelligence.
• The leadership shall commit to ensuring that the principles of D&I are embedded in decision-making, encouraged in employee behaviours, and to this end, ensure adequate resources are available.
• Formulate an integrated diversity and inclusiveness policy that explains the benefits, and the strategic fit of defined diversity goals with the organisation.
• Declare that accountability for D&I within the firm rests with the leadership and clearly delegate responsibility for the execution of the D&I programme.
• Ensure that the responsibility for the achievement of D&I objectives and inclusive behaviours rests with managers.
Planning: Section 6
• Map the potential benefits and risks of greater D&I in the organisation and establish monitoring processes accordingly.

(continued)

NS11201:2018 Explanation of Topic & Document Reference

• The leadership shall establish coherent D&I objectives in all relevant functions at all levels of the organisation.
• In formulating D&I objectives, the firm should establish achievable goals, deadlines and metrics, allocate required resources, responsibility, monitor and evaluate outcomes.

Support: Section 7

• The D&I policy objectives must be adequately resourced regarding finance, staffing, competencies and leadership commitment.
• Personnel development programmes and recruitment objectives should be aligned to the D&I objectives of the firm.
• Map existing diversity of culture and skills to desired D&I outcomes and establish recruitment and training strategies accordingly.
• Ensure D&I policy and objectives are clearly enunciated and supported by the leadership.
• Make public the D&I values and behaviours to be exemplified by managers and employees.
• Ensure awareness of all managers and employees of the D&I policy, the benefits of its implementation and the consequences of any breach of policy.
• Define a D&I policy communications strategy on its implementation and maintenance.
• Make provision to ensure that all documentation relating to D&I is clear, relevant, accessible and up to date at all times.

Operations: Section 8

• The organisation should review processes and procedures to ensure that D&I principles are correctly embedded.
• Attention to and monitoring of the risk of unintended consequences needs to ensure rapid mitigation when required.
• Particular attention should be paid to the D&I policies, processes and procedures of external suppliers and partners to ensure they conform with internal policy objectives.

Performance Evaluation: Section 9

• The organisation must define concrete goals relative to D&I policy.
• Individual performance criteria must be defined, assessed and have an impact on promotion and reward systems.
• Performance must be systematically documented and stored.
• The organisation must establish the traits, competencies and behaviours to be expected of staff and leadership.
• Diversity at all levels should be monitored relative to achieving diversity objectives over time.
• Internal audit programming should be equipped to perform and include social auditing of the achievement of D&I policy.
• Social audit reports and conclusions must be communicated to the directors and executives of the organisation.
• The board of directors and executive shall be subject to a complete evaluation of their behaviours relative to their function as role models.
• The leadership shall play their full role in evaluating D&I performance and outcomes, the monitoring and fulfilment of continuous improvement objectives.

Continuous Improvement: Section 10

• When D&I policy is found not to be correctly implemented, non-compliant behaviours detected, or the D&I programme is found to be ineffective, the leadership must investigate, assess and take necessary action(s) to mitigate and rectify the failings permanently.
• As a matter of principle, the organisation must strive for continuous improvement in the management of its diversity and inclusiveness.

References

1. Accessed February 8, 2021., from www.iso.org
2. (2015, April). Roundtable on Benchmarks and standards. *Journal of Business Compliance*.

18

Change: No Longer a Matter of Choice

The third decade of the twenty-first century risks becoming remembered as a time that heralded much change. From a social perspective, it was a time when the world stood up against racism, and ex-colonial populations started to look over their shoulders—at their past legacies and at changing demographics. An openly trans-gender athlete made waves by competing in the delayed Olympics in Tokyo 2021. A pandemic thrust workers all over the world into a mode of working from home. Climate change started to become climate chaos as heatwaves, wildfires and floods hit normally climatically stable regions of the world. ESG (environment, social, governance) is growing in stature as non-financial reporting requirements are being formed and promoted in the regulatory sphere. Organisations need to increase their resilience and sense of direction in the face of change.

This book is about encouraging a new generation of leaders focused on outcomes and organisational cultures that bond its members in relationships of trust that promote innovation; an openness of mind and agility to meet change head-on; and a grassroots dialogue that shares knowledge and develops ideas without hesitation. In this book, these imperatives of sustainable culture change have been applied to the ambition of achieving diversity and inclusion, yet have everything to do with the ability of the organisation, any organisation, to face a future of dynamic change.

Reaching for the Stars Is Not Enough: You Must Know Which Stars

In the pursuit of culture change, there is no one-size-fits-all recipe for success. There is no single definition of what constitutes "good" diversity or an ideal state of inclusion. Deciding on what diversity, equity and inclusion mean to the individual firm is a question that needs asking and elaboration in its boardroom.

To embark on a complete diversity and inclusion programme to achieve culture change and reap the benefits of diversity is, it should by now be evident, an enormous undertaking. It requires carefully selected staff, a communications net-work that reaches into the far corners of the organisation, a governance framework that ensures that both accountability and empowerment are placed in the hands of the right leaders, and that the full commitment and interest of the board and the

A. Smith-Meyer, *Unlocking the Potential of Diversity in Organisations*, Diversity and Inclusion Research, https://doi.org/10.1007/978-3-031-10402-2_18

executive is maintained. If all of that is the cart, then the horse to be placed before it is the conscious understanding of why the organisation should pursue the objective. If a D&I programme is launched due to external "woke" or ESG pressures, then the risk is that of creating a "tail wagging the dog" bureaucracy.

Shelly McNamara is the Chief Equity and Inclusion Officer and HR Executive at P&G. Her title of E&I officer is interesting in itself and reflects what we mentioned in the introduction regarding the labelling of the exercise. She explains that her task is to focus on the two operational outcomes of what can sometimes be called Equity, Diversity, Inclusion and Belonging. In her dictionary, belonging is a part of inclusion, and diversity is a part of equity [1]. P&G made a conscious decision to reflect all the consumers they serve around the world, requiring a diverse representation of employees. This worldview creates a diversity objective, but the emphasis on equity and inclusion is intended to ensure that the system is fair for all employees, irrespective of whether you find yourself in the "ingroup" or the "outgroup".

The first question to answer is: "what do we want diversity to do for us?" In a very homogenous region, where society already produces multi-cultured employees who share similar values, we may be less expectant regarding the innovation and inspiration minority groups might bring to the enterprise, because even they belong to the same educational and social background as the majority. In another region, there may be historical bias and prejudice against a former slave-class that appears threatening to a dominant social grouping. Not only is the task in these two circumstances very different, but the range of outcomes of successful equity and inclusion initiatives will be very unalike. Are we seeking to find and employ the best talent available from the entire, diverse employment pool? Or are we trying to introduce some out-of-the-box perspectives to our product development, sales and decision processes?

Inclusion Is a Human Objective
Diversity, equality, equity, inclusion and belonging, leadership, authenticity, trust, dialogue and reconciliation: these are all very human concerns. D&I is not a science and never will be. It is spiced with emotions of fear and hope. Nothing is stable. Everything is volatile, but when diversity is managed correctly, it is vibrant, innovative and adds up to a total far more than its individual parts.

To break through to a new mindset, we must break free of our anchors. We have to liberate ourselves from conventional wisdom and presumptions that what has been, is also what is right. We have to learn to be curious and to listen to other worldviews; be ready to see different realities and embrace alternative futures. This requires confidence. We are primed to protect what we have, to risk leaving this behind on the promise that the "grass is greener" elsewhere means that we must feel convinced that the promised return is worth the disruption. Change is something that requires not only a strong culture of trust within the organisation, but also a society that is accepting of change. If politicians do not provide leaders who instigate change, then corporations must lead by example. Increasingly, our younger Millennial and GenZ generations, pushed by what they observe as a declining and unjust world, are expecting them to do so.

If our political systems will not deliver necessary change, or we do not trust it to do so responsibly, then we cannot pretend that change is beyond us. It is down to each and every one of us to educate ourselves and determine what behaviours, values and beliefs best serve our social or organisational well-being. To achieve this, we need to leverage the stability of the society around us to allow our curiosity and openness to new ideas to flourish. As an organisation, we are uniquely placed to create those conditions by showing leadership, promoting transparency and fairness in the workplace, and generating a grassroots conversation leading to reconciliation. As a commercial or industrial business, there is pressure to succeed. The more we recognise that we are being judged by our actions, and that the verdict will determine society's valuation of our product or service and our employees' willingness to go the extra mile, the more we will understand the importance of our conduct and words on the sustainability of our enterprise and long-term success. Board members and executives have a greater responsibility than most in this regard.

Inclusion Is for Everyone
There is a growing number of people, including leaders, who believe in the benefits of diversity and inclusion. Still, we have discovered that, as humans, our motivation and appetite for change is often driven by what we perceive to be the path of least resistance. The push towards a more inclusive society or organisation will encourage many to shout and argue their case with greater urgency and passion, but we must not forget that persuasion tactics do not always succeed at convincing the recalcitrant. Rather, the most successful path to change is to ease the fear or pain associated with new opportunities.

Barak Obama, the first African-American elected to the office of the President of the USA, pursued an aim of breaking racist glass ceilings and walls. "That was part of the reason I was running, wasn't it—to help us break free of such constraints? . . . I wanted to be neither a supplicant, always on the periphery of power and seeking favour from liberal benefactors, nor a permanent protester, full of righteous anger as we waited for White America to expiate its guilt". He realised that to be elected President, he needed to appeal to all Americans. He used language that "spoke to all" and "propose policies that touched everyone—a topflight education for *every* (sic) child, quality healthcare for *every* (sic) American". President Obama believed that to lift the cloud of injustice that beset People of Colour in White America, the solution lay in adopting a progressive agenda that would tackle injustices across the board, thereby helping Black Americans to achieve a fairer and better life. By acknowledging that social injustice affects all hues of Americans living today, he sought to focus minds on systematic solutions rather than injustice inflicted on one part of society to the exclusion of another. To achieve fairness for one need not dismiss fairness for all [2].

The benefits of diversity are embedded in our culture with phrases like two heads are better than one. Sometimes it is only a matter of removing the barriers to its implementation. The definition of what we expect from diversity provides the fuel that powers and directs our efforts at equity and inclusion. However, as seen in the discussion of the ISO 30415 guidelines, much of what is recommended is little more than fairness, equity and inclusion measures that you would best implement irrespective of any consideration of diversity amongst employees. Many of the lessons learnt can relate to so many forms of discrimination, as yet less explored. In her book, "The truths we hold", Vice-President Kamala Harris mentions the many struggles we face within our communities. We have struggles "against racism, and sexism. Against discrimination based on religion, national origin, and sexual orientation". To her list, we must add the fight to acknowledge the physically disabled or cognitively impaired as complete and capable human beings. Harris goes on to quote Martin Luther King: "Our separate struggles are really one—a struggle for freedom, for dignity, and for humanity" [3].

Where There Is a Will There Is a Way

Building an equitable and inclusive workplace is a time-consuming journey. There are many pathways to be developed concurrently, and progress must be tracked and reported on following an accepted map of milestones and points of maturity to be reached. Using the Norwegian Standard 11201:2018 or equivalent recommendations, the D&I function can start to determine both the distance to be covered and focus on weak points in the chain.

There is a business case for diversity and inclusion, equity and belonging. There is, however, also a moral imperative that cries out for individuals to be allowed to find equality and equity in their access to education, opportunity and reward. As you, the reader, end your reading of this book, take a moment to return to the testimonies of Elisse Daley, David Chukwujeku, Melanie Onovo, Chieka Okadigbo, Jack Callow, Liza Bilal and Dylan Kawende in Chap. 1. Then, ask yourself if it is not in your power to act, as an individual or an organisation, to change the perspectives of these people on what it means to be a member of a minority community. Look around you, and question the status quo, the narrative and the prejudices that stand in the way of inclusion at your place of work and within your community. Do not look for the example of others to follow, but be yourself the leadership role model that others crave to observe and emulate.

Where the business imperative is pressing, the moral imperative to move on from our prejudice-induced slumber is long overdue. In the words of James Baldwin [4]:

What is it you wanted me to reconcile myself to? I was born here almost 60 years ago. I'm not going to live another 60 years. You've always told me it takes time. It's taken my father's time, my mother's time, my uncle's time, my brother's and my sister's time, my nieces and my nephew's time. How much time do you want . . . for your progress?

References

1. (2021, August 3). *Moving the needle on DEI*. Podcast interview of Shelly McNamara on HBR Ideacast episode 812.
2. Obama, B. (2020). *A promised land*. Viking.
3. Harris, K. (2021). *The truths we hold: An American journey*. Penguin Random House.
4. NPR. (2020, October 30). *James Baldwin's shadow*. Abdelfatah and Arablouei on the Throughline podcast.

Index

© The Author(s), under exclusive license to Springer Nature Switzerland AG 2022
A. Smith-Meyer, *Unlocking the Potential of Diversity in Organisations*, Diversity and Inclusion Research, https://doi.org/10.1007/978-3-031-10402-2

Milton Keynes UK
Ingram Content Group UK Ltd.
UKHW022206041023
429923UK00001B/6

9 783031 104046